DESTINATION D.C.
A Modern-day Jonah?

FOREWORD BY DEAN BRAXTON
Author of *IN HEAVEN! Experiencing the Throne of God.* Guest of
"It's Supernatural" with Sid Roth, and the Christian Broadcasting Network (CBN)

DESTINATION D.C.
A Modern-day Jonah?

*Has America received a Reprieve?
The true story of Don Duncan's
obedience to God*

Ann Rich Duncan

Ann Rich Duncan
Donald W Duncan

XULON PRESS

Xulon Press
2301 Lucien Way #415
Maitland, FL 32751
407.339.4217
www.xulonpress.com

© 2019 by Ann Rich Duncan

All rights reserved solely by the author. The author guarantees all contents are original and do not infringe upon the legal rights of any other person or work. No part of this book may be reproduced in any form without the permission of the author. The views expressed in this book are not necessarily those of the publisher.

Unless otherwise indicated, Scripture quotations taken from the Holy Bible, New International Version (NIV). Copyright © 1973, 1978, 1984, 2011 by Biblica, Inc.™. Used by permission. All rights reserved.

Printed in the United States of America.

ISBN-13: 978-1-54566-869-6

TABLE OF CONTENTS

CHAPTER 1: Just Like Jonah 1
CHAPTER 2: Led by God 10
CHAPTER 3: Feeling Like Noah. 14
CHAPTER 4: Basking in Wellness 22
CHAPTER 5: Serpents in the Dirt 27
CHAPTER 6: The Power of Faith 32
CHAPTER 7: Starting a Faith-based Life 38
CHAPTER 8: An Amazing Healing. 47
CHAPTER 9: A Healing and a Prophesy. 52
CHAPTER 10: North Carolina Here We Come. 56
CHAPTER 11: Why, God . . . Why? 59
CHAPTER 12: Your Will, Not Mine 71
CHAPTER 13: The Husky Caper & the Devil's Face 81
CHAPTER 14: Miracles and God's Creatures. 88
CHAPTER 15: Godly Connections 95
CHAPTER 16: Angels in the Sky 98
CHAPTER 17: The Heal America Walk Begins 103
CHAPTER 18: A Guiding Light 122
CHAPTER 19: Visitors and Answers. 127
CHAPTER 20: Blisters and Miracles. 136
CHAPTER 21: A Glowing Report. 141
CHAPTER 22: A Spiritual Lift 145
CHAPTER 23: Detour to Rejection. 154
CHAPTER 24: Miracles and Memories. 165

CHAPTER 25: Troubles on the Road 171
CHAPTER 26: Meeting Rabbi Jonathan Cahn 177
CHAPTER 27: The Redneck Reverend............... 183
CHAPTER 28: A Tough Witness.....................191
CHAPTER 29: A Magnificent View 195
CHAPTER 30: The Missionary 198
CHAPTER 31: The Grace of God 203
CHAPTER 32: My Friend from Utica................ 208
CHAPTER 33: Praising the Father Saves the Day 212
CHAPTER 34: Encounters on the Road 223
CHAPTER 35: Getting Closer....................... 237
CHAPTER 36: Declaring God's Grace 243
CHAPTER 37: Congregations Pray for America......... 248
CHAPTER 38: Destruction or Reprieve 254
CHAPTER 39: Shaking up America's Leaders 259

FOREWORD

Don Duncan's book *DESTINATION D.C. A Modern-day Jonah?"* gives readers a journey of one man's love for his Lord and Savior. Along with his love for his country. By reading this book you will be intrigued with Don's travels from death to life, from disobedience to obedience and from his walk to Washington, D.C.

In reading this book, you will come to a new understanding of God's love for the United States of America. The things he saw and experienced are described in this book in many cases in detail. I myself have enjoyed reading his story of his walk with Jesus—and I believe you will.

After my experience of dying and visiting heaven, I came back with a zeal to see people come into awakening in the knowledge of God. In this book you will know Don has the same passion to give people in the United States and around the world the knowledge of our Lord and Savior, Jesus. I pray you will enjoy *DESTINATION D.C.*

DEAN A. BRAXTON
Dean Braxton Ministries

INTRODUCTION

When I was asked to write the Introduction for *DESTINATION D.C.*, I decided to do more than say what a good book it is. Don and Ann Duncan are members of the church that I Senior Pastor and Don is an Ordained Minister with our Corporate Ministry, Living Waters Evangelistic Ministries. Both Don and Ann are strong Christians who have matured in the Lord over many years through service to our Savior. I decided to share how my wife Cindylee and I were affected by this wonderful story as we read it together.

When Don first told me of hearing from the Lord that he was to carry a Cross on a walking journey to our nation's Capital, I was skeptical. Not skeptical about whether Don had heard the Lord, but skeptical about his ability at his age to do it. Of course, anything we do for God is not by our strength, but His. Don is a man who has witnessed God's great power in his life over and over. From a difficult childhood to dealing with stage four cancer, Don has learned to depend on the Lord and how to hear His voice. Ann, his wife, is an author and strong woman of faith in her own rite.

DESTINATION D.C. touched Cindylee and me deeply. We laughed, we cried, we shook our heads in amazement as we read how God directed Don to Divine Appointments, one after the other. The blessing of Don's trek to D.C. is not mostly in the end goal where he proclaims God's goodness, grace and power, but in the encounters along with way.

DESTINATION D.C. A Modern-day Jonah?

As you read *DESTINATION D.C. a Modern-day Jonah?*, be ready to be moved, excited and encouraged in the Lord and in one man's journey into truth.

PASTOR TIMOTHY A. BOHLEY
Senior Pastor, Jacob's Well Family Fellowship Center
Founder, Living Waters Evangelistic Ministries

DEDICATION

This book is dedicated to
JESUS CHRIST, man's greatest blessing.

And to my wife, Ann Rich Duncan.
Ann has not always been what I thought I wanted . . .
yet, she was always what I needed:
Loving, Loyal, Generous, and Committed.

I LOVE YOU BOTH.

Don Duncan

ACKNOWLEDGMENTS

Words cannot express our appreciation for all the assistance and encouragement we've received from the people listed in this book, including friends and family, and everyone else who helped to support the creation of the House of Angels, the walk to Washington, D.C., the writing of this story. We've made list after list, each time realizing someone had been left out and we finally determined there simply are too many to name! Suffice to say, we appreciate and love you all. That being said, we could not have succeeded with the publishing of this manuscript without the excellent guidance and attention we received from our pre-production rep Nick UnThank, Project Coordinator Alexandria Zaldivar, Publications Consultant Toni Riggs, and Editorial Consultant Greg Dixon Salem Author Services. But, the one, most important thank you of all goes to God the Father, who led us to this life and has given us the strength and ability to accomplish what He directed us to do.

WRITER'S NOTE

This book is filled with real-life miracles and the belief that God is still working in our lives today. Sometimes you can experience events and not learn from them until much later; and as I worked to weave my husband's notes and his walk of faith into a fact-based story, I concluded that this was true for me. I have learned that God has been leading us both. He brought us together, knowing we'd end up here in Vermont where Don would create the House of Angels, become an ordained minister and trek by foot over 500 miles on his Heal America Walk.

Life with Don led me toward a path of faith and authorship. He had an idea for a book, I had the experience of writing for others, and a hero (my eldest brother, John—a real-life treasure hunter) whom I'd always wanted to write about. With Don's encouragement, and after attending a few writers' conferences, I wrote and published five books. All of them have been endorsed by educators and/or clergy and have positive messages about America and our Christian heritage, so I guess you could say those years were, like my second eldest brother, Bruce, said, "warm-up sessions" to get me equipped for this endeavor. And what a necessary endeavor! After all, so many these days do not realize or believe that God continues to be involved in the lives of His people. After reading *DESTINATION D.C.*, you'll understand why Don and I can say without hesitation that God was, is, and forever will be, involved in our life; and if we can experience it—you can have a relationship with Him, too.

DESTINATION D.C. A Modern-day Jonah?

**OTHER BOOKS BY
ANN RICH DUNCAN**
www.Annrichduncan.net
anrichduncan@gmail.com

*The SEED
Travel With Johnny Vic
Johnny Vic's Nautical Adventures
Johnny Vic's Plymouth Adventures
Buried Alive*

PREFACE

I've experienced miracles in recent years even though for much of my life, I felt something was missing. As a typical person, I tried many things on this earth to fill a huge void in my heart, but nothing worked. And the sad thing is, deep down I knew what was missing: it was God. As you'll see in this book, I fell in love with Jesus as a young child, feeling comforted by the love I learned He had for me. That comfort was especially necessary because of pain I suffered during my childhood. Thank God my mother introduced me to Christ by bringing me to Sunday School. That's where this great, new love blossomed; but somehow it started to wither. After all, it was so hard! I mean, following God's word is a difficult thing to do, especially if you're a young emotionally tortured guy in a secular world, ready and determined—you think—to take on the whole world. But the world fought back, and the hole in my heart grew.

Unaware for years, I was in danger of being lost forever. But not anymore!

DESTINATION D.C., a Modern-day Jonah? is the story about my growth in faith, written with the hope that you'll realize redemption is available—for yourself or for someone you love. It comes from having a relationship with Jesus, the Great I Am, the one true Savior, who is willing to forgive you and bring you back to His fold, no matter what you've done. It's wonderful. It's amazing. Sometimes even miraculous and unbelievable.

I should know, because during my return to God's grace, I've had experiences that even I find hard to believe! This book is all about listening to God's voice, and how I got up from my deathbed to do what He told me to do. He's given me the strength to wrestle with boulders and fell humungous trees to create Christ's House of Angels; and to walk over 500 miles to proclaim His message—even though I was 65 years old and suffering with major health issues.

Why me? If God only worked through the greatest, richest, most able people on this earth, it wouldn't be miraculous! He often works through those who seem to be incapable, not having the ability to accomplish great feats—therefore revealing that God was in command and made it happen. And for me? It began after I had strayed from His Word for about 40 years. Yes, 40 years!

But, the most important reason for this book? It's to verify how the Bible is a true document that is filled with the knowledge that your soul can survive, no matter who you are or what you've done, because God wants you to be saved. But you have a part to play to determine your fate. You must obey His word. He wants a relationship with His wondrous creation: you! He can talk to you. He can direct you. And if you learn to recognize His voice, He will fill you with joy. Just as He did with me, a regular, hard-working guy who lives in a trailer, and is not what "the world" thinks of as a successful man.

It is my prayer that the faith of current believers will be strengthened and that seekers will find the gifts that God has for them.

I know I've got something that is more precious than silver or gold, more admirable than a million-dollar mansion, more valuable than an oil gusher. I've got the joy of the Lord and this book—I believe—will help you to believe it, too; so that you may receive that which He has prepared for you!

Don Duncan
ministerdonduncan@gmail.com

CHAPTER 1
Just like Jonah!

At the age of 65, I walked from Vermont to Washington, D.C. It was my Heal America Walk: a 500-mile journey during the summer of 2015, in obedience to God's will and with His help—help needed because even before starting out, I had diabetes, horrible recurring cramps in my legs, and feet with deep cracks and excruciating nerve damage.

Then again, the muscle-crumpling cramps couldn't hold a candle to other experiences over the past few years—like shovels of snakes, snowfall creating a demonic face on a car, and near-misses from life-threatening encounters—not to mention wonderful experiences like multiple sightings of angels, swirling winds around a sphere of stillness, bright auras; and most importantly the fact that I was given the gift of healing that ended with some cases that baffled doctors! The exciting events during my 500-mile journey from Vermont to Washington, D.C. are only half the story, though, for God had previously told me to build an outdoor sanctuary for prayer and healing we call The House of Angels where some of these miracles and puzzling incidents have occurred.

Receiving the message to walk to D.C. was truly an honor, and it made me feel a little like Jonah because I had to leave my home, my wife and The House of Angels, to travel to a city that, like Nineveh, had been backsliding against Godly principles. I had labored at The House of Angels until the dark of night—mostly with hand tools—for seven years, and as you can imagine, I was reluctant to leave it; but I am glad I did! The Heal America Walk was filled with divine and distressing encounters, prayers and healings; and more importantly, the joyous feeling of the Lord's presence throughout the entire journey.

One of the distressing encounters still causes chills to creep up my arms. It happened close to the Maryland state line near the end of my lengthy Heal America Walk. And to be honest, it was more than disturbing—it was frightening! The summer of 2015 was hot—a record breaker for sure. I'm talking heat waves shimmering-from-the-tarmac hot, but on this day, during this encounter, I forgot about the heat. I was thinking, *Is this it? Am I going to die now, Lord? Murdered on the side of a remote stretch of highway in Pennsylvania?*

I was watching a car that stopped on the narrow shoulder of the road at a place where you'd think no one would want to stop. Earlier in the day the same type and color of vehicle, traveling in the opposite direction, soared close and slowed to a crawl so the driver could thrust an obscene hand gesture my way. I remember thinking, *this guy could be violent.* I mean, his face was contorted with rage when he glared at me and the six-foot wooden cross I carried! And now, the same guy was apparently parked up ahead.

Like the roads along vast cornfields in the mid-west, this stretch of highway was unobstructed; so, I first noticed the familiar-looking car from quite a distance. My brain raced from one scary question to the next, all the while worrying that I was not going to make it to Washington, D.C. after coming so far. And then, when he stepped out to get something from the back seat, I really thought it meant trouble: the object he retrieved was long and slender, hidden beneath a multi-colored cloth.

Rifle! My brain screeched. *Does he have a rifle? No, it couldn't be that.* I struggled for a better, safer answer; but I had to accept the possibility that it was a concealed firearm. After all, there has been so much violence against Christians in this world, I was on guard. *What should I do*, I wondered; but it did not take long to find an answer: Prayer! I prayed for God's protection, even as I continued to ask, *why'd he move it to the front seat and climb back in? And why is he just sitting there? Should I get closer? Will he shoot if I walk past him?* That's when I prayed for forgiveness and confirmed to God that just as I told Him when I was a child who first came to know Him, I would willingly die for Him (just as He died for me) if that was His will. I also called upon the Lord for salvation.

Moments later, the mystery man got out of the car again, returned the thing to the back seat, slipped behind the wheel, and before I could blink, his taillights popped on and he sped away. I was sure he'd been thinking about shooting the man with the big wooden cross and then lost his nerve. I mean, why would he go to the trouble of moving something from the back seat of his car to the front, only to put it back again—still concealed? Did he feel God's impending judgment? Could it have been a gun? With so much hatred in the world for people who publicly practice their religion, and so many horrible atrocities against us, it was smart to be prudent; but I happily realized violent action was not going to be my fate today. I breathed a sigh of relief and thanked God for his protection and intervention.

The presence of the Holy Spirit during my Heal America Walk was so real, I am extremely grateful to have those memories; I truly desire that everyone could feel His presence so powerfully. I'm telling my story because I genuinely believe it is possible for anyone. For you! The simple truth found in the Holy Bible—that God wants to build a relationship with us all, no matter how we've sinned—was proven to me. I've spent a good share of my life feeling unworthy, but I now know without a doubt: if you truly want a relationship with God; if you desire it with a pure heart; if you listen for His voice, you can experience joy beyond anything else you'll ever experience on this earth.

As I tell you about the House of Angels and my Heal America Walk, it's my hope that you'll come to believe the good news that Jesus Christ brought to this earth is real, truly real; or, if you already are a believer, I pray that my experience will help to bring you closer to Him.

I started to create the House of Angels in 2004, in obedience to God's will after I was miraculously healed from my second life-threatening cancer. I worked on the site for seven years. Seven years! And as I said, the Heal America Walk was a second mandate from God.

When I received the directive to walk to D.C., I was excited, ready to take off; but I also wondered, *how can I possibly manage to walk all that way in the shape I'm in?* I quickly decided God would equip me no matter what the challenge. And, the more I thought about it, the more I realized I was ready for that challenge. Thoughts of the barbaric attacks that were occurring throughout the world often swirled through my head, like the horrific shooting incident in Charleston, South Carolina. Nine innocent people were gunned down at the Emanuel A.M.E. Church—an historic place of worship known as the oldest black congregation south of Baltimore. Plus, the thousands of people slaughtered in 2014, by members of the Nigerian group Boko Haram and by ISIS. Not to mention the unrest in America, and the fact that our own president encouraged rioters to "hold their ground" against the police in Ferguson, Missouri after many press members erroneously reported upon the infamous shooting. All these incidents and more have caused me to look to God for answers, and to be mindful that this country became great because our founding fathers looked to Him for guidance and direction. My wife, Ann and I often ask ourselves, *why don't people realize this?* Too many are living complacent lives, not bothering to fight against the downward spiral of morality. Corrupt politicians? People just say, *that's the way it is.* Increased use of drugs? *Nothing we can do about it.* Sexual immorality? *Nothing wrong with that!* Going to church? Being religious? Promoting Christianity? *Not on your life! Those religious nuts are prejudiced and narrow minded.*

Unfortunately, the world seems to be topsy-turvy: what once was wrong, is now okay. What once was right, is now wrong. Our politicians seem to be candidates in popularity contests—more interested in gaining votes and wealth than improving the nation.

The cause of this? I believe it's the fact that, as a nation, we've turned our backs on God. We've lost faith in Him and the legacy of our founding fathers.

But, what can I do, I have often asked the Lord; and then, He answered my anguished question with a new mandate—I felt unworthy of the challenge, but I knew the Bible was filled with stories about unlikely people doing extraordinary things; and, I recalled a recurring message that helped throughout many difficult times, especially the years of hard work throughout the creation of the House of Angels: 'If God gives it to you to do, He will help you see it through'.

After hearing the message to walk to D.C. it was easy to visualize an exciting march into our nation's capital; however, those triumphant thoughts ended abruptly a few days later, when I got up to get a drink. That's when I realized God was saying, "Slow down, Don. Now is not the time," because I rammed my foot into a chair—and broke my toe. I was not going to walk over 500 miles quite yet—it seemed that I needed to wait for confirmation on when to go. Did it come in a few weeks or even a few months? No. A couple of years passed before the confirmation arrived. I mean, it took so long I became puzzled, wondering if God changed His mind; but then I declared, "No! I don't believe He changes His mind! *I've got to be patient. It'll happen in His time.*" The wait was frustrating, especially when people were asking, "Are you still going to walk to Washington, Don?" I'd say, "Yes, but I'm not sure when I'm supposed to go," and sometimes I'd joke around, with thoughts of Jonah, saying, "Of course I'm going: I'm afraid of big fish," and I'd add, "I don't know how God would get a whale into Vermont, but I'm not taking any chances!"

Confirmation did finally come. It arrived through the course of several messages that solidified the need to take the walk, and amazingly revealed how it could be accomplished, and even indicated exactly when to begin this trek to Washington, D.C. It was revealed to me that the "Heal America Walk, should start on June 29th, in 2015.

DESTINATION D.C. A Modern-day Jonah?

Recollections of the oppressive heat of that summer-time journey somehow remind me of my mother's stories about my very first journey into this life. While aspects of my birth journey were on the opposite end of the spectrum, it was also filled with similarities to my trek to D.C. I was born on a frigid January day in 1950. Of course, I don't have any memories of those first days as an infant, but my mother spoke about them. She said it was incredibly cold when she and my dad brought me, their first-born son, to their humble home—a tiny shack spanning only about 12-feet by 12-feet, with just a cooking stove for heat; but I must have felt warm and protected at the time. I mean, I was healthy, and I never suffered from frostbite! And before long I had a younger brother and then a sister. But soon after my sister was born my family changed. Forever.

Our dad left. He made very little effort to keep in touch. And so, I watched as my mom labored to give us the best life she could. Sometimes she struggled just to feed us. Every so often we walked miles just to purchase chicken necks on sale. Chicken necks don't contain much meat, but my mother would pick at them until the bones were stripped bare like white skeletons in a museum. All that work, just so we'd have a bit of protein to eat! She had quit high school to get married just three weeks before graduation, believing she'd have a wonderful life with the man she loved. Instead, it had become a life of disillusionment, and sometimes I found myself in the middle of their disagreements. While I was still a child in grade school, she even sent me into local bars to track him down, so he could be arrested for non-support. All this anguish must have affected her, and sometimes she took out her frustration on me. I still loved her and respected the effort she made to improve herself and provide for us; but she often beat me.

As I think about it now, I wonder if she saw a bit of my dad in me. Of course, that abuse profoundly affected my self-esteem. It was incredibly painful, both physically and emotionally. And confusing! I mean, my mother often would tell me she loved me; but then at the slightest provocation—sometimes from unfounded suspicions—she would hold me down on the floor and pound on me. As a young child, I'd cower in a fetal position as she struck me with a belt or broom or whatever was handy. It happened throughout my childhood until I was in my late teens and could defend myself. It was during these beatings that she'd say ugly things like, I was a stupid son-of-a-bitch. It was totally degrading and affected me throughout my life, well into my adult years. Even to this day it has underlying effects. I literally despised her during those times. Who wouldn't?

And to add to the confusion, she would bring me to church; but, I'm profoundly grateful for that. It's where I learned about Jesus and His love for me. And so, now that she's gone, I still have conflicted feelings about my mother. It's hard to admit these things, but I believe it's important to tell the truth and to stress how confusing it was to be degraded and abused like that by someone who would then turn around and introduce me to God. "He loves you," my mother would say. "God truly loves you, and I love you, too." But those wonderful utterings would soon enough be followed by other abusive episodes. And yet, I must give her credit for working hard to provide for us. She obtained her G.E.D. and put herself through nurse's aide training which helped her to be hired by the local hospital where she finally landed a great job with the Physical Therapy Department.

I also faced other challenges as a child. I was tormented by neighborhood bullies and sexually abused by an older boy who was often charged with the care of me and my brother. The guilt I felt about those days also pummeled my self-esteem. As I disclose these sad moments, it's my hope that anyone who reads this who experienced similar abuse, has been able to overcome the lack of self-worth that can occur. It might seem crazy, but sometimes I think it was good that I experienced that pain because it led me to the point where I came to realize the best, most effective way to develop a positive sense of self-worth is to have a close relationship with Jesus.

I do have happy memories for sure, especially the companionship of my brother. We had lots of fun together, like the time we ventured into a field across from our home to feed the deer. They were busily munching the grass and we wanted to give them some torn bits of bread. I smile at that memory. I was around 5 years old. We were slowly approaching the deer, talking softly to them, stretching our hands out, trying to show them our offerings. The deer did not bolt. They seemed to be curious about these two tiny humans. But they did not let us get too close either. I believe the experience was a great lesson in life: an approach with an open hand in kindness and caring is so much better than advancing with a closed fist and a hardened heart.

It's funny that one of my fond early memories focused on deer, because as an adult, well over 50 years later, I still have wonderful experiences with the deer that roam throughout our property and inevitably feast on the flowers I plant at the House of Angels. While I'm not at all happy about the loss of the flowers, I cannot help but maintain fond feelings for the deer. Especially when they stop at the sound of my voice, and sometimes even step closer toward me for a few fearless moments before they finally bolt away, or I head on past them.

Other fond memories include the times when we went on camping trips with my mother's best friend and her kids. And one year, our mom scrimped and sacrificed to give me and my brother a race track for Christmas. We had admired it and chattered about it for weeks after we first spied it in a store window. I don't know how she managed to purchase it, but she did, despite the scarcity of money!

Yes, I have memories of a very humble life—but most importantly, they include the discovery of Jesus! You see, I was truly influenced by my experience at Sunday School. I mean, there was this picture of Jesus and I believed what my mother said about Him—things that were confirmed, expanded upon and validated by the Sunday School teachers. It felt amazing to think that He loved me. So much so, that He died for me. For me! And I loved Him back. And, somehow, that discovery coupled with those humble beginnings helped to influence my feelings about God. It was during those Sunday School years that I started to become aware of the cruelty that was occurring throughout the world. I sadly learned there was so much suffering, *not just by me*. And when I realized how Jesus suffered during His life on earth so that we could be saved from sin, I told Him that I wanted to be like Him. Those feelings of faith that developed during my childhood ran deep into my soul—even if I did stray for many years before coming back to Him.

As I recall so many painful memories, I now see it is important to tell people that no matter what you are facing, no matter who you are, you are worthy. Worthy of God's love.

And so, in 2015, I embarked on my special journey. Once again totally dependent. But this time? It was on the opposite end of the temperature scale and I was not leaving the security of my mother's womb, totally reliant upon her nurturing skills. This time I was leaving my wonderful wife and home, dependent upon my loving Father in heaven.

But, before you learn more about the miracles, the dangers, the struggles, and the heartwarming events that occurred on my Heal America Walk, I would like to tell you about the creation of the sanctuary we named Christ's House of Angels; how my faith was strengthened and tested, molded and solidified, and how I had to complete one special addition to the sanctuary's design before I received the confirmation and information that revealed God was finally saying, "It's almost time, Don . . . here's when you should start that journey."

LISTENING FOR GOD'S GUIDANCE: "You guide me with your counsel, and afterward you will take me into glory." Psalm 73:24

DON'S NOTE: Despite humble beginnings, it's good to remember that God uses regular people for extraordinary purposes!

CHAPTER 2
Led by God

The House of Angels is in the middle of our heavily wooded property in Southwestern Vermont. The scene of several healings, the sanctuary is comprised of about one acre of our 14-and-a-half-acre parcel. It includes a twenty-foot cross on top of a rocky ledge. At the base of the ledge three low stone walls support a grassy patio-like area. It also includes a small valley that resembles an outdoor amphitheater, along with shrubs, perennials, annuals, benches and statuary; and as I said before, it's the result of seven years of hard work—mostly with a chain saw and hand tools like a pick ax, a shovel and a rake. While I had been told by God during the summer of 2003, to put a cross upon that ledge, I was not obedient to begin work on it until the following spring—after I realized I had been miraculously healed from my second life-threatening cancer.

Here's how it all fell into place.

Several personal issues caused my wife, Ann and I, to move from Massachusetts to Vermont in October of 1998. We adjusted to our new surroundings over the next few months and the following February I was hired by a commercial electric company. Life in the Green Mountain State was pleasant enough, but as the next few years passed, I became more and more overwhelmed with fatigue. I'm not talking about the bone-weary tiredness that comes from a demanding construction job. It was more than that. I'm talking about the soul wrenching exhaustion that fills your heart with the fear of a life-threatening infirmity. I had not said anything to Ann about it, even though I'd been having troubling symptoms including bloody bowel movements, even before we moved to Vermont. I was reluctant to check into it after the move because we had just started to get back on our feet, and I did not want to disrupt our lives again; but, I was forced to face the reality of it one workday in 2003, when I felt so tired I couldn't even get into my truck. I slumped over the hood, trying to work up the strength just to open the door to climb in and drive home.

As believers we all know we should not be afraid to face reality. We should trust God to lead us on the right path; but as mortal humans, we often cannot overcome our fears. How foolish we can sometimes be! However, by early December, I just didn't have the strength to continue and was forced to see a doctor. A colonoscopy was quickly scheduled and after the procedure, I awoke to find Ann standing close by with tears in her eyes. She said, "You have colon cancer, Don. A big tumor. The doctor wants to operate today."

What? Operate today? My still fuzzy brain resisted that suggestion even though the doctor said it was a good time to perform the operation. He explained, "You're as clean as a whistle—all prepped, so we can take you right into surgery."

I did not like that idea. I was remembering the instructions I had received that morning, before the colonoscopy—instructions warning patients not to make any major decisions right away. I decided the surgery would have to wait.

Now, we had not met many people we felt we could turn to at this point; but Ann had called my employer to tell her the bad news, so when I woke up a second time the two of them were at my bedside. Seeing the compassion and caring attitude my boss displayed started me to think about the first few days when Ann and I had arrived in Vermont. Once we found a place to live, we spent the fall and winter months earning a few dollars selling items at craft shows and flea markets, but I knew this money could not sustain us for long. I eventually had to find a job; so, I purchased some local newspapers and reached for the telephone when I spied a couple of job listings that looked promising. This woman who was now at my bedside had been the first employer I had contacted. I had been doubtful about landing the first job I applied for; but she seemed pleased with my background and hired me right away. Although I didn't have any experience with commercial electric work, the starting pay was at a good rate. I believed it would take care of the rent and essentials in life. So, we were on our way to a better situation! Praise God!

Those recollections came to a screeching halt when I suddenly felt compelled to focus once again on my situation: I was in the hospital; had just received the news of colon cancer and my employer was at my bedside, talking. She was assuring us she would do what she could to help us get through it. I wasn't so sure since I had already experienced stage four skin cancer years before and at this moment, I did not think there was much probability that I'd survive a second life threatening bout with the disease. It was the 18th of December and I was expecting the birth of my first grandchild around Christmas time! Besides, Christmas was Ann's favorite time of the year and I wasn't about to spend the holiday season in a hospital bed, let alone go into surgery with the possibility that I might not survive to hear about the birth of that first grandchild.

Throughout the days that passed before the surgery, Ann and I tried to put on a brave front. It was nerve-wracking, but I realized how blessed I had been in the past, having survived a stubborn patch of melanoma that I had carried for about 15 years. You might wonder how I could have melanoma for so long without doctors becoming alarmed; but back then, skin cancer was not as well-known as it is these days. When I had a back injury, a doctor had written the spot off as a black and blue! I took the lack of concern as a sort of confirmation that it wasn't anything to be worried about.

I was in my 30's when the melanoma had finally been diagnosed. At first, they said it was a stage two; but after performing surgery with a local anesthetic, the doctors determined it was a stage-four cancer and I had to return to surgery to have a bigger area removed along with lymph nodes under my arm. Once that was done, they were amazed to realize the cancer had not spread. How could it be, they wondered, that a spot of melanoma had grown to the size of a quarter over a period of 15 years without killing me or spreading? At my last follow-up with that surgeon, he proclaimed, "You must be one of the luckiest people I know. The melanoma had not spread!"

He remained baffled, but I was not baffled at all. I knew I was not lucky. I was blessed, and I told him so, explaining, "A guy I knew asked me about the spot. He said I should have it checked out; but I decided to put it in God's hands instead." I went on to say there were times when I'd get out of the shower and look at it and say to God, 'If this is the way You're going to take me, there's nothing I can do." So, I put my faith in Him along with the destination He had for me on this earth.

GOD's PROMISE: "How great is your goodness, which you have stored up for those who fear you, which you bestow in the sight of men on those who take refuge in you." Psalm 31:19

DON'S NOTE: What we receive comes from God whether it be fortune or healing. My recovery was not based on luck. I knew I was blessed because I put my destiny in my Creator's hands.

CHAPTER 3

Feeling Like Noah

So, here I was, well over twenty years later, facing another case of life-threatening cancer. This time it was a big ugly tumor in my colon. Before agreeing to anything, I had a few questions for the doctor who would be performing the surgery. Ann and I looked him up and we were satisfied with his credentials; but other concerns were important to me: I asked him if he believed in God. He seemed puzzled by the question and wanted to know why I would ask such a thing.

I said, "I don't want a surgeon who thinks he is God or feels he does not need the guidance of God to perform an operation." After he assured me that he was a man of faith, I asked if he had grandchildren. When he said yes, I knew he'd understand that I did not want to be in the hospital during the time my first grandchild was due to be born. After those issues were settled, I agreed to have him perform the surgery—after Christmas.

So, I celebrated the rest of the holiday season at home and happily received the news of the birth of my first grandson. As I tried to prepare myself for the operation, I realized I'd been in preparation for a long period of time, because I clung to the belief that God's hand was directing my life—even though there were times when I was not obedient. Often, on my way to and from work I would pray, "God, I want to be closer to You than I ever have been." I also wanted to stop the habit of smoking. I knew it was causing havoc to my body, which I recognized was created by God as a physical container that houses my soul and spirit and other eternal aspects of life, like my will and my conscience. After all, I Corinthians 6:20 says you should glorify God in your body. "I want to be the person You created me to be," I often prayed. "A person more like You."

How does this relate to the House of Angels? Well, about four months before I realized I had the colon cancer, a curious thing happened. While we were in a Bible study at a pastor's house, I lost track of the discussion that was going on because I heard a message to, "Put a cross on the ledge in the woods behind your house." It was loud and clear, and it wasn't coming from any of the people in the room.

"What?" I murmured, feeling kind of startled.

"Put a cross on the ledge in the woods behind your house," repeated the voice that only I could hear. I felt overwhelmed. To have heard it once was kind of weird, but to hear it a second time? It was hard to focus on the discussion going on amongst the other people in the room. I didn't say anything about it until Ann and I were in the car and on our way home. We hadn't driven far when I said, "I have something to tell you, hon."

"Yeah?" she said. "What?"

I was both excited and hesitant. I wasn't sure what she would think, and to be honest, I wasn't sure what I thought about it myself; but I had to tell her. "At the Bible study tonight," I said, "I was told to put a cross up on the ledge in the woods. Up behind the house. I'm pretty sure it was God." At that point I thought, *Now I think I know how Noah felt when he explained to his wife that God told him to build a boat in the desert where it never rained.*

"What ledge?" she asked, and I told her it was about 200 yards or so up in the woods, just beyond where the dirt road on our property circles around. "Oh, the hillside. It has so much dirt and brush, I didn't realize it was a ledge," she said. After a brief discussion about the message, I was amazed for a second time that night—instead of snickering and telling me I was nuts, Ann said "Well, I guess you'd better do it then, if God told you to do it."

Just like that! She didn't question it. But I questioned it. For several months, actually—right up to the time the test revealed that I had the colon cancer; and, for several months after that, I asked over and over, "Why, God? Why would You want me to put a cross up there where no one would be likely to see it? Will a deer hunter come to it and be saved?" And as I thought about this, I realized that, *yes, it would be worth it to erect a cross up there, even if it helped to lead just one person to God and ultimately to his or her salvation.*

So, now, a few months after receiving that message, there we were: my wife, one of my sons, David, and I, sitting in the car in the hospital parking lot. It was almost time to have major surgery to have part of my colon and that big ugly tumor removed. Of course, we prayed. And I admit, I smoked a cigarette. My last cigarette, because, when I snuffed it out, I quit. Cold turkey. After all, I knew it was important to take better care of God's vessel—the body He had given to me. Ann and David were both fighting the tears, trying to control their fears, but I was telling myself that I'd been in this position once before and God had protected me. I had to believe He would do so again.

It took about four hours and the operation was a success. But certain things had to happen in recovery to determine how long I would have to stay in the hospital. It took nine days. On one of those days when the surgeon came to see how I was progressing, I asked questions about the recovery and the after-effects of the surgery. He remarked how the staff in the hospital didn't look at me as being very sick at all. Even so, it was no picnic. It felt like forever and I had to remind myself the comforting hand of Christ was with me and was healing me.

Finally, after nine long, frustrating days, I was released and told that after two or three weeks I should return to the Cancer Unit to start receiving radiation and chemo treatments. They said I would need 30 radiation treatments and six months of chemo. So, I went home, my recovery progressed, and I started to gain a little in strength and stamina. Before I knew it, the time had come to begin the prescribed treatments. I was scheduled to start both the chemo and the radiation on the same day.

I had received some orientation about how these things would be done and how they would affect me, but it still was hard to accept the fact that my health immediately started to decline. I mean, the next few days were unbearable! Before the time came for the second set of treatments, I was going into the bathroom about 60 or 70 times a day, thinking it was for bowel movements. It was the closest thing I would ever experience to match what a woman must feel when she's having painful contractions while giving birth. I really suffered! On top of this, I spent several hours each day between the trips, in the bathtub, trying to sooth and comfort my body with hot, hot water. I really didn't know how I would be able to continue to cope with the total lack of energy. Not to mention the pain. All I could do was lay on the couch between the tormenting contractions that led me to the bathroom and/or the tub.

While this was going on, one big blessing was the companionship of one of our cats. Mr. Mistoffelees. He was a big fluffy black part-Coon cat, and he was my constant companion for most of the time when I was suffering. Ann and I have been blessed with special pets. Lucas, our dog, and our cats, Mister, LucyLou and LillyGirl, never ceased to provide comfort and peace for the two of us. No wonder—for the Bible says that when God created animals, He said He was pleased!

If Mister could talk, he might have mentioned a strange thing I did one day. At least it was probably strange to him and most likely it would have seemed strange to non-believers as well. We had set up a bed in the living room, so I could watch TV and not feel isolated throughout the recuperation. Being a cat, Mister was quite happy to stay next to me on the bed and do nothing but snuggle and sleep. At one point, my eyes were scanning the room when they rested on the front door and the angel that was hanging above it. The angel, having golden wings and a flowing green and burgundy dress, had been a Christmas present from Ann's eldest daughter, Elizabeth. When my eyes shifted downward, to the door frame, I thought about a conversation I'd had with a Greek man from my past. I had worked for him and his wife for many years and had come to be very fond of them both.

I was thinking back to the day when he told me how the Greeks would scratch a cross over their door, so the Devil or other evil entities could not enter. At the time, I thought it was just a superstition. I asked him how it could keep the evil ones out since there are windows they could enter through. He explained the belief they would only enter a building or a room through doorways—like humans. He said it was considered a great protection against the harm they could inflict upon you. So, as I lay there, I thought, *Why not?* I was feeling like evil had invaded my body and I wanted to do something. Anything! So, despite my weak condition—and Mister's disapproving glare for being disturbed yet again—I got up and scratched a cross on the door frame above the front door and above the back door. As I did so, I recalled the story about the Passover in the Book of Exodus in the Bible, when the Israelites who were still in Egypt, were told to smear lamb's blood on the sides and tops of their doors so their first-born male children and animals would be protected when the angel of death passed by. As I recall this, I am reminded that I was the first-born son in my family.

I cannot say these crosses have helped or not helped my household, but there have been many times in my home since then when I've felt blessed with the presence of the Lord.

Despite the comfort I received from Mister's soft warm body each day as he snuggled next to me, I still suffered terribly. Just prior to returning to the hospital for the third chemo and radiation treatments, I told Ann I didn't want to continue the radiation. Since the first treatment, I could feel that my strength and stamina were greatly declining. The removal of the lower intestinal tract had caused stomach acid to be released, creating a painful irritation that was like a diaper rash. It had become so raw and red, it bled. I tried ointments and anything and everything we could think of, but nothing helped to relieve the pain and discomfort. And then, there were the horrific contractions. Unbearable! I was only getting about two hours of sleep each day and I knew I was dying. I was sure it was caused by the treatments.

I remember at one point in the tub, I said, "Thank you, Lord. Thank you for the pain." And when I felt compelled to say it again, I began to wonder, *what is wrong with me? Are both ends gone—my butt and my head?* But I did understand I was being led through this process for a purpose. A few months later the purpose would become clear: I was going through the illness and the pain, so I might better understand what Jesus did for me—and to have greater compassion for others who are sick; but it took a while to understand the message that water heals.

Each day I grappled with the question: should I continue the treatments or not? Well, I decided against radiation. Of course, the medical staff tried to convince me to continue those treatments. They spent about 30 to 40 minutes, insisting it was in my best interest to receive the radiation. But I said, "No, I am not going to continue this," and they finally gave up on that and told me to go across the hall to receive the chemo treatment. As I started toward the chemo area, I was told, "You don't need this, either."

What?

I questioned the message, but I heard it loud and clear a second time. "You don't need this, either." Well, I'm not a medical professional, and I certainly didn't know much about cancer, despite the experience I'd had with it. My first reaction was to wonder if it was God or the Devil telling me this, so, I decided to accept the chemo treatment that day; and I thought, *if this message is from the Devil, he should get lost!* But I qualified my reaction by thinking, *if it's truly a message from You, Lord, I need confirmation!*

After the third chemo treatment, I told the doctor I might not want to continue with it, either. He very strongly advised against that decision and suggested that I set up an appointment for the next session and plan to come back for it; but if I still wanted to decline the treatment, I could. So, I went home and wondered, *what should I do? I had that message to put a cross up on the ledge behind the house—which I had not done—and now, the same voice is telling me I'm to say no to medical treatment.*

I had asked for confirmation, so I decided to wait to see if it would come. One day went by and nothing happened. Another day, and nothing. But on the third day? It came in the mail—it really did! Our mailman delivered a video tape about cancer, chemo therapy, radiation treatments, and faith. It had been sent by a cousin I had not seen nor spoken to for almost six years. The doctor in the video said chemo and radiation are not always the best choices. I took it to be the confirmation I had asked for.

I talked with Ann about it and we both agreed the film had to be a sign from God—a message to also stop the chemo—but she said it was my choice. She would not push me in either direction. So, after making the decision to refuse the chemo, we went back for the appointment and the first words that came out of my mouth were, "The Lord told me not to do this anymore, so I will not be continuing the chemo treatments."

The doctor looked at me as if I was crazy. He insisted the treatment would only help. I told him what I had seen in the film and it made sense to me; but most of all, I said I was going to listen to Christ. The doctor did not try to push me into taking the chemo that day, but he asked me to make an appointment to be tested in the months to come to see if there was a sign of cancer. While I felt there was no real need to check for the presence of cancer, I did agree to the test. I believed it would be important for men (like my doctor) to see that my faith in Christ would overcome the disease. On the way home, I wondered how the next few days would go. After all, I was still very weak, and I was still suffering terribly.

Three days later something had changed. I awoke to discover the pain and discomfort were gone; but I still wondered what the rest of the day would bring. After all, on the first two days after saying no to the chemo, the contractions had continued. But, on this third day? The contractions stopped and the trips down the hall dropped from 60 or 70 times to just two or three per day. Praise Jesus!

My mother had come from Massachusetts to visit while I was in the hospital and she had also visited a couple of times after I returned home. She said she wanted to be informed about any changes in my condition, whether they were big changes or small, painful or recuperative; so, I thought I should give her a call. It had been on my mind throughout the cancer ordeal that she had lost my brother David while he was serving in the military, and she had said she did not want to live long enough to lose another child. You can imagine how great it would be for her to realize I was feeling so much better. After hearing my voice for only a few seconds, she exclaimed, "You're better, aren't you? I can tell."

"Yes," I said. "On the third day after saying no to the chemo and yes to God, I knew I'd been miraculously healed!"

DECISIONS: "Show me your ways, Oh Lord, teach me your paths; guide me in your truth and teach me, for you are God, my Savior, and my hope is in You all day long." PSALM 25:4, 5

DON'S NOTE: We should always seek God's wisdom first in any big decision. I am so grateful that this is one lesson I learned during my topsy-turvy life

CHAPTER 4

Basking in Wellness

For the first part of the day when I realized I was healed, I just sat around crying with relief, thanking God and basking in my wellness; but, it didn't take long before I remembered the message I'd received at the Bible study several months before: to put a cross up on the ledge behind our home. I now had the strength to start doing it and I knew I had to be obedient; so, that afternoon, I began to shovel my way into the snowbank at the bottom end of our driveway. The snowbank was blocking access to the dirt road that led up to the site that included the ledge. As I shoveled the snow, I recalled this was the third day since I chose to follow God's direction, and the number three was an important number in a Biblical sense. Three in the Hebrew text means resurrection. And, here I was, on the third day after refusing treatments—and having faith in God—feeling as if I'd been resurrected to a healthy life.

I couldn't believe the strength I'd regained—the strength to lift a shovel full of snow, never mind the second, third, and many more that were to follow. I did not spend a lot of time at it that day, but I did make a surprising dent in the snowbank, all the while feeling amazed at the strength God had given back to me. It was only the day before this, that I lay on the couch with Mister, unable to do anything but make my way to and from the bathroom . . . over-and-over again.

The next day I arose, once again feeling better than the day before. Once again realizing I had been healed from the pain. And as I proceeded to work on the snowbank, I praised Jesus, overwhelmed with emotion, in tears because of God's mercy, love and grace. I was truly anxious to accomplish what I had been told to do.

As I labored to remove the snowbank, I wondered about a message I'd received while I was sitting in the tub, hoping for relief. I was told, "Water heals." It was a persistent message. "Water heals. Water heals." *What does it mean?* I wondered hundreds of times. All I had prayed for was that Christ would forgive me and that I would receive salvation through Him. Despite my experience with the melanoma, I hadn't even thought about being healed this time—convinced I would surely die from my second cancer—the pain was so great. And to be honest, in my ignorance of the Bible, I didn't know about the healings that can be found in the Good Book.

On the third day when I was making my way through the snowbank to gain access to the ledge where the cross would go, I still didn't understand why I was supposed to erect a cross up in the woods. I asked questions as I worked, and I remember telling God, "I'm being obedient! I'm doing it!" but I could not help but wonder, *what is it to be for, God? It's so far in the woods.* The only answer I could come up with was the possibility that a hunter might see the cross and be saved. We have almost 15 acres and people do hunt here. Despite the questions, I continued to work and said, "Lord, although I don't understand this, I'll continue to obey."

On the seventh day of shoveling, I found myself about a hundred feet from the ledge. There were trees everywhere. "Trees, trees and more trees," I muttered as I realized I'd need a chainsaw. *Time to feel like Noah again,* I thought when I approached Ann.

"I think I need to go out and buy a chainsaw," I said. "It's time to start cutting trees to clear the area in front of the ledge."

"Well, if that's what you need, then go and get one," Ann replied. This was the beginning of seeking her approval on many facets of the development of the House of Angels. And although to say we did not have an abundance of money was a huge understatement, she always said yes to whatever was needed for the site.

I soon got busy cutting the trees. Each day feeling astounded that so soon after so much suffering, I was able to do this work. Some of the trees were 50 feet tall and 12 inches across! I cut them into 20-foot lengths and managed to maneuver them out of the way to a place where they could be chunked for firewood or be discarded.

After a couple of weeks of this strenuous labor, I realized I would soon be able to return to work for my employer. It was late spring, and I did return to my job; but I also continued to work on the House of Angels each night when I returned home, and on weekends. For years, from early spring until late fall, without taking any time off, I felt compelled to develop the site. There were stumps to pull, boulders to move, soil to loosen and enrich, statuary to be set in place, and of course, flowers and shrubs to plant. I'm still amazed that I was able to do it and that Ann was so agreeable. I mean, for us, vacations were unheard of and she asked for very little. I was simply driven by a need to work on the site and to serve God who had blessed me so greatly.

No matter how hard I pushed, throughout all the months and years I struggled with the manual labor, it did not seem like drudgery. But eventually I realized I would need heavy excavation equipment. I couldn't accomplish what I had visualized for the site without heavy equipment or more help to pull stumps and perform the more strenuous duties that often are required with big landscaping projects. When I showed the area to my friend, Roscoe Jones, I asked him, "How am I ever going to do this?" He replied, "You're already doing it, Don. Look, you've cleared almost an acre of wooded land already. By yourself! It's incredible considering what you felt like just a short time ago!" On those nights when the completion of the site seemed impossible, I'd been buoyed by his words and by the knowledge that God had given me the image of what was to be accomplished. As I think of this, I get goosebumps and I can't help but remember one of my favorite phrases about faith and one's goals: "His will. Not mine."

It was amazing to realize I had been able to clear the site that first year. I mean, that's a lot of trees, but there were problems with the project: Mother Nature had a way of adding roadblocks; the trees and shrubs grew back. I had worked a lot of overtime hours at my job to get enough money to pay for things I needed for the sanctuary, so, I couldn't keep up with everything. And then, one year, my mother had a stroke and came to live with us over the summer months. It's not an overstatement to say she needed care 24/7. Ann's job at the radio station required her to be live, on the air every day with interviews, so most of the care of my mother was left to me. And, of course, Mother Nature was at it again. To make a long story short, before the site was truly cleared and ready for the final plantings and other aesthetic additions, I cleared that acre of land three times—including hundreds of saplings that had to be clipped and reclipped!

Despite these setbacks, I was not going to quit. I was determined to do as God had directed!

You might ask how the name, House of Angels, came about. Many pastors refer to their churches as the house of the Lord, but, I had always looked to nature, the Earth and the out of doors beneath the stars as being the house the Lord had provided for us since the time of Adam and Eve. The angels came into the picture on December 18th, the day I had the colonoscopy and was diagnosed with the colon cancer. Our friend, Linda Nye Knowlton, who lived a few miles away who knew I had gone for the colonoscopy, realized it was a serious situation. She had driven to our house to see if we had returned home. When she reached our property, she saw an amazing sight, but realizing that we had not yet returned, she headed back to her own home. Half way there, she recognized our car, but she decided not to turn around—she'd call us instead. So, she continued her way home. And called us right away.

Ann answered the phone and listened as Linda described the experience she'd had on her trip to our driveway. "I've never seen so many angels, Ann," she said. Ann thought she meant Christmas decorations in the form of angels along the road. After all, Christmas was just around the corner. But when I got on the phone, I realized what she meant. She had seen angels hovering over our property! With a voice filled with amazement, she said, "There were angels all around your property, Don. Real angels! Hundreds of them and it's a very good sign! You're truly blessed, you two."

My belief that this earth was given to the first man and woman to be their home, coupled with our friend's report of the presence of the angels, brought us to the decision to name the site Christ's House of Angels.

THE WILL OF GOD: "Trust in the Lord with all your heart and lean not on your own understanding; in all your ways acknowledge Him, and He will make your paths straight." Proverbs 3:5-6

DON'S NOTE: One thing about these last several years? I've learned to obey while not understanding God's reason for me to do whatever He asked of me. I had to trust that He has given me the strength to do His work.

Some of the crew who helped to raise the cross at Christ's House of Angels.
Left to right: Dana Jones, Leo Fowler, Rick Jones, Roscoe Jones, Chad Jones, and founder, Don Duncan.

CHAPTER 5

Serpents in the Dirt!

The days were flying by. I felt stronger and healthier with each week that passed and had gone back to work. And each night when I came home, I spent as much time as possible up back, clearing the land and preparing the site; but there was no cross yet. It was about the middle of summer when I felt the need to get one up on the ledge. At that point, it had to be a temporary one.

The desire to get a cross up was intense. I wanted to do what God had told me to do. After all, He had said to put up a cross on that ledge. Another reason? I wanted to have one up for Bryan Anthony Tressler, the son of two members of the church we were attending in 2007. He was in his early teens, suffering from a deadly childhood cancer that had first been diagnosed when he was only about five years old. His parents, Bob and Mary Lou were wonderful people. Strong believers. And I thought that putting up the temporary cross would be a focal point to pray more intensely for his healing.

Bryan was a very special young boy who melted the hearts of everyone he met. His courage and his fearless way of facing his disease were inspirational for scores of people throughout our region. Most children who face the form of cancer that Bryan had been diagnosed with, did not survive into their teens; but he would not let it keep him down. He loved to participate in outdoor winter sports and showed a growing creative skill by creating an ever-growing miniature Christmas village—with moving parts, no less. Bryan's life and courage were an inspiration right up to his sudden death in 2007, and his parents' faith and ability to cope with his condition and allow him to live as full a life as possible, were no less than extraordinary.

Not only did Bryan's life make a huge impact on the people he dealt with during his life—he played an integral role in my witness at the House of Angels. One day while I was working on the site, I was feeling immensely sad. It was shortly after Bryan passed. I thought, *why, God. Why did You tell me a few weeks before this that he would be healed—and then take him from us so suddenly? I received Your message so clearly!* As I was pondering this, I felt a presence at the site and when I turned, I saw the most wondrous vision one could possibly hope to see. I saw transparent silhouettes of a boy with a larger adult figure. I knew instantly that it was Bryan and he was with Jesus! The joy they exuded was far beyond any earthly joy I could ever witness in life. It was clear to me that Jesus was showing me that Bryan had received the ultimate healing.

Shortly after that I realized that I needed to tell Bob and Mary Lou that I had felt Bryan's presence and that they should know that their son did receive the greatest healing of all. Shortly after that, Bob and Mary Lou came up to the site and I told them about seeing Bryan and Jesus. During that visit, they told me that a few weeks before he died, a person from the church also received a message that Bryan would be healed and told them about it. But after his passing, they were concerned that they had given the Tresslers false hope. As I recall the experience, I hope my witness gave Bryan's parents comfort.

That first summer the temporary cross was firmly planted on the top of the cliff, but I was anxious to put a final one in place. It would be made from two solid pieces from a Hemlock tree I had cut down because it swayed in the wind and was too close to our home. Cutting that tree was a dangerous, labor intensive project. It was a massive tree and there was only about eight feet between it and our home, so I had to use some ingenuity like laying down logs to use as rollers to pull it between our home and the storage trailer out back, inching it out foot-by-foot with my Jeep Comanche.

Steve Schinski, a neighbor who had a wood-mill on his property agreed to cut and fashion the logs from the Hemlock into both the upright and crosspiece. The logs were massive. I couldn't wait to get the finished pieces back. But, of course, I did have to wait. And wait ... for several months. But, finally, the pieces were delivered. Soon after that happy fall day, I had to figure out how to get them up to the site and assemble them. The upright piece was 25 feet long and the cross arms stretched out about 14 feet. It was October and I realized I did not know many people in the area who would be willing to help. Most of my time had been spent working alone up back or at my job, so I thought I'd have to wait until the spring. After all, I reasoned, it could snow at any time; but as it turned out, I guess God did not want to hear any more excuses.

One day, when I prepared to take a shower, I was thinking about all the reasons why I had to put off setting up the cross, and I heard, 'By the pagan holiday'. I wondered if it was my own thought and said to myself, "I really don't see how I can do that," and got into the tub. Then, as the water started to flow, I heard those four words again. "By the pagan holiday." I once again pondered the message, convinced it was my own desire to get the permanent cross up before Halloween; but when I pulled the shower curtain aside and stepped out of the tub, I knew it was not my own thought. The mirror in our bathroom, which measures about three feet by four feet, was covered with steam—except for the image of a cross that glistened on it. Spanning about 18 inches, it was hard to miss this visual message. "Alright," I said with determination. "I'll get it done ... somehow."

After telling Ann about it and thinking about it for a while, I made plans to rent a gas-powered jackhammer to break into the top of the ledge. After all, a hole would have to be drilled deep enough into the ledge to support such a heavy load. That weekend, I studied the area, hoping to find the perfect spot for the hole. After choosing what appeared to be the best spot, I realized it would be a good idea to remove the surface dirt by hand, so, I grabbed a shovel.

I still shiver with goosebumps at the thought of that first shovelful of dirt. It was solid dirt and it contained a snake! I could barely believe it when a snake emerged from the dirt I'd cast aside. It was eerie! I'd done a lot of digging for construction jobs, and in my own yard and gardens, and I had never dug a snake out of a solid mass of dirt. And then? I took a second shovel of dirt and cast it onto the same pile and a second snake slithered out! What a freaky thing for someone like me: I absolutely do not like snakes or what they represent. And, if that wasn't enough, the next three shovels of dirt each contained a snake. I accidentally killed one of them with a shovel. As you can imagine, I was really freaked and yelled, "Okay, Devil. I don't like you, and I don't like snakes and I don't like the number six and I'm not going to dig up a sixth snake. And, you're not going to stop me from putting the cross up!"

So, I moved over about a foot and a half and held my breath as I sunk the shovel once again into the dirt on top of the ledge. *Great! No snakes!* I managed to clear enough dirt off the area, so I could get busy with the jackhammer; but first, I just had to go down and tell Ann about the slithering serpents I had dug up. She quickly came up to the ledge to see the snake I had killed, and I was glad she would be able to corroborate my story. After all, who'd believe I dug snakes out of solid dirt? I barely believed it myself!

Help did arrive, thanks to my friend Roscoe Jones. He brought his sons, family members and friends to help get the cross pieces up to the top of the ledge. They were so massive, it took eight men to carry them up. A fellow church goer and the pastor of our church also showed up that day and offered their help. All I can say is, "Thank you God for bringing them all to me!" There's no way I could have done it myself.

OBEDIENCE: "Have I not commanded you? Be strong and courageous. Do not be terrified; do not be discouraged, for the Lord your God will be with you wherever you go." Joshua 1:9

DON'S NOTE: I think the evil one wanted me to give up when he put those snakes in my shovel! I don't like to deal with snakes, but I knew I was working for God, and I was determined to put up that cross, no matter what the Devil threw at me! To this day I believe the Devil tries to stop me from accomplishing the things I know God wants me to do. But God often uses what is bad for good purposes—and it took some time, but I eventually noticed that by moving the cross over a short distance, I was placing it next to three pointed outcroppings of rock that I later came to recognize as representing the Father, Son and Holy Spirit. I am so glad I did not break them off as originally planned

CHAPTER 6
The Power of Faith

I was glad the permanent cross was in place; but thoughts of erecting it bring back memories of Bryan's cancer and some of the health troubles one of my own sons had experienced. One incident was very memorable. My boy was only about eight years old when he had a bad cold. I was giving him a bath, getting him ready for a visit to the doctor when I noticed one of his feet was covered with warts. I'd seen a few warts on his foot over the past year or so, and occasionally asked if they bothered him. He'd always said no; but now I was really concerned: his foot seemed to be covered with them and some were bigger. This time when I asked if they hurt or bothered him, he admitted they did. I made a mental note to ask the doctor about the warts; but I also said a prayer, asking God to please heal my son from this condition, or at least to ease the discomfort.

With a reassuring smile, the pediatrician told me what to do about my son's cold and asked if I had any questions or other concerns. I told him about the warts. "His foot is covered with them," I said, reaching for his sneaker. "There must be a hundred or more."

"Let's have a look," he said, and off came the sneaker. After a few seconds to indulge my boy with a playful kick and grab game, I carefully peeled off the sock and stared. You can imagine how

The Power Of Faith

surprised and puzzled I felt: the warts were gone! I could not see a single wart on his foot! The doctor's eyebrows arched upwards as he looked back at me. My face grew a few shades brighter as I studied the little wartless foot: I was sure the doctor thought I had made it up.

Thoughts of my son's warts bring me even further back in time, to my own experience with one wart. I was about 14 years old; and at that age, of course, I was self-conscious: especially since this one was big and ugly, and it was on my hand where other kids could see it and pester me about it. After all, your hands are always visible.

I spent most of that summer with my grandparents at their home in Maine. My grandfather was a wise man, and he seemed to have an answer for everything. Even warts, as it turned out. When I showed him my ugly wart, he said to break off a piece of milkweed and rub it on it. He said I had to do it every day; and if I believed it would work, the wart would be gone by the end of summer.

"You have to believe it'll work," he stressed. "Belief's important—if you want results."

I was determined to get rid of that unsightly bump on my hand, so I agreed to try the milkweed remedy. Day after day, I found a milkweed plant and rubbed a piece of it all over the area; but then, there was one day when I forgot to do it. I thought the reward of healing was suddenly out of reach; so, I ran to tell my grandfather how I messed up. He said, "Don't worry. It's okay to slip up, or forget once in a while, as long as you didn't deliberately try to get out of doing it." Then he looked me in the eye and asked, "You still believe it'll work, right?"

My head bobbed up and down and I said, "Yes." *After all*, I thought, *I know I wasn't being lazy or thoughtless*. I immediately felt better, and promised to keep up with the milkweed treatment every day after that—and you know what? By the end of summer, the wart was gone! I believe this was one of my first lessons regarding faith and sin. With the right attitude and not letting a bump in the road become more than a mere bump in the road, we can be successful. Especially if we hold on to our faith and repent.

DESTINATION D.C. A Modern-day Jonah?

The story didn't end with the disappearance of that wart—it reappeared over 25 years later, after my grandfather died. It brings tears to my eyes when I think about it. You see, as a young adult, I had been angry with him for quite a while. It meant a great deal to me that my grandfather believed in me but unfortunately, because of a misunderstanding, he seemed to have lost his belief in me as a person of good standing. It hurt. It truly hurt, and we had very little to say to one another for quite some time. He was on his deathbed and unconscious when I finally told him I forgave him. At the time, I didn't know if he understood or even heard what I was saying; but the wart came back after he died, and I accepted it as a sign, a message from heaven. You see, I believe in the spirit and that sometimes God sends messages to individuals through the spirit, messages that are meaningful and personal. The re-emergence of the wart was a reminder of a lesson learned about faith, a personal reminder that only I could understand. I had been so concerned that my grandfather had not heard me say I had forgiven him, it was emotionally debilitating. By reappearing, the wart awakened memories of the lesson my grandfather taught me about going forward in faith. And somehow it helped me to believe he had heard me and knew I had forgiven him and still loved him. That wart pretty much disappeared again a short time later; but to this day, there is a slight trace of it that is barely visible—just enough to be a constant reminder of the love I shared with my grandfather, and not enough to be an ugly blemish.

Thoughts of my own childhood herald in memories of children I've known. And one memory still gives me chills down my arm. Good chills! But, wow, if I only knew then what I know now, perhaps I'd have traveled a straighter path toward following God's ways. It happened while I was charged with watching a 1 & ½-year-old toddler. A cute kid. And as I watched him do what toddlers do, I wondered about his future and what role I might play in his life; for I truly loved this little boy and as he played, I recalled a scene from the movie series, "Roots."

A slave in the scene I was remembering, went outside with a baby boy one night and held him high over his head, under a star-lit sky, saying, "Behold the only thing greater than yourself." The stars were shining brightly outside my living room window just as they had in the scene from the movie. Now, at that time of my life I was working as a mason and my foreman was a pastor who had been somewhat of an influence on me. He often talked about Christ and His mercy and grace and the blessings He brings to us. Although decades would pass before it became a reality, those talks were effective enough to cause me to consider becoming a pastor or minister myself; and on that starlit night, I had the sudden desire to re-enact the scene from "Roots."

It was the powerful love and concern I had for this boy that drove me to take him outside to ask that he be protected and made safe. I had some comprehension that, perhaps, if someone saw me holding such a young child high over my head out on the front lawn late at night, they might get the wrong idea—so I hastened out to the back yard. Moments later I took a deep breath, lifted him high over my head toward the star-skittered sky and said, "Behold the only thing greater than yourself." And then I said, "God of the heavens, the universe and the sky, keep this boy safe and protected."

What a feeling! To be standing under the stars, knowing they were created by a great, loving God with unlimited, unbelievable power. Knowing in that moment that this Creator, this Benevolent Being, loved me. Me! And He loved this little boy! Overwhelmed, I pulled him back into a tight, teary hug. I stood in silence then, not wanting to break the spellbinding awareness of the vastness above us and the unknown possibilities that lay before us.

Time passed, day-to-day life took over and I never did tell anyone about my Roots re-enactment. In fact, for decades I never gave it a thought. I had seen this boy from time to time and continued to care about and love him even though it was from a distance. But one day, many years later, my mother came to say he had enlisted in the military and was probably going to be deployed to Haiti during a serious conflict. Not even remembering my re-enactment from the scene of Roots, I prayed for him. It was more than a prayer that I undertook then—it was more like begging God to please, please, protect this young man, and keep him safe.

Many years passed again before I was able to talk with him. It was after he left the military. I went to his house and he told

DESTINATION D.C. A Modern-day Jonah?

me something incredible. He said, "While I was in the service, I jumped out of a plane at 800 feet and my shoot didn't open."

"What? What do you mean your shoot didn't open?" I stammered, and he repeated his astonishing news with a dull utterance that belied his own amazement. "My shoot didn't open."

"What did you do? How did you . . ." my voice faded. I couldn't get the word "survive" out. And before I could finish my astonished response, he said he did what they told him to do in training. He said, "They told us all, if our shoots failed to open, we should just do what we'd do if we fell on any other occasion. You just must hit the ground and roll."

"How bad were you hurt? How many bones did you break? How can you still be alive and talking to me?"

"I just had a slight concussion and I got up and walked to my troop. They were about two miles away."

He also revealed to me that he and his wife had not been able to have children. They'd tried several times to be parents through artificial insemination and he said it was the third time at this point and they didn't yet know if it was successful. They expected to be finding out in a week or two, so I asked him, "Give me a call and let me know what happens, will you?" He said he would.

While I didn't really expect to hear from him, I did receive a call a couple of weeks later. He said, "I'm calling to tell you we got the results and we're still not expecting a child." I told him I was sorry, and hoped they'd get better results in the future; but he said they weren't going to be able to do it anymore. The process was just too expensive.

I often pray and talk to God and listen to religious stations while I'm in the car. And at that time, I did so each day as I drove to and from work. And the day after I heard the discouraging report from that young man, I recalled my sadness that he and his wife could not have children. But I also remembered God had said we were to go forth and multiply. So, after remembering that, I prayed, "God . . . let that be for this young couple. After all, those are Your words!"

The Power Of Faith

The days continued to come and go, and after a couple of months passed, I received a very happy call! He said, "My wife has conceived! We're going to have a baby!" They ended up having a healthy baby girl and as the years passed, they were blessed with three more children.

I believe God had heard my prayer. And answered it.

It was a few years later when I thought about the story that young man had told me about his parachute not opening, and I finally recalled the time I had brought him outside, lifted him to the sky, and asked God to protect and keep him safe. It was incredible. I thought, no wonder he had survived that perilous fall. It had been arranged many years before, and God was faithful to answer all those heartfelt prayers. Thank you, God. Praise You Jesus!

Ever since that memory returned, I wanted so badly to have a prayerful service under the stars at the House of Angels. So, after my Heal America Walk, we held a singalong service at night. It was especially incredible because our guests were camping out overnight and the weather forecast predicted rain, lots of it, but as we huddled under a dreary sky in front of the fire, one star appeared, then another, and then we suddenly found ourselves singing and praising God beneath a beautiful starry sky.

GOD ANSWERS PRAYERS: This is the confidence we have in approaching God: that if we ask anything according to His will, He hears us. I John 5:14

DON'S NOTES: Sometimes we treat prayer as if it were a magic formula to get whatever we want. But an important part of prayer is discerning God's will and accepting His will. Our prayers should also include our gratitude for what we have, and for the sacrifice Jesus made for us. And to be thankful when God has granted our requests.

CHAPTER 7

Starting a Faith-based Life

One's journey into a life of faith often follows a path of ups and downs, with choices and the results of those choices. Sometimes we persevere and grow, like I did with my wart. Sometimes we give up and we fail. And sometimes, a couple grows together, even during troubled times. It helps if you are equally yoked in faith, and that's what I was hoping for regarding my marriage to Ann which took place in May of 1994, in Massachusetts.

At that time, she was not a churchgoer, nor had I been for quite a long time. I did go occasionally throughout my adult years, but my attendance at Sunday services was sporadic. And, I knew very little about the Bible. As a boy, I truly had fallen in love with Christ, but when I got into my teens, I strayed from Him. I thought I was going to kick the world's butt—however, like many others in this world, I found it was my butt that would be kicked. As mere humans, we don't always realize we do not have the power within ourselves to maintain, sustain or direct our lives in the right manner and so we fall into trials and tribulations when we don't make the right choices.

But, getting back to the start of our venture into a faith-based life: soon after Ann and I were married, I began to remember the love I'd had for Christ during my youth; I yearned to resurrect those

Starting A Faith-based Life

feelings of faith; and, naturally, I wanted my new wife to feel the same way. However, while I did not know much about the Bible, I did remember that you should not push anyone into Christianity, so I secretly prayed that she'd become interested at least in going to church. I believe if you pray for something with a righteous heart, God answers your prayers, and I was quite hopeful for this prayer to be answered.

It didn't take long.

After the ceremony, I moved into Ann's house in Williamstown, Massachusetts. Her three daughters, Elizabeth, Alison, and Johanna were friendly and curious and welcoming but just a little wary. We did seem to fall into a family routine; and a couple of weeks later, I quit my job to join my new wife in building up her business. She had created The Snack Box, an honor-system vending service before we met; but she was struggling to get more customers so the business could support the family. And then, soon after I joined her in running The Snack Box, she was inspired by one of my aunts to create a second business—making cinnamon ornaments. Suddenly we were running two money-making ventures! One too many we soon realized, so we decided to sell The Snack Box and focus on the newer effort called, Simply Cinnamon. I was amazed at how easy it was to sell the gingerbread-type ornaments we were making. It was quickly becoming a successful enterprise.

Around this time, my prayer for Ann to develop a faith-based life was answered! We were in the car when she unexpectedly turned to me to say, "I was thinking, maybe we should start going to church: what do you think?" I was amazed. And happy. Of course, I said, "Yes." So, we soon took a tiny step in the right direction. She became active with the local Methodist Church and before long, she had designed a special cinnamon ornament in honor of the church's anniversary celebration.

We were putting an extraordinary amount of time into the business and it had a great deal of potential. Still, there was a financial strain—a big strain, actually—and right in the middle of these worries, Ann received sad phone calls from two of her brothers. She says it was one of the worst weeks in her life.

Her brother, Jim called, saying their mother had to be put into a nursing home. During exploratory surgery due to internal bleeding, she had been found to be so full of cancer the doctors were not going to try chemo or radiation: they were just going to ease her pain. And she was showing signs of dementia. A day later, Ann's brother, Bruce called. He said their father just received news that he had an aggressive form of lung cancer. It was more important than ever to find time to spend with them, but it wasn't easy—we were too far away.

We had been putting a hundred hours or more into Simply Cinnamon each week, working at home and at the plant, plus we were trying to make time for family; and while my son, David and Ann's two oldest daughters, Elizabeth and Alison had all entered college within a couple of years after our wedding, her youngest daughter, Johanna, was still with us. Then, during the same week when Ann learned about her parents' plight, we suffered an unexpected financial loss connected to the business. Her heart was no longer with it. We were going to have to move; and to top off all of that, Johanna did not want to move to a new town in Vermont or upstate New York and decided to live with her father in Rhode Island. Before we knew it, almost everything was gone; the house, the business, furniture, and even our youngest daughter. And so, we moved what was left of our meager belongings to Vermont.

Ann says I was her rock. She is not afraid to admit that she retreated emotionally. How can you blame her? She was feeling a sense of loss on so many fronts and she was also struggling with her own chronic, painful illnesses—three of which had not yet been diagnosed. Basically, we both decided it would be best to be closer to her parents who were living in upstate New York, not far from Lake Champlain.

We had searched for affordable housing in New York and Vermont within an hour or two of Elizabethtown where her mom's nursing home was. Affordable housing? We didn't know what we'd be able to afford, or even how we were going to secure an income.

And, we both desperately wanted to keep our animals: Lucas, our amazing white German shepherd, and the family of black cats, including Mister Mestofelees, LucyLu, LillyGirl, and RoseyBud. The search seemed daunting. Totally impossible! But as we would discover—God had a plan. After searching for hours one day in Vermont—feeling like we had searched everywhere we could—we stopped at a small store near the town of Addison, where her brother Bruce lived. We picked up a newspaper to look for home listings that would suit our needs. And there it was!

"Hey, look at this," I said. "Here's one near Poultney that has two bedrooms. And it's out of town, so maybe they'll let us keep the animals."

"I hope so," Ann said, declaring that she would live in the car before giving them up.

It had been a long day and we were going to have to find it in the dark. We were tired and not familiar with the Poultney area; but, fortified with a drink and a sandwich, we agreed to try. Thank God it wasn't hard to find, and upon arriving we were pleased to see the place was clean and had a large yard—with no immediate neighbors. We asked if we could have animals and let the owner know about the dog and cats and he said it would be fine. We still thank the Lord for that, because Lucas saved Ann's life a few years later. While I was away, working for my employer on a temporary project in Maine, she had been attacked by a swarm of bees and the guys in the rescue squad said if Lucas had not thrown himself on top of her and brushed the bees away, she most likely would not have been able to reach the telephone to call for help soon enough. As it was, they had to make a stop half way to the hospital, so a police officer could intercept the ambulance and administer a shot: the squad members were from a nearby town in New York, and none of the guys on duty that day were certified to administer the shot within the state of Vermont. And one amazing thing about Lucas? He was so protective toward Ann, he would not let strangers anywhere near her, yet, when the rescue squad arrived, he was completely compliant and let them lock him in the house and take her away. Ann remembers that as she sat, feeling slightly woozy, waiting for help to arrive, she hugged her heroic dog and checked him for stings,

DESTINATION D.C. A Modern-day Jonah?

but he did not seem to have even one. He was fully functional and knew the crew was there to give her the help she needed!

When we checked out this new place and discovered the rent was doable, we asked if it was possible to get an option to buy the place. He did not render an immediate answer on that; but we did return soon after, to give a deposit and to make the first month's payment. After seeing the property in the daylight, we asked again about an option to buy. The owner said other people had asked for the same option, but he had refused. He said he just did not want to sell the place; yet, for whatever reason, he did agree to give us the option.

Eventually, thanks to some generous bonuses from my employer, we had been able to follow through with the option to purchase our home. Of course, we did not know the extent of God's plan when we first moved to this property. It was perfect for us in many ways and we know as we look back, it's because God was in charge.

We can see God's hand was surely at work! After all, He knew this property was destined to honor Him as the site of a wonderful outdoor sanctuary for prayer and healing! And, He was not just planting *us* here in this area. Over the course of the next few years, we met several people who said they had recently come from other regions of the country because God had directed them here. By the end of the first week of October in 1998, we were able to settle most of our legal and financial obligations in Massachusetts, Johanna had gone to live with her father, and we moved what few belongings we had, plus our pets, to Vermont at the property that was destined to include the House of Angels.

Shortly after the move, we started to attend a Methodist church in the area. A few months later I'd become quite comfortable with my job and Ann was hired by a local radio station. She did not expect to go on the air—but her experience with writing news stories and working within the realm of public relations helped her to ace the news-reading test. It didn't take long for her to become comfortable in front of a microphone; and she was soon asked to host the station's daily morning talk show. For about nine years she interviewed "people of interest," like politicians, educators, medical specialists, community leaders, and even a few artists and authors. Some of her guests were famous, including Gloria Vanderbilt, Governor Jim Douglas and Pulitzer Prize-winner Ron Powers.

One of Ann's on-air guests turned out to be the son of a woman she had worked with years ago. He was a pastor in a nearby town. Not even knowing that Ann was a former friend of his deceased mother, he asked to be a guest on her morning talk show. They soon realized the connection and with a desire to get to know his mother's old friend and of course a desire to bring a new couple into his church, he invited us to his home. We soon found ourselves attending an introductory, faith-based program he was organizing and before long we decided to attend his church. It was at his home during a Sunday night Bible study when I received the message to put the cross on the ledge. And it was in his church that Ann had her first experience with an evangelical type of worship. She says without the connection to the pastor's mom, she might not have been receptive to that form of worship; but she also adds she appreciated the fact that it was more about faith and a relationship with God, and less about religion and man-made rituals. Isn't it amazing how God leads us!

My mom enjoyed going to this church when she visited us, and after my cancer was miraculously healed her visits became more frequent. She also loved the fact that I was working on the creation of the House of Angels. Even at the age of 74, she helped as much as she was able to clear the site, removing small rocks and small armloads of brush. I know she was pleased to be able to help, if even a little, with the creation of a faith-based sanctuary. Over the next few years, as the site became more and more developed, and Ann and I had amazing experiences, I would see my mom marvel as she listened to our stories of witness. She was with us on the Sunday that we were baptized. Ann and I had agreed to the ceremony because Christ said we are to be born again as adults. After all, Christ himself was baptized by John the Baptist and in the Bible, He says we are to be like Him.

On the day of our baptism, the three of us attended church as usual, then went home to take care of a few things before heading to the lake where the ceremony would take place. On the way there, my mother couldn't contain herself. She said, "I have a surprise for you."

"What is it?" I said.

"I'm not telling you. You'll see when you see."

"Come on, mother. What is it?" I coaxed. And coaxed. And of course, she caved.

"Okay. I'll tell you: I'm going to be baptized today, too!"

She had spoken to the pastor, who agreed to keep it a secret. Of course, my mother had been baptized as a child, but she had never received the Holy Spirit as an adult. Had never been born again—until she was baptized with us!

I am so thankful that at the age of 74 my mother received baptism and was born again in the spirit, and that it had come during the stage of her life when she was still of sound mind and knew what she was doing. Soon after this, she had two major strokes that, sadly, brought confusion and hardship and memory loss. The second stroke was the worst. We were told she had a hole in her brain from a previous stroke and more damage from another one caused her speech to become greatly diminished. She was not able to be alone and needed to be transported back and forth to therapy. So, Ann and I brought her to Vermont to live with us. That's when Mother Nature sprouted more trees and sections of brush onto the cleared patch at the House of Angels. After about four months mother was able to once again live on her own. Her ability to speak was still a big problem and she could no longer drive a car. So, every other week for a couple of years one of us drove about an hour and a half to her apartment in Williamstown, Massachusetts to help with her shopping and errands and appointments with health care providers.

Eventually, my sister arranged for our mom to live closer to her near the Cape in Massachusetts. At that point, my sister obtained power of attorney and took care of most of my mom's needs and continued to do so until it was just too hard. After being placed in a nursing home, our mother's health declined and eventually took a turn for the worst. She was in a lot of pain and the time finally came when I realized she probably was not going to be around much longer.

The doctor was in her room one day when I stopped for a visit. She dozed off to sleep while he and I spoke, and I started to witness to him, explaining how I'd been healed of life-threatening cancer twice and how I had a healing gift and would be praying for my mom. We talked a little longer and he finally revealed a little about himself. He said he'd had a leg injury for quite some time. It created an indentation in the muscle of his leg and one of his feet was affected so he could not bend it in certain ways. As a result, he could not jog or run anymore, and he missed being able to do that.

"I miss it a lot," he said; and I said if he ever wanted me to pray for him, I would. "Just let me know when you want prayer, and I'll be there," I said. He surprised me by saying, "Right now would be a good time," so we both got down on our knees at the foot of my mother's bed and I prayed for him.

On my next visit a few weeks later, the doctor exclaimed that he was able to jog again; the indentation had disappeared and he had regained the ability to bend his foot! During that visit, he showed me something that I thought was great. "You – God – Me" was engraved on the back of his stethoscope. He said when he was with a patient, he was aware that they were not the only one's present: God was with them.

My mother died soon after that, but life in Vermont continued to go well.

BAPTISM: "Peter replied, "Repent and be baptized, every one of you, in the name of Jesus Christ for the forgiveness of your sins. And you will receive the gift of the Holy Spirit." Acts 2:38

DON'S NOTE: What a wonderful day it was, to be baptized along with my wife and my mother. I wasn't aware of the dramatic change that had occurred in my spirit during the Baptism, until I noticed people's reactions to me. Suddenly people were smiling and waving at me from passing cars, and people in general were much more friendly, as if they were aware that something good had occurred. What else can I say but, "Thank You God!"

CHAPTER 8
An Amazing Healing!

As I've said before, God never gives us work to do without giving us the means to do it. That's a great motivator, for sure, but I haven't mentioned the greatest motivation of all that I'd received. Talk about the mercy of God, the grace of God, and the blessing of God! Usually I would go to bed and fall asleep quickly. And usually, I remained sound asleep. There wasn't much that would wake me up, while Ann was a light sleeper and would be awakened by almost anything. But on one special night? I was awakened while she slept soundly. Awakened and amazed, because, standing at the foot of the bed was what I believed to be an angel. I have never experienced such fear and such peace at the same time.

Terrified? Yes; but I was also aware of a great peacefulness. I told Ann the next morning I had seen an angel. An angel with a face as bright as the sun—so bright I had to turn my eyes away and could not look at it again. And behind the angel I sensed there was a bluish sky filled with white clouds. This Being wore a gown that was whiter than any white I'd ever seen—so brilliant, the only way I can describe it is to say it glowed like a fluorescent white light.

That had been a Friday night and by Saturday afternoon, I realized I had seen the apparition on Good Friday. I was totally amazed. I couldn't believe that on the anniversary of the day Christ had been crucified, He would find the mercy and blessing to send to anyone—let alone me—the presence of an angel. When I told Ann about it, I asked if she realized what night it was, and reminded her it was Good Friday, the day we remember as the day Jesus was crucified on the cross.

On Easter Sunday, after we went to church, I received a wonderful message. There was no visual visitation this time, but it still was a very specific, very special message: I was told the cancer was gone. Now, as I said before, the pain had disappeared three days after I decided to end the Chemo treatments; but I did not know for sure if the cancer was truly gone. *Wow*, I now thought. *First, I was visited by an angel on Good Friday, then on Easter Sunday I was told the cancer was gone.* How gracious can God be, to resurrect your body to be cancer-free on the celebration of the same day that Christ was resurrected. A couple of years would pass before I would fully understand the true extent of that Good Friday visitation.

Right after I was healed, I was told by the Lord to, "Go forth and witness." I was obedient in doing so verbally. Several years passed before I attempted to pick up a pen and write a book; but like so many aspiring writers, I did not get very far. Something was holding me back. I did not know it, but many things had to be accomplished before I'd be able to take pen in hand and write this book.

Isn't that the way God works? We can try and try to accomplish things in our life, but one big lesson I am still learning is, it will happen if it is within His will—and it will happen in His time. And as I put this story into print, I realize the number of years I put into constructing the House of Angels was significant. We held early Easter services there on an annual basis and when I realized the seventh Easter was coming, I got excited. In the Biblical sense, the number seven signifies completion and I thought, *this next Easter service is going to be special. After all, it's the seventh one!*

Nothing significant happened before or immediately after that service; but then as the eighth Easter service approached, I realized while this was the eighth service, *it signifies the completion of the seventh year after we began to hold the Easter services!*

An Amazing Healing!

"Maybe something special is going to happen now," I said. And something sure did happen! Shortly after our eighth Easter service, I received a message from the Lord. It happened while I was splitting wood up at the House of Angels.

"Walk to Washington," I heard.

That's strange, I thought. And then I heard it again. "Walk to Washington, D.C." And then I was told to bind a Bible to my chest and to declare God to be the power the blessing and the grace that made this country great. I stood in amazement. *Stupefied* might be a better word according to my authorly wife, because I often seem confused and ask, "What?" and then I hear the message being repeated.

If you recall, I've already explained that right after this message arrived, I broke my toe and had to wait for it to heal before I could start the walk. But winter was coming, and it would not be sensible to attempt such a journey during the winter months; so, after my toe healed, I attended a local gym, trying to get into shape, thinking I would start out the following spring, or early summer.

Memories of the time I spent in the gym are bitter sweet. A tragic accident became a lesson, or should I say a reminder, from the Lord. I'd met a young woman who often walked the treadmill next to mine. I learned she was close to her sister, and she was going to enter the military. I also discovered that she did not know Jesus and told her it would be better to learn about Him before she found herself in a foxhole or some other dangerous situation and needed Him. I felt I should give her a Bible, so Ann and I gave her one we hoped she'd carry during her time of service. As the weeks passed, when I asked if she and her sister had read from it, she said they had not. Shortly afterwards, she was killed in a two-vehicle crash. I felt so bad for this young soul, fearing she was truly lost. And so, I asked God, "Why would You have me meet her and give her a Bible? She hadn't even looked at it!" His reply? "Do I have you do anything, or direct you in any way, without a reason?"

Eventually, I saw her sister while running an errand and she told me that, yes, she and late her sister had read the Bible a few times before the crash. Her answer coupled with God's response gave me the hope that my young friend very well may have come to know Christ and the timely gift of the Bible had not been without reason after all. I thought perhaps when she read the Good Book, she saw something that helped to lead her to accept Jesus as her Savior. With this sudden insight, I was able to explain to her still-grieving sister that I believed she was okay and in a good place.

After my winter stint at the gym, I developed nerve damage to my feet and required medical help from a podiatrist. I'd have to wait even longer before I could start my trek to D.C.! At that point, I thought perhaps it was time to create a walkway up to the cross itself. I didn't have to wonder for long about it, though. As you might guess, confirmation came. It was connected to a visit from a young boy who arrived at the House of Angels with his grandmother and her companion.

She had driven to the House of Angels in a truck with a man, and at first, I did not realize the boy was with them. As they drove back down from the site, she stopped to say thanks for allowing them to visit the sanctuary. Then she explained that her grandson was in the back of the truck and although he was only about ten years old, he had glaucoma and other problems with his eyes, and could possibly go blind. She said, "I hope it was okay for my grandson to go up and touch the cross and ask for healing."

I was immediately moved to tears because just before she explained how he had climbed up to the cross, I was about to suggest that he do just that. I then described an experience Ann had when she went up to hug the cross and received a healing from shingles that had affected one of her eyes. I thought it was amazing that right after I considered the pros and cons of constructing a walkway to make it easy for people to climb to the top of the cliff and approach the cross, these people came, confirming the need. As I think about it, I realize it was as if God was giving me a slap on the back of the head, telling me to, "Get busy!" After all, the walkway had been prophesized to us a year or two before this by Dottie Stevens, a friend at church. And her prophesy had occurred right at the time when Ann needed to be healed from an excruciating case of shingles!

DO NOT EVER GIVE UP HOPE: "I revealed myself to those who did not ask for me; I was found by those who did not seek me. To a nation that did not call on my name, I said, "Here am I, Here am I." Isaiah 65:1

DON'S NOTE: While so many of the people mentioned in Isaiah were considered a "stench in the Lord's nostrils," I find the first verse comforting when I think of my young friend who died in the car crash. Perhaps she did ask about the Lord in time! After all, He let me know that He did not have me give her a Bible without reason!

CHAPTER 9

A Healing and A Prophesy

One blustery fall afternoon, Ann felt a strange tingle on the top of her head. Although it persisted for a couple of days, she ignored it. A few days later, we were heading toward a special evening session at our church when she showed me a rash that was starting to spread onto her forehead. When I saw the line of red spots my first thought was, *shingles*, but I was not sure about it; and Ann said they hurt a little, but she didn't say too much more. I didn't realize it was worse than she was letting on, but it became very clear that evening when a female prophet was speaking at Jacob's Well, the church we attend in Cambridge, New York. Ann says the woman looked just like one of the angels from the old television show, "Touched by An Angel." After she had prophesied over several people, this woman suddenly hurtled down the aisle toward us. We were sitting about four rows back, in the middle of the row.

She stopped. She locked eyes with Ann. And she bellowed, "Not today. The Lord God says you are not going to die, and you are not going to give in to your illness." Then she reached out and took my wife by the hand and led her up to the front of the church.

The thing you need to understand is, Ann had not said anything about how badly she was suffering. She did explain later that just

A Healing And A Prophesy

before the prophet approached her, she had been thinking the pain had become so unbearable, she was going to swallow a handful of pain killers when she got home if she had to. *Anything to stop it—even the whole bottle,* she thought, *even if it kills me!* She has said since then that it was more unbearable than the worst migraine headache that had landed her in the hospital, or even the excruciating pain during one childbirth session when the contractions spread to her back. She described it as being hit by the white-hot flame of a blow torch every few seconds. *Wow,* I thought. *That's gotta hurt! A lot!*

The prophet called all the women in the audience to come forward to lay hands on Ann and to pray for healing. Ann says while the women were praying for her, she felt a curious flutter on her eyelid. "All I could think," she said later that night, "was that while they were praying, it felt like angel wings touching my eye." One of the women was Dottie Stevens. She and her husband, Paul, were visiting from North Carolina. They were well known to our Pastors, Tim and Cindylee Bohley and to many members of the congregation. We soon learned that not long after this event, they would be moving back to the Cambridge area and Paul would become an Associate Pastor at Jacob's Well.

When Dottie approached Ann that night, she whispered in her ear, "You should go up to the cross your husband put up. Go up and wrap your arms around it and ask the Lord for healing. Remember, you must touch it." She told me a short time later how she had experienced a vision about our cross. She said in the vision she was ill, and she went up to the cross and when she hugged it, she was healed. Then she pronounced to me, "Ann needs to go up and hug that cross, and you need to put a path up to it as soon as you can to make it easier for people to go up and touch it."

The next day, it was Sunday. Despite her pain, Ann did not want to miss this day at church. The prophet was scheduled to preach the sermon, and it was our congregation's Thanksgiving Dinner event. Ann was so sick by the time the meal was served, she could not eat. At one point, she slipped away into one of the Sunday School rooms and just sprawled onto the floor. She said it felt like a blow torch was hitting her forehead and eye over and over. When she

DESTINATION D.C. A Modern-day Jonah?

returned to the food tables, it was obvious she was in tremendous pain. Once again, I worried about shingles and when he saw her condition, Pastor Tim agreed that she needed medical help. He urged us to go. "Go right now," he said. "There's an emergency clinic not far from here that's open on Sundays."

Without hesitation, we rushed out the door and soon the doctor confirmed Ann had shingles. By that time, her eyelid was swollen and as stiff as cardboard. The doctor said it might be too late for the medicine to work because it should have been taken within three days of the onset of the symptoms. She also explained that when the rash travels down your forehead it follows the path of the nerve endings and goes to the eye, jumps to the nose where it continues to the tip of the nose, then reverses itself, heading back along the same path up the forehead.

"You need to see an ophthalmologist tomorrow," she said. "This is serious. It's recognized as one of the most painful areas to have shingles, and it could quickly blind you." Then, she sent us home with a prescription for a pain killer and antibiotics—and with the slim hope they would work. The next day, the ophthalmologist confirmed what the emergency physician had said. He directed Ann to continue taking the pills and urged her to call if there was any change, especially if it got worse. Over the next few days or so, she remained about the same, setting the alarm clock as a reminder to take the pills every five hours. It was terrible to see her flinch over and over from the pain. By Wednesday morning, the day before Thanksgiving, she was worse.

I told her to call the doctor and make an appointment, and to call me at work so I'd know when I should leave work to head home to take her. By the end of my lunch break, I hadn't heard a word, so I called home, wanting to know why she hadn't contacted me. She told me she was healed, but I didn't quite catch what she said, and I started to lecture her about not taking care of herself.

"Don't you love to read, and paint and do crafts? Do you want to go blind? Don't fool around with this," I continued in the way that only an irate, worried husband can, until she finally got my attention.

"You don't understand," she said. "It's gone. My eye is better." And then she said a miracle had occurred when she decided to

A Healing And A Prophesy

do what Dottie Stevens had suggested. It was the day before Thanksgiving and it was a cold, stormy day, with hail and sleet and rain. There already was one-and-a-half inches of cold, wet sleet that she had to slosh through. It swirled in the air and stung her face. But that did not stop her. Thinking she could not feel any worse, she was determined to get herself and her half-closed, cardboardy eyelid up to the cross.

At the top of the ledge, she wrapped her arms around the base of the cross and pressed her cheek and swollen eyelid against its cold, hard surface. She explained later, how the wet sleet continued to hurl itself out of the sky as she prayed for healing, clinging to the wooden cross that stretched to a height of 20 feet. And then it happened. She said she was bracing for the next brutal flash of pain to strike and was suddenly realizing it didn't happen. Her eye popped open, her vision was almost clear, and the fiery blasts had morphed into warm flushes and then disappeared altogether!

She thanked God for His mercy, then made her way down the icy edge of the ledge, up the slippery grass slope, then skittered down the sloppy roadway back to the house. The first thing she did was peer into the bathroom mirror. Sure enough, her eye was pretty much normal, although it was blood shot. And then, as she continued to tell me about her experience, her voice cracked when she said that when she went to hang up her coat near the woodstove to dry—after all it was an old one made of corduroy and she'd been in the sleet and rain for more than 45 minutes—she realized it was not even damp. It was completely dry!

Thank You Jesus! Thank You for the miraculous shelter from the storm and for the healing!

HEALING: "Be merciful to me, Lord, for I am faint; O Lord, heal me, for my bones are in agony." Psalm 6:2

DON'S NOTES: The above passage tells us that prayer is a powerful source of healing because it puts us in touch with our Creator. Who can argue with that? Especially when your prayer is followed by a healing and a miracle?

CHAPTER 10

North Carolina Here We Come

Before Paul and Dottie Stevens returned to North Carolina, I told them about my healing and all that had been happening since then: there was so much to tell! After hearing my witness, they said they often assisted a woman who hosted a Christian television program that focused on faith-based healings. The show aired on Direct TV from her studio in North Carolina.

"I'd love to be on that show," I said, excited about the possibility of sharing my experiences with millions of people. *What a great way to proclaim the power of Christ*, I thought, and to explain how He appeared before me and how He wants to be active in people's lives.

Paul and Dottie agreed to connect us with the host of the show and before long, Ann and I were both on the phone with her. After hearing a bit of my testimony and learning about Ann's books, she agreed to interview both of us. A few months later we were on our way to her beautiful southern state!

We stayed in North Carolina over the course of a long weekend and after taping the interviews, we had a chance to visit several interesting sites, including Moravian Falls. The water flows down a slanted ledge of solid rock in the foothills of the Brushy Mountains. Angels have reportedly been seen in the area and many people believe there's an open portal to heaven somewhere there. Ann

North Carolina Here We Come

and I can say for sure that, like the House of Angels, the waterfall at Moravian Falls exudes a feeling of peace and tranquility. It was named after the Moravian Unity of the Brethren, known locally as the Moravian Brothers, a group that settled there in 1753. The Moravian Church is an international entity that became official in the mid-1400's. The Moravians believe what makes one a Christian is not the doctrine you follow, but rather, it's about living your life according to the teachings of Jesus, with an emphasis on gentleness, humility, patience and love for your enemies. They have a northern American headquarters in Pennsylvania while their southern headquarters is in North Carolina. America has one of the smallest numbers of congregations in the world because the Moravian mission has focused on bringing the good news of the gospel to the poorest and most despised people of the world.

At the falls, we met a woman who was also visiting the area. After taking a few photos, we wished her well, and our host continued to drive us on a tour she had thought we would enjoy. Dottie and Paul were with us.

About 15 miles from the Moravian Falls we visited a beautiful Christian retreat. High on the hillside, it offered a spectacular view of the valley below and while we were checking out the scenery, we recognized the woman we had met at the falls. She was quite energized. Filled with the Spirit. And soon she began to prophesy over us. When she got to me, she spoke about seeing a big tree and a road. I immediately associated her message with the tree I had cut down and used for the cross at the House of Angels. And then she said she saw me speaking to people in stores and gas stations. She was unsure of the timing of it and wondered if it had already happened. I told her that ever since I started working to develop the House of Angels, I did often witness to people and spoke of Christ wherever I could—in stores, gas stations, our bank, and other places. I figured she was referring to my encounters during those errands.

Of course, I now believe her vision of the tree was a reference to the cross I would carry on my Heal America Walk! After all, in the Bible, the cross was sometimes referred to as a tree. And I witnessed to dozens of people in stores, gas stations, parks, and along the road during the Heal America Walk!

DESTINATION D.C. A Modern-day Jonah?

AFFIRMATION: "... being confident of this, that he who began a good work in you will carry it on to completion until the day of Christ Jesus." Philippians 1:6

DON'S NOTE: While we did not understand what our new acquaintance was really talking about, I felt a sense of encouragement that she was confirming I was due to do more work for God.

CHAPTER 11

Why, God . . . Why?

Ann's healing from shingles was just one of many, many healings connected to the House of Angels. And while I did not know it was meant to be a place for healing when I first started to work on the site, it did become evident after about a month into my efforts to clear the area. I was in the car running errands and had not gone far when I was instructed to go to the hospital.

"The hospital?" I asked. And just like it happened with most of these messages, I heard it being repeated. "Go to the hospital."

"Why should I go to the hospital? Will I have a heart attack and You want me to be where I can receive immediate care?"

There was no reply, but the message had been so explicit, I decided to be obedient. Then I wondered if I was supposed to see a nurse who had treated me with such kindness, I thought she had a gift from God—a healing touch beyond an earthly ability. I had visited her before and told her how I was miraculously healed. But during my hospital recovery, she had revealed that her husband had been very sick, and I now wondered if he had fallen ill again and if I was supposed to comfort her and reassure her about God's mercy and His willingness to work in these matters.

There were many times when I would ask God, "Why am I building this place? Why should I go there? Why should I do this?

DESTINATION D.C. A Modern-day Jonah?

Why are You speaking to me?" Or, just simply, "Why?" There were many times when I did not hear a response, but recently it seemed like God was saying the House of Angels was for prayer and healing. Perhaps the answer would be revealed at the hospital; so, I proceeded to the nurses' station on the third floor where the duty roster was posted.

The nurse I sought was not listed on the board. So, I asked, *why, then, God? Why am I here?* Without knowing what to do, I headed back toward the elevator, but when I passed a patient's door, I heard my name being called. I didn't recognize the voice, but as quick as you can snap your fingers I thought, *Okay, God, if what I'm building is to be a place of prayer and healing, please show me!* And then it happened: before I could take one step back and enter the doorway, the message came loud and clear: "Touch these people and pray for them."

I need to explain that if God had said, "lay hands on them," I would not have known what it meant. Sometimes I joke around, explaining that for me, laying hands on someone means to fight them. I'd never heard about the laying on of hands during prayer for healing.

In the bed lay Tim Mead, a parishioner from the church we were attending, his wife Dawn, at his side. After our initial greetings, he said he'd been sent to this hospital from one in a nearby state because they could not find the cause of his problem. They weren't having any luck in diagnosing his illness here, either; and planned to run a cat scan later in the day and then send him to a third, much bigger facility. Tim said he had a blockage that was so extensive, they could not use a scope to see into or beyond it. I asked if I could pray for him. He said it would be fine, so I reached to hold his wrist and his wife Dawn's wrist and I began to pray.

That was on a Friday, and on Sunday when Ann and I went to church, we realized he and his wife were seated behind us. After the service, he explained that he'd been discharged from the hospital Saturday morning—the day after I had prayed for him. Talk about a confirmation! God showed me the House of Angels *was* to be a place for prayer and healing. This was the start of my healing ministry—and the confirmations just kept coming. "Thank you, Jesus!"

A couple of weeks later, our pastor said a woman had suffered for quite some time with a severe blood issue and she had suddenly become more ill than ever with it. They thought it might be cancer or some other serious blood disease. Our pastor and his wife were very concerned for her and they asked the congregation to pray for her.

When Ann and I were on our way home, I received a message that the woman our pastor mentioned would be okay. I turned toward Ann and said, "I just got a message the woman we prayed for will be healed." I wanted to call our pastor and tell him about it, but I had not yet revealed my experience with the healing prayer in the hospital to anyone except Ann. I simply was not sure how to explain it—but it seemed that now would be a good time to tell the pastor about these happenings. When I called, he agreed to meet for a talk, and I asked about the woman he'd mentioned in church.

"Pastor," I said. "You know the woman you were talking about in church? The one who needed prayer? Can you tell me who she is?"

"She's one of my wife's relatives," he said. "Why do you ask?"

"Well, I received a message that she would be healed." Then, I described what had happened in the hospital the previous Friday, and how the work I was doing on my property was in obedience to God's will and these experiences confirmed to me it was to be a sanctuary for prayer and healing. He thought it was great and it might be a good idea to work together to organize a healing service. I agreed, and I'm happy to say that even before we started the first one, we received confirmation that the woman with the blood issue was fine and she merely needed to build up her blood with vitamins. Once again, I had the opportunity to say, "Thank you, Jesus!" But there were so many healings and other memorable events around that time.

On my way home from the hospital one other day, I came upon two boys who were frantically waving for help. It was only a quarter of a mile or so from my home and I wondered if they were up to no good; but as I got closer, I could see panic and fear on their faces. When I stopped, they pointed toward the embankment, yelling that a woman had crashed her car into a tree down at the bottom. They thought she had a serious head injury, and I quickly realized I didn't have the first aid skills to help her, so I said I'd go home and call for help. When I dialed 9-1-1, they confirmed an ambulance was already on its way.

Back at the scene, I clambered down to the crash site to check on the victim whose pulse was barely discernable. Then I heard sirens and saw a constable was making his way down to us. *Thank God.*

"I felt a pulse," I said. "It's weak, but it's there." Worried that I should have done more, I said, "I haven't had time to do anything for her." He said it might be good if I would help deal with traffic and explain to the delayed drivers why the roadway was blocked. On my way up the bank, I started to pray for the girl and asked God to send His angels to help her; then, to my amazement, when I glanced back toward the mangled vehicle, I saw angels! Many, many real angels were descending toward her!

Still in awe of the sight I was seeing, I managed to head back up the slope to assist with the traffic. Eventually, I had a chance to speak with the constable and he said, "You know, sometimes people can still have a pulse, even though . . ." His voice trailed off. He didn't have to say more. I got it. "You mean she'd passed," I said.

"Yes."

My heart was broken. It was a young girl, about the same age as my youngest stepdaughter, Johanna. And what made it worse? I had just been tested for signs of cancer, confirming the miracle God had blessed me with after I quit the treatments: and at the cancer unit, I had seen several people waiting for their chemo and radiation treatments, including a little girl; so, I was already in the midst of a strong sense of survivor's guilt.

On my way home, I had been praying for them. Praying that God's mercy would fall upon them and they might all be healed. And then, when I saw the young crash victim, the same age as Jo, it felt as if the Devil was in my face, laughing, sneering, full of contempt. Even so, it did not take long to realize the Lord had triumphed! He let me see the angels that He had sent to her, and to this day I believe she's gone to a better place. A few days after the accident, I noticed the boys had put a cross on one of the trees at the crash site. It had her name on it. I knew they lived close to the scene of the accident, and I thought perhaps they were feeling sad that they had not been able to save the girl.

I wanted to tell them about the angels—that it was a sign she was in a better place, but they were not at home—so I told the adult who came to the door about my experience and asked that the message be relayed to the boys. I admit, my survival guilt still looms up at times, but I do thank the Lord for reminding me of His promises. One of His reminders during those tough days still lingers in my memory. Most of my worktime for the commercial electric company was spent in a plant that produces calcium carbonate. A bit like talcum powder, the stuff covered almost everything for hundreds of yards, and it was not exactly filled with the scent of flowers or perfume; but, about two days after that fatal accident, I was feeling sad about the young girl's death when I was overwhelmed by a sweet fragrance at the work site. I guess you could say it was a bitter sweet moment with a smell, unlike anything I'd experienced before. I took it as a reassurance that the young girl was truly in a better place, with her maker, our Lord, Jesus Christ.

It was amazing how many times my prayers would be answered, and healings would take place. One of our friends had a son who suffered a severe head injury in a four-wheeler accident. He was diagnosed with brain damage and he was in a coma for several days, but they were not sure of the extent of the brain injury. After I prayed over him, his awakening and recovery were much speedier than expected, and he recovered almost completely.

Other recoveries following prayer included a man who was seriously injured in a snowmobile accident. He had been hospitalized for quite a long time and was not expected to leave the hospital, but he did experience a full recovery. Another person I prayed for became healed from a serious drug addiction. One prayer did not result in a healing, but it did include an interesting prediction that came true. A woman named Marge, from Jacob's Well, was scheduled to receive a cardiac procedure, and after praying for her, I said, "You never know. It's possible that you'll get there, be on the operating table, and they might not do the procedure and just tell you to get up and go home. The next time I saw her, she said that is exactly what happened. The surgeons needed more information before they could operate. While the procedure was eventually done, and she recovered, I can't help but realize my prediction about getting off the table and not being done the first time the procedure was scheduled, did come true. I mean, how often does that happen? It was a first for me. And for her! Time has passed, and she has continued to do well.

One healing came in what I call a "delayed action". A family from a nearby town had an autistic son, and one day when I saw the boy, I thought I should pray for him. I received an answer right away that was puzzling. I was told, "Not yet. Not now." About a month or two later, Ann said she felt we should pray for the autistic boy. I said I wanted to a while ago but was told to wait and I was still receiving the message to wait. So, we waited. And waited. A couple of months went by and a healing service was held at one of our local churches. I was glad to see the boy was there and he was going forward to be prayed for: I felt it was time. After we prayed for him, I suggested that, perhaps he should pray for his mother and he did so.

Amazingly, we soon realized both prayers were answered! Not long after the healing service, his mother received a report that his teachers saw such a huge improvement in his abilities they were awestruck. With tears of joy in her eyes, his mom told us no one believed her son would ever be able to function on his own; but, following that healing service, he continued to improve to the point where she believed he might even live in his own apartment one day. What a blessing it was for the boy to realize that his own prayer—asking for his mom to be happy and able to stop worrying about him—had been answered by God. Not to mention his own improvement in cognitive abilities!

There's another story I just must mention. After all, it also includes a delayed reaction! A one-and-a-half-year delay, at that! This time, God used the telephone to transport my message to a co-worker a few years after I made the call.

My employer had taken on a new project that involved the construction of a new addition and the hiring of new employees as well. One of the new guys stood out because he had a good work ethic and a good attitude toward life in general. We teamed up a lot of the time. When the building was completed, he was laid off.

Soon after that I was working on the House of Angels when I thought I'd give him a call to see how he was doing. Then I thought, *isn't it strange I had never given him any of my testimony or witnessed to him about faith or things about the House of Angels?* That was not like me, so with these thoughts, I decided to give him a call. He was not there, but his answering machine recorded my message. I had asked him how he was doing and how a certain project was coming along that he had told me about. I left my phone number and asked him to give me a call.

Time went by and I didn't receive any messages from him. We weren't exactly close friends, so I did not think too much about it; plus, I knew we were both very busy. And then one day as I was entering the house the telephone was ringing. I answered. It was him.

He said, "Hi. How are you doing?"

"What's up," I asked.

"I'm returning your call," he said, "but I have to admit not much is happening." Then, after a few seconds of silence, he finally added, "Well, there was one thing. I had cancer."

I responded, "You don't have it now."

"That's true," he said. "That's right, it's gone. I had only one treatment for it and I was healed." I paused a moment, thinking to myself that it was a miracle. Then I said, "I did tell you I had cancer, right?"

"Yes, and you were healed, correct?"

"Yes, yet you had never been told how, or anything about the House of Angels." It was more of a statement than a question.

"No, so what's that about?"

That's when I told him that God had led him to make this call.
"Why's that?" he asked.

"Well, I think God set this up a long time ago so you would know He was the healer who had blessed you with your healing and determined it in a way that would be shown through this call."

"What are you talking about?" He queried with skepticism.

"Do you have faith," I asked.

He said, "I guess I believe a little." And I said, "I believe this call to me that you just made was to show you in a most unusual way how the Lord works. You need to understand something: I made that call and left that message to you well over a year ago—maybe even a year and a half ago."

"But I check my messages all the time," he said, "and I just got this message today. Come to think of it, I wondered why you asked about that project I was working on since it was so long ago."

I took that moment to invite him to the House of Angels. "I think you'll love it and it's a great place to thank God for your healing." As far as I know, he never did come, and I haven't seen or spoken to him since. It's my hope that God has gotten through to him. Perhaps he now answers Christ's call.

If I haven't said it already, I must say it now: these things are not of me, they come through me from Jesus Christ. He has given me a gift of healing, one of the gifts listed in I Corinthians 12:28 that has been given to many, many people. No man can bring about healing through prayer on his own: it only happens when Jesus Christ answers his prayers. Jesus alone is the great healer, the great physician. Each time I witness healings following prayer, it reinforces my belief in the message in Mark 9:23, that says, "Everything is possible for him who believes." With a glimmer of a tear that morphs into a bright light of joy, the passage produces thoughts of my grandfather and his insistence that, "It's important to believe."

Wherever I go I seem to end up talking about Jesus. It happened one day in a restaurant. I struck up a conversation with a woman. While her friends were not interested in what I had to say, she clearly was interested; and when I mentioned the House of Angels and had photos in my car, she agreed to look at them. She studied the photos as I told her about some of the amazing things that had happened. She then said she had a friend who was struggling with an illness who might benefit from a visit. My first thoughts? *It's January! There's snow! It's not a good time!*

There was quite a bit of snow on the ground, and I told her we don't usually plow the road that leads up to the site, but she did not care. She said she would still like to bring her friend as soon as possible. To my surprise, they knocked at our door about a week or two later and said they wanted to walk up to the cross. I didn't feel comfortable having them struggle two hundred yards through the snow alone, so I agreed to go with them and grabbed my boots and a warm hat and coat.

I was happy to realize that although the snow was knee high, there was a firm crust that could hold our weight most of the time. Even so, we'd occasionally sink to our knees. I felt a little concerned about the woman who had been sick. She struggled behind us by a few feet. I mean, halfway up to the cross, I was breathing hard; but she seemed to hold her own and did not complain at all. Her tenacity was admirable.

As we approached the point where we could see the cross, I started to tell them about some of the experiences Ann and I have had. But you know what? I quickly stopped talking. The woman who had been ill had already caught up to us before I could say much. She had one of the biggest, happiest smiles I'd ever seen. I mean, she was beaming, and with arms outstretched she exclaimed, "It's gone! My pain is gone! I can breathe, and I feel great!" She then explained that she had been left with residual pain after suffering from pneumonia. She had been diagnosed with COPD and suffered serious pain that would not go away. Until now!

One day as I was returning from the Wells Town Dump, I passed a man who was limping along the side of the road on crutches. I thought it was a bit strange to be traveling that way on a busy road; but as I slowly passed the guy, I heard a message. Loud. And clear. And beyond my comfort zone. "Stop and pray for him."

"What?" Thoughts of praying for a stranger on the side of the road made me feel self-conscious and I just continued to drive; but I started to feel guilty. Finally, I suggested to God that I'd go to a certain spot on the road I live on and turn around. If the guy was still hobbling along, I'd stop and pray for him. I never had any trouble when people asked me to pray for them in a store, at a healing service, in church, or at the House of Angels; but to stop and initiate a prayer session with a stranger on the side of the road? Not comfortable. Not comfortable at all. *It doesn't make sense*, I argued, but I had to remind myself that God always has a purpose.

Of course, he was there, so I parked a little way down the road from him and approached him on foot. When I got close enough, I told him I was a minister and asked if he was a man of faith. He said he was.

"You might think this is strange," I said. "But when I passed you in my truck, I was told to stop and pray for you." I told him I felt I had been given a healing gift and my prayers had been answered on many occasions, and a lot of people had been healed. When I asked why he had to use the crutches, he said he had an operation and he'd been told to walk with them to get a bit of exercise. By this time, we had reached my truck—directly across from the gas station and an intersecting road. He agreed to let me pray for him. Of course, it was at a place where there were people watching.

I told this stranger that I would kneel to pray because I felt I was directed to exalt people I pray for to a higher position than myself. I asked if he knew about the laying on of hands during prayer for healing; and when he said he did, I put one hand on his hand as he supported himself with the crutch and I prayed. At the end of this, I noticed there were three vehicles waiting to enter the road. The first vehicle was a truck driven by a bearded man. I could see a scowl beneath his baseball cap and my first thought was, *maybe he never saw a prayer session on the side of the road.* A few hours later, while I was sitting at home thinking about it, wondering about the trucker's expression, I had to laugh. It struck me that he might have thought I was proposing marriage! Even so, I was glad I had been obedient—and I was completely clueless about the fact that

Why, God . . . Why?

I'd end up praying for a lot of people on roadsides several years later, on my Heal America Walk!

For a long time, I wondered about the experiences at the House of Angels, and all that had happened since my recovery from the colon cancer. Why me? I truly did not feel deserving of God's grace, or to have been chosen to do His bidding. But, on one occasion, some of it became clear through a special message.

Shortly after I was healed from the colon cancer and the pain had disappeared in such a miraculous way, I heard a message. Repeatedly as I woke up, I heard, "Deuteronomy. Deuteronomy." The word ran through my head as I walked from my bedroom toward the kitchen. It was a strong message, but it made no sense to me, so I returned to the bedroom where Ann was just starting to wake up and asked her, "What's Deuteronomy?"

"I don't know what it's about," she said, "but it's a book in the Bible. Why?"

"From the moment I woke up, and as I headed toward the kitchen to get my coffee, I kept hearing it," I said. She shrugged and raised her brows as if to say, 'look it up.'

I want you to understand as you read this, that Ann and I had only been going to church for a few years, and before that I had been away from church and had not read or studied the Bible for a good 40 years or so. I really didn't know the Bible much at all and decided to check it out—even before I got that much-needed cup of caffeine. So, I pulled a Bible off the shelf and flipped for the page that lists the books. Sure enough, Deuteronomy was the fifth book in the Old Testament.

"Yes," I said. "That's it." And when I opened the Bible to where I thought the fifth book of the Old Testament might be located, I found it. My eyes immediately fell upon verse 8 in Chapter 23. I don't know which version of the Bible I had picked up, but the way I interpreted the message was: 'those of the third generation in a new nation would receive their own congregation.' It immediately struck me that in this country, I was a third-generation child. My grandfather had come from Scotland, making my father a member of the second generation. I was overwhelmed at how God works.

Not long after this experience many more things began to happen, and I attribute most, if not all of it, as evidence of a path that had been written down by the Lord for me to follow. And even though the path was not visible, I believed I was being led toward certain positions, from learning the importance of faith and belief during the summer in Maine with my grandfather's remedy for my wart, to working as a mason with the foreman who was a pastor who advised me, to meeting Ann in North Adams, and praying for her to yearn for a Christian life. These events and encounters have helped to direct me to do certain things. All of it prepared for me by God! And now, as I chronicle these experiences, I am certain I've been following the blue print for my life. Could my life possibly be a paradigm connected to Jonah? It's beyond belief, unless you understand it could only be of God and from God; and I am certain that He does this for everyone who takes the time and effort to listen to and hear His voice.

All I can say is, He certainly got my attention!

OUR PURPOSE IN LIFE: In Philippians 3, Paul wrote that he lived in eager expectation and hope and Philippians 3:12 begins with an apt headline: '*Pressing on Toward the Goal*.' "Not that I have already obtained all this, or have already been made perfect, but I press on to take hold of that for which Christ Jesus took hold of me."

DON'S NOTE: I heard the message to put up the cross, and I heard the message to walk to Washington. I did not know the purpose of those mandates, but, like Paul, I lived in eager expectation and hope, that first, I would accomplish what Christ wanted me to do, and second, that I would eventually understand the end result of God beckoning me to have faith in His instruction such as praying for people like the man on the side of the road, and others. That kind of understanding came, and the process of waiting for God to reveal His objective helped me to grow in faith . . . and to develop a greater sense of patience.

CHAPTER 12

Your Will, Not Mine

One day while I was working on the site, two women came to see the House of Angels. One of them explained her husband of many years was sick with cancer. She had heard about us and was curious. I gave witness to some of the things that had been happening, like my healing and other healings. She eventually commented on a song that was on display up at the worship area. She admired the message it revealed, and I said the first time I heard it, I felt the song was special. Entitled, "Let Your Light Shine", it had been written by Karen Gallagher, a worship leader from a local church. I was so happy when Karen gave me permission to have her song etched onto a large slab of slate that stands at the site. The lyrics of the song can be seen at the end of this chapter.

Eventually I asked if my visitor would like me to pray for her and for her husband.

"Yes, please," she said, and beckoned her friend to join us.

It was a cloudy day. I hadn't seen the sun at all, which was okay because it's easier to work on gardening and landscaping when you don't have the hot, bright sun bearing down on you. The three of us stood together and closed our eyes as I began to pray. Suddenly, I felt the heat from a ray of sunlight. I mean, it was intense, and the

DESTINATION D.C. A Modern-day Jonah?

brightness pierced through my eyelids . . . lingering throughout the prayer . . . and ending with my silence.

"Did you feel that?" one of the women asked. She didn't have to explain what she was talking about. The other one said, "Yes. It was amazing! The sunray hit us the minute you started praying, Don, and I could feel it right up to the point when you stopped speaking; and then, in that instant the heat vanished, like the click of a switch."

"Yes, it was truly amazing! We've got to go back and tell my husband about it."

As I recall this event, I remember feeling as if we were in a spotlight. The sun never did reappear that day; and this type of thing has occurred several times over the years. She called me soon after that day and asked if I would pray for her husband at their home in Rutland. He was agreeable, she said, and I certainly was happy to do so. I remember when I finished praying for him, he questioned why I asked for forgiveness at the start of the prayer. He said he had not done anything wrong: he was a good person.

That was a difficult moment. I was being confronted by someone who was a loving husband and father who had provided a good living for his family. I learned he had done many kind things for others before being overcome by his illness; but like so many people who have not focused on Jesus and the message of salvation, he did not understand the biblical definition of or connection between sin and salvation—and the need for forgiveness no matter how "good" one is. A study of the Bible reveals that sin is anything we do that takes our focus away from God and leads us farther from Him.

The only person who has never sinned is Jesus Christ.

You are not saved just because you are a good person or by the good things you do. Jesus the Christ said, and the Bible clearly states, you cannot be saved by works—the only way to salvation is to believe Jesus Christ is your Savior. Good works are important. And as I understand it, the Bible reveals that you will be rewarded for the good works you do. But salvation? It comes freely through your faith.

I'm sad to say the man from Rutland lost his fight with cancer soon after we met. It's so hard to see a good person like that pass on.

Hard for the family for sure, but it's truly heartbreaking for a believer to see someone pass when you're not sure of their salvation. And while it hurts to lose someone, I've come to know God has a purpose for all that He does, and I've come to believe the greatest healing will be received through the death of the physical body. The last time I spoke to that man he still did not understand why he needed to be forgiven to obtain salvation, but I hope in the last moments of his life, he could have had the opportunity to accept Christ. After all, during their last moments of life, Christ forgave and promised salvation to one of the criminals who died beside him on Calvary.

Good things continued to happen throughout the years as I worked to develop and maintain the House of Angels. Especially the healings! One day I attended a Christian music festival in a nearby town. During that event, I heard that three people in attendance had cancer. Two pastors I knew were also at this festival and I asked if they would pray with me for the three who had cancer. Soon after that event, I learned our prayers were answered: all three cancer victims received good reports from their doctors.

Some of the people who visited the House of Angels were those whom I met by chance at local stores and supermarkets. First, we talk about the best deals of the week, then before I know it, I'm mentioning the House of Angels and inviting them for a visit. One was a young woman at the checkout counter. We only saw each other at the checkout line, but we sometimes had a few minutes to talk. There were things that deeply troubled her, and she said she appreciated our talks. At one point I said she should come and visit the sanctuary. Well, time passed, and she didn't come—at least I didn't see her but realized she might have driven up to the site. We often tell people they can just enter our driveway and proceed up the dirt road. We know they do, because we hear about their visits after the fact.

In this case, it was a few weeks after I invited her when another woman who worked with her led her to the site, then stopped to tell me our young friend, who was about 19-years old, was up at the sanctuary. Of course, I went up to say hello and offered to pray with her, suggesting it might be good for her to climb right up to the cross. While she admitted she was not strong in faith, she went willingly. Minutes later, we were both standing with our hands touching the base of the cross. The sky was blue, the trees were still. There wasn't a breeze to be felt—until I started to pray. And then a light breeze began to blow.

I stopped praying long enough to say, "This may not be the wind—it could be the Holy Spirit passing by us." As soon as I said this, the wind at the cross totally stopped and it was as if we were encased in a sphere of calmness. But my young friend was not calm. It's hard to describe what was happening, but it's as if the wind was swirling faster and faster beyond our tranquil little spot, like a tornado gaining in power. I guess you could say it was like being in the eye of a storm. My trembling friend said she was so frightened by the sounds, she had to open her eyes. She could not believe the way the wind near us had stopped, yet she could see it swirling around the outskirts of the sanctuary. She also said she noticed the air had changed as soon as I mentioned the Spirit.

A week or two later, a woman approached me and said, "I want to thank you for taking the time to talk to my daughter. Her experience up at the cross was amazing." Weeks and months went by, and as far as I know, the young girl's troubles and trials were decreasing. I was glad to hear it because I felt a strong bond with her—I believe she is a very caring person who is always trying to help others. Ever since our experience at the cross, she would come to give me a hug and I'd ask, "How are you doing, sugar?" After the first time I greeted her with that expression, she said, "You know what? The only other person to ever call me Sugar, was my grandfather." And, of course, the bond became even stronger when she came to me one day to explain how much our talks had changed her life. She said she had developed the habit of repeating a simple prayer I had taught her. A prayer with just four words: "Your will, not mine."

Those four words are the ones I most often repeat in my daily prayers. But, after she had proclaimed that I had changed her life, I quickly said, "It wasn't me. It was Christ." I advised her to continue to pray each morning for His will to be done, not hers. The last time I saw her, she said she was going to be moving out of the area. I told her to hold Christ in her heart and to continue to pray. I sincerely believe if she does this her life will continue to improve; and, it's my prayer that her troubled spirit would fully recover and she will continue to be

Your Will, Not Mine

a great, loving person who will help others—and even more importantly, to be a great witness to Christ and His work in her life.

Another time at a supermarket I struck up a conversation with a man I'd never spoken to before. When I asked if he was a man of faith, he said he was, but he also told me he was feeling hopeless. He had cancer. I told him I had been diagnosed with life threatening cancer twice, and both times I was miraculously healed. I also explained that I felt I had been given a healing gift and before we parted, I asked if he would let me pray for him. He agreed and so I did.

We came across each other only a few times over a period of about six years when he finally said his prostate cancer had been gone for several years, despite his doctor's pronouncement that it most likely would come back in five years. Even so, it seemed like he would never be in good shape because he was now diagnosed with Lyme disease. I said I would continue to pray for him and reminded him that he had been healed of the cancer and prayer could lead to a complete healing. The last time we met, we sat at a booth in a local convenience store and I took his hand and prayed. He commented, "You know what people are probably thinking when they see us holding hands like this," and I said, "I don't care what they may think. I don't believe we should hide behind closed doors when we pray for someone. Shouldn't we do so out in the open? As for me, I refuse to be a closet Christian!" I hope the next time I meet this man his health will be much better. I do believe he has faith. I do believe he will continue to become healthier.

One day our church hosted speakers from a group called "Jews for Jesus". Members of this group believe in Christ and His resurrection. The speakers were a dynamic husband and wife team. Ann and I had the chance to talk with them after the service, and we invited them to come to the House of Angels. They were genuinely enthusiastic about seeing the site and we were interested in learning more about their faith.

DESTINATION D.C. A Modern-day Jonah?

At the time, there was a lot of hay on the ground—35 bales of hay to be exact—spread around to protect a major part of the site where I had planted grass seed for the first time. The woman asked how I was going to water it. My answer? I pointed to the sky, saying I believed God would take care of it. They could not stay long, but after an enjoyable visit I prayed for rain. As I had hoped, a day or two later, rain was in the forecast. Trouble is, a hurricane was coming up the coast and remnants of it were heading straight for us. I thought, *Oh no! All that work. All that hay!* It covered almost an acre, including a gentle slope that makes the area resemble an outdoor amphitheater. I could picture high winds snatching up the blanket of hay and heaping it at the bottom of the hill like a giant bedroll. There was nothing I could do but wait and pray.

Later that day, I flipped the TV back and forth between a show we were watching and the weather channel. The destructive storm was continuing its northward trajectory, heading straight toward us. I expected to find my hard work undone in the morning, but I should not have worried. To my amazement the early weather report revealed how the hurricane split in half, veering to the east and west as it approached Vermont. My immediate reaction? "Praise God!"

And the grass grew.

There was a wonderful little congregation in a neighboring town called the Cowboy Church. Ann and I attended from time to time. It was there that I heard about a man who desperately needed help on many levels. He was suffering greatly from the advanced stage of cancer; so of course, I agreed to go and pray for him. At his house I met a woman who was his friend and was acting as his caregiver. During one visit, I brought a picture showcasing the House of Angels when the flowers were in full bloom. She stared at it with a look of astonishment.

"I've seen this before!" she exclaimed, and I wondered when she had visited our place. But then, my own expression morphed to amazement when she explained that she had seen it in a very vivid dream when she was just a child. She said, "The ledge. The flowers. The cross. They're all there just like I saw in my dream!" I thought it must have been a powerful memory for her to recognize the details so well after so much time had passed.

A couple of months later, she called to say her friend had passed and she wanted to visit the House of Angels. She also announced that she was going to leave the area and move to Texas. When she came, we planned to spread his ashes and ended up doing so shortly before her move.

It helps me to handle the passing of the sick and elderly when I focus on the hereafter. A few years later, I would be blessed to meet Dean Braxton, a man who had been clinically dead for over an hour, who had gone to heaven and returned to tell of it. His story helps to reinforce my belief that we do move on to a better place when our physical bodies fail. He has an amazing story for sure, because the medical establishment had documented the fact that Dean Braxton had been pronounced clinically dead for one hour and forty-five minutes—a length of time that is considered clinically impossible, yet he recovered 100-percent. Might it have been that his experience, including his full recovery, is proof that we receive a new body in Heaven? His talks and his energy are truly inspiring, and his memory of heaven is astounding! You can read about it in his books, including: *In Heaven: Experiencing the Throne of God*; and *Deep Worship in Heaven*.

I love Christian music, so whenever an area church opens its doors for a night of worship and praise, I try to attend. For several years, Ann's work schedule prohibited her from attending most of these concerts, but she insisted that I go as often as possible. One of these concerts featured a young woman named Laura Hawthorne who had an extraordinary voice and an incredible story. In my estimation her talent was off the charts. That concert was quite a distance from my home, so I was pleased to hear she would be singing again that week at a church situated only a few miles from us. Of course, I introduced myself and invited her to come and see the House of Angels. After hearing Laura's story, I was sure she would be blessed by a visit. She had told the audience that it was her first performance in over a year and a half because she had been tormented by a problem with her vocal chords; and this concert was special because it was her first return to the first church she had performed in.

I was happy to be able to attend her next concert and once again, I invited her to the House of Angels. She explained she was pressed for time but would love to stop for a quick visit; so she followed me home after her performance. Ann welcomed her and the three of us headed up back. It was not surprising to see her reaction. Most people who come to the House of Angels say they can feel God's presence. After a heartfelt prayer session and a visit that we all agreed was too short, our new friend headed for home and preparations for her next performance. Neither Ann nor I expected to hear from Laura again. That's the way it often is and we're alright with it. But we did make contact about 12 days later. I had felt this extraordinary need to call her. I did not know why, but I believed she had been blessed by something. When I called, she recognized my voice and exclaimed, "Don! I have great news and I cannot believe you're calling me at this moment! I went to see my doctor, and the report was wonderful. It's the first time I've had such an encouraging medical report. I wasn't sure I'd be able to continue singing, but my doctor said there's no longer anything to worry about as far as my vocal chords go. I'm healed! I'm truly healed!"

But that was not the only time she gave a great report over the phone. She eventually went to Nashville to do a recording session, but she had a cold and wasn't sure she'd be able to proceed with it. She called to say she kept the handkerchief I'd prayed over, and with her belief in the healing power of prayer, she persevered, and the recording was a success. We kept in touch for a while, and she sent Ann a beautiful silver angel as a memento of our friendship. We've lost touch since then. Even so, I still love to listen to her CDs—her voice is so incredible. To this day, Ann keeps the silver angel on her bedside shelf; and I know that while our Christian singer has been blessed by God with an incredible gift, we've been blessed by her friendship.

As promised at the start of this chapter, here are the lyrics to Karen Gallagher's song.

LET YOUR LIGHT SHINE
Lyrics by Karen Gallagher, 2006

Let Your light shine on my world today
Let my words reflect the mercy of Your ways
Let my heart be broken by the lost I see
Let Your light shine on my world through me
Let Your light shine on my world through me.

All around me there is suffering; Hidden pain I cannot know
They are searching for living water; Lord, through me let it flow.

Those who need You, Lord, they turn away
They are blind and will not see
That the chains they have chosen
Can be broken to set them free!

Let Your light shine on a world of illness;
Let Your light shine on our fear and shame.
Let Your light shine on all bitterness and anger,
So the world can see why Jesus came.

POWER OF THE HOLY SPIRIT: "But you will receive power when the Holy Spirit comes on you; and you will be my witnesses in Jerusalem, and in all Judea and Samaria, and to the ends of the earth." Acts 1:8
"Suddenly a sound like the blowing of a violent wind came from Heaven and filled the whole house where they were sitting." Acts 2:2

DON'S NOTE: Our experience at the cross was unforgettable. It's hard to describe how the wind swirled as we prayed, leaving us untouched and safe, while the air rushed and gushed and raced and swirled around the perimeter of the site. My young guest was frightened. I was awestruck, believing it to be The Holy Spirit, dancing, reacting to my heartfelt prayer and this young woman's heartfelt need to reconcile with God and her destiny. I was reminded of the outpouring of the Holy Ghost at the Azusa Street Mission, in LA that had begun in April of 1906, and grew to include thousands of believers within the next five years. It was such an amazing event where believers of every race and nationality were slain in the spirit.

CHAPTER 13

The Husky Caper ... And the Devil's Face

Petunias don't come back on their own in our region. Well, it does happen occasionally, maybe one or two, here or there. But one year, when we didn't have enough money to purchase the plants we wanted for the House of Angels, a multitude of petunias grew. On their own! I was in the planning stage for a new season and I wanted lots of flowers. The petunias lining the stone walls in front of the ledge had been spectacular the year before. We loved the way almost four dozen of them drooped over the stone walls, spilling color and softness down the slate and granite. But money was short. As much as I wanted to repeat the effect, we couldn't afford to purchase so many plants and I decided we'd only be able to focus on the flowers at the base of the ledge.

I guess God wanted those stone walls to be colorful again, too, because as the plants we put in started to take hold that spring, I realized the petunias were coming back along all three of the stone walls, just as full and colorful and healthy as they could be, with no bare spots. They resembled a joyful reflection of God's gift—a reminder to enjoy what you have and to know that when one door closes, God will have another door waiting for you to open, if you praise Him in your hour of need and watch for it: whether you're in need of love, a home, a job, or a bed of flowers . . . or the companionship of dogs.

Ann lost both of her parents during our first few years in Vermont, and I suffered with my cancer. But we also experienced another heartbreaker: Lucas was in so much pain that could not be relieved, he had to be put down. Five years would pass before Ann would even think about "replacing" this beautiful white German shepherd that had saved her life and had been a daily companion for ten years. And when she was ready, God opened a new door, alright—a door that revealed two lovable blue-eyed huskies!

Around that time, every couple of weeks, one of us would go to my mom's apartment in Massachusetts to help with grocery shopping and chores and repairs. And sometimes we'd bring her back to Vermont for a visit. On one of these trips, I noticed a pack of dogs fenced in at a field along the roadside. I'd driven this route many times and had never seen any dogs there, let alone a dozen or two of them. I wondered if they were available for adoption.

I drove past the dogs without stopping and picked up my mother, but on the way back I just had to stop. When I pulled over to get a better look, I saw a sign that made me believe it could be a rescue place. I wanted to see if the dogs were available. Mom was game, so I got out and knocked at the door. The woman who greeted me said most of the dogs were huskies and there was one lovable boy that had been abused and she hoped to find him a good home. With a hopeful heart, I received permission to enter the field and visit the dogs. The male dog she had spoken about caught my eye. He was beautiful—a typical white and caramel Siberian Husky—with blue eyes. As soon as I bent down to say hello, he kissed my face. That did it. Instant bonding.

The woman then threw a curve, saying there was a female back at the house. "She's had to stay out on the deck because she, umh—well, she has a problem—she messes in the house." *Oh, oh,* I thought. *Not good.* But she wanted me to see this female, so I did. She was a pretty dog, with soft, fluffy white fur that was longer on her legs—like the long hair on an Irish setter. And her eyes? Big, blue . . . and sad. "Her name is Ginger," the rescuer said, "and I want to get her placed in a good home first. She was also abused; but she's lovable!"

"Oh, boy," I said, realizing Ann was still reluctant to replace Lucas. But the poor little thing was irresistible. So, when my mother and I got back to my place, we told Ann about the dogs.

"No," she said. I could see it wasn't anger that sharpened her voice. Her eyes grew shiny. She was remembering Lucas, the dog who saved her life. The dog who knew hundreds of words and tried so hard to speak, sometimes seeming to echo her greeting, "Hellooo," as she arrived home from work. The dog, who I'm sure I heard murmuring words like, "I love you," as well as any dog could. But my mother and I talked Ann into going back with us to see the huskies.

"We don't have to get a dog if you really don't want to, but I want you to at least look at them," I said. "And it's only about ten miles or so down the road." We must have been convincing, because she did finally agree to check them out. "Just to look," she insisted with eyes glistening brightly with memories.

All this time, I was thinking about Ginger. I decided she was just confused and sad. I mean, there she was, about three or four years old and not spayed—in a new place where the people already had their own dog who recently gave birth; and there were all those male dogs out in the field. I decided that maybe, just maybe, her "problem" stemmed from a hormonal imbalance and her confusion and fears about her strange new surroundings after being so badly treated.

It took Ann about three seconds to fall for Ginger. When she sat down on the deck to get a better look at this fluffy white dog with the big, sad eyes, the dog just ran to her and snuggled right up into her arms. Of course, she was hooked. So, while she was bonding with Ginger—who we believe is part Samoyed—I went down for another look at the male dog; and now, when I think about the moment when I approached him, I'm not sure which one of us was happier to see the other.

We went home with both dogs. Ginger and Gabriel have been wonderful, loving companions ever since, and it seems that Ginger has a healing touch, too. Whenever we hurt, she zooms right over to lick the spot, instinctively knowing where the pain is. Of course we feel better! And Gabriel? This blue-eyed, four-footed angel has his own way of speaking. He says, "Go out," when he's in dire need, and, "Right now," when he's in a demanding mood. And boy does he make his demands known to Ann: he practically shouts, "right now!"

God has a way of intervening in our lives on many fronts. Even with decisions about cars! We'd been thinking about getting a bigger car, although we were not ready to purchase one. But an opportunity came along that we could not refuse. A car was being offered to us for free by a family who knew about our work at the House of Angels. One of the in-laws wanted to get rid of a vehicle and she was willing to give it to us because of our faith-based life. Now, we weren't ready to be a two-car household. A second car did not seem necessary, so we decided to sell the car we already had, especially after we learned that the book price was more than what we had paid for it!

We put it up near the road with a for sale sign and it wasn't long before people stopped to check it out. One of these people was a military man who had just returned from a tour in Afghanistan. He was interested, but he admitted he was kind of low on cash. He said he'd come back if he could scrape up the money. He did show up the next day and after talking with him, I headed down to ask Ann what she thought we could do price-wise.

Before I reached the front door, I received a message, loud and clear, that I should give the guy the car. *What?* That was a message I did not want to hear. There was a lot I could do with the money from the sale of that car. After all, I was thinking, *God gave us this other one. Why not make the most of this impending sale?* Anyway, Ann was right there in the living room when I entered the house and I said, "The military guy came back, and he made an offer. He doesn't have much money, but there's something I should tell you."

With a thoughtful look she said, "I know. God wants us to give it to him, doesn't He?" It wasn't a question. She had heard the same message and of course, as always, she agreed. It could have been easy to come up with lots of excuses why we should sell the car for the highest offer; but we also had to recognize that before this and ever since, we've received what we need. And, no matter how much we give, we receive even more so we can give more. That is one of the truths about God's way that is so important to learn: the more you give, the more you receive. But it's not a revolving door: you must give joyfully with a desire to help others; and you don't get rich by doing it. At least not rich money-wise. It's a richness in spirit.

And now, as I look back to that occasion, I realize Ann and I often receive the same message. It's like a confirmation that, yes, we are on the right path; or, as is sometimes the case, we need to switch gears. But we have another car story!

After a few years passed, we decided to shop for a better vehicle. It did not take long before we found a spotless car at the right price at a dealer's shop. After a quick inspection we agreed the previous owner must have taken very good care of it, but we decided not to jump too fast. We went home, thinking if we felt the same the next day, we'd go back for it. And we did. But just ten minutes out of the sales lot, there was a problem. When we stopped a short way up the street to fill it up, we could not get the gas cap to open; so, I scrambled across the road to ask the dealer to help us out. He did. So, heartened by his cheerful assistance, we headed home.

A couple of days later, it seemed the battery was dead. We called the dealer and even though there was no warranty on this used vehicle, he replaced the battery. Great! It was going to be a sweet drive after that. Or not. Before we knew it, we had a major break-down and the dealer even agreed to put in a new transmission and to pay for half the cost. "That'll do the trick," he said."

Or not. By this time, we were calling it the car from Hell.

It stalled again. And we got another transmission! And then there were electrical issues, causing it to stall again and again. The car from Hell was living up to its name, and after only a few months, that "new" transmission completely died. At this point, we brought it to a different shop where we were told that after all the replacements and expensive work we'd already put into it, we'd have to spend another fifteen hundred dollars to fix it—with no promises.

We said, "No," and had it towed to the junk yard.

Enough is enough, right?

Or not.

A few days later we found another car. I mean, this one looked great. Really great, but we were leery of getting stuck again. Very leery. So, I decided to ask for another opinion, but we would have to wait a few days before the mechanic would be free to lend his opinion.

Time for God to step in, correct? All we had to do was ask and that's exactly what we did. After all, it's a real hassle to go without transportation and we were tempted to at least go and put a down payment on the car so no one else would snatch it up; but we decided the best thing we could do was to pray about it. So, we said a prayer and then popped open the Bible and there definitely was a message for us. The NIV Touch-Point Bible we used had sidebars with examples of how the Bible verse relates to current times, and wouldn't you know it? This sidebar dealt with decision making and referred to decisions about cars! It said to pray for guidance and act accordingly. After doing so, we received confirmation on what to do alright. And it came in a very unusual way.

The next morning, I happened to glance out the window and saw that the night had released a blanket of freshly fallen snow; and right there, on the hood of our car, was an image that without much imagination revealed an evil, demonic face. I instantly wondered, *are we about to purchase another car from hell?* I called to Ann and pointed toward the car without saying another word. Her eyes bugged when she saw the demonic face. We decided it was a message saying, "Don't purchase the car in question." This is something no one would believe, so to prove it happened, I snapped a few pictures. I started from about 50 feet away from the car and continued to snap pictures as I moved closer. I wanted to prove there were no footprints in the fresh snow, and there was no way we could have drawn that face.

I called the garage again and this time he said he could look at the car as soon as we could get it to him. Well, his inspection revealed too many expensive problems that a lay person like me would never have seen. For instance, no matter how good they looked, the car floor, the brake lines and the gas lines were all rotting out. I still thank God for His direction and I still remember the lesson to seek the Lord's help when you have important decisions to make. Even with cars!

GIVE WHAT YOU CAN GIVE: "Bring the whole tithe into the storehouse, that there may be food in my house. "Test me in this," says the Lord Almighty, "and see if I will not throw open the floodgates of heaven and pour out so much blessing that you will not have room enough for it." Malachi 3:10

DON'S NOTE: You can't out-give God! Ann and I have given money and food and a car, a bed and heaters and furniture, to numbers of people in need and we've ended up better off after each generous action. How can this be? We believe it's because we give with cheerful hearts. And when you think about it, God's promise has rung true for us many, many times. The more we gave – in a fully, cheerful, "happy-to-help-you" way, the more we received. We are not trying to boast about our good works—we hope this information will help people to understand it is simply better to give than to receive. And we are not wealthy. We live in a trailer. We can't afford to take yearly vacations. Our clothing is mostly second-hand. But, we have more than we've ever had before! God wants us all to be content with what we have and where we are in life. You can have all the money you need and not be content. Think of the stock market crashes where millionaires found themselves penny-less.

CHAPTER 14

Miracles and God's Creatures

When we first moved to Vermont, Ann was not sure what she was going to do. She had experience with public relations and with newspapers, but it had been so many years since she had worked for someone else, those jobs required computer skills that she didn't have and did not want to pursue. She did end up with the job at our local radio station, but as we talked about other job opportunities, I remembered conversations we'd had about her experience with writing: she'd always wanted to write a book. I had a good idea for one and her radio job left time for her to focus on writing and to do research on the subject.

I'd been concerned about the food industry. "Supermarkets have fruits and vegetables with patent numbers on them," I said. "More and more they're filled with genetically modified foods. Not only that, there are fewer and fewer companies that sell heirloom seeds. They focus mainly on hybrids. She did not want to write a scientific book about seeds. She was more into adventure stories and thrillers, so she decided to write about the food industry in a novel of suspense filled with real information. She'd also wanted to write about her brother, a treasure hunter who lived in Alaska and traveled across the country with his metal detector, so she decided to combine the two concepts; and before long, she was penning a thriller about John Victor, a treasure hunter who stumbled upon a plot to control our food supply. She called it, *The SEED*. Over the course of the years, she also wrote three children's books, featuring a magical metal detector that propelled the hero back through time.

Little did we know, but God was leading Ann toward a life of writing. It became evident one day when she decided to take what she calls a "power walk". She had been suffering with asthma and other health issues for a while and she was quite out of shape, but she felt better one day, so, she headed toward the dirt road on our property. This was a couple of years before we discovered that I had the colon cancer—before we ever knew that we'd be creating a site called the House of Angels beyond the top of the road. Anyway, Lucas, our shepherd was always happy to walk with her. As I mentioned earlier on, Lucas was a special dog. One of the most intelligent dogs I'd ever known. And, he was very protective toward Ann. If she was not feeling well and was wheezing and struggling to breathe, he would stay very close to her on their walks; but when she was feeling well? He'd meander off on his own. But on this walk, she suddenly stopped short and grumbled, and Lucas came straight back to her. She was grumbling because the roadway was strewn with dozens and dozens of little, bright orange salamanders and she couldn't take a step without possibly squishing one; so, she started to complain, "Here I am, finally feeling well enough to exercise, and I have to stop for these little buggers." Well, the grumbling ended fast when she sensed a voice that said, "You wanted a woodland full of salamanders."

Ann froze, and Lucas sat down and looked toward the sky. It was as if he heard what she was hearing. Instantly, she flashed back to a time long forgotten, when she was about seven years old. Her family had moved to a house on the outskirts of Fort Ann, New York, and she was on her first excursion alone into a nearby wooded area. She had turned over a log and had found a little family of orange salamanders, and when she turned over another log, she found another family of them. It was a significant moment, she now realizes, because it was the first time in her life when she acknowledged God and His creation. She also thought the people who owned that piece of woodland were the luckiest people in the

DESTINATION D.C. A Modern-day Jonah?

world, and she wished she could have a woodlot full of salamanders someday. Kind of a typical reaction for a seven-year old, right?

Well, after that flashback, she was quite bewildered, but endeavoring to avoid the little critters she crept slowly and carefully around them. After she got a little further up the road, she asked one of the questions she'd always had about faith: "God, how can you talk to me, and to so many other people in the world at the same time?" The response was: "You can communicate with millions at once, so what do you think The Almighty God can do?" When she asked, "What do You mean," the answer was clear: "You can communicate throughout the world with the click of your computer. So, don't you think the Creator of all, the God of the Universe, can do even more?"

She continued up the road and asked more questions and got more answers. And she was told to write a book about John. *That's weird*, she thought, *after all, the Book of John had already been written*. She knew without a doubt that she could not even remotely become a biblical scholar. And then, when she got to the top of the road where it circles around, she asked a final question. But she did not receive an answer to that one at that time. She had asked, "How God, how can I believe in You when You allow my mother to waste away with cancer?"

Her mother was in a nursing home. She had been found to be full of cancer over a year before this during an emergency surgical procedure and had to be transferred to the nursing home in upstate New York. She was so full of cancer the doctors had not even tried to treat it by the usual means—they were just medicating her for the pain. She was also slipping into moments of dementia.

Lucas remained close by throughout the walk, sitting and tilting his head as if he was listening each time Ann received a message. Well, when she did not receive an answer to what she thought was the most important question, she started to trudge back down the road. Halfway down, she spied a white rock. Oddly shaped, about the size of a softball, it was a solitary rock in the middle of the road where there usually are no rocks. She was told to pick it up and give it to me and she did as she was told. I was sitting in the living room when she came through the front door and I could

Miracles And God's Creatures

immediately see that something profound had happened. I mean, her face seemed to be drained of blood and she was weeping and shaking when she handed me the rock, saying, "I was told to give you this. I think God told me."

I was bursting with questions: "What? Who? Are you sure? What's wrong?" But even before the stream of questions poured out, I began to tear up, too. That's because I had seen a movie once that depicted Jesus as saying, ". . . split some wood and you will find me, turn a stone and I'll be there." I had always wondered if the movie was revealing God's truth. The stone confirmed the belief that the church is not a man-made structure of wood or brick and mortar, and those who discover the true meaning of that message will find life forever after. So, the rock that was so emotionally dropped in my hand was my answer! I forced myself to calm down and concentrate on why she was so upset. That's when she told me the whole story, starting with the salamanders and ending with the question about her mother, and the order to give me the rock.

No more than ten days passed when we received a call from Ann's brother, Bruce. He said, "Annie, I've got some news about Ma." She immediately thought the worst and braced herself. Sensing her nervous silence, he hurried to say, "Well," the doctors are scratching their heads. They did their usual tests, and then they re-tested, 'cause, well . . . her cancer is gone. They can't find any evidence of cancer anywhere in her body. It just disappeared!"

"Of course," I said as soon as I heard Bruce's message. "God didn't just answer your question with words. He answered it by curing your mother's cancer!"

Within a few years, Ann published her first children's book and her first novel, *The SEED*. We framed the first copies and hung them on the living room wall. Several months would pass before realization struck. She suddenly turned toward me and said, "The book of John! I was told to write the book about John! And I did!" She was looking at, *Travel With Johnny Vic*, and *The SEED*. "They're both about John! That must be what God meant. Remember? The day the salamanders stopped me?

Since that time, she published two more Johnny Vic adventure books, and a second novel, called *Buried Alive*. All of them have positive messages about America and our country's Christian foundation. While they have not become best sellers, they have been endorsed by educators and/or clergy; and she's received a 5-star rating on Amazon.com. She also has happily framed a letter from First Lady Laura Bush, who sent a hand-written note that says, "I think you have talent as a writer," and a letter from Mary Higgins Clark that agrees *The SEED* is a great idea for a story.

Although the cancer Ann's mother had suffered never returned, she did eventually pass. A few years had gone by when we received the call that no one wants to receive. Ann's mom was coming close to the end of her life. We had to go to her. Of course, Ann's four brothers and their wives also spent those last few days at the nursing home.

We all took turns at her bedside, making sure someone was with her all through the day and night. When it was possible, we would make the two-hour drive home to tend to Lucas and the cats. We had been on the night-time vigil a couple of times. One evening when we offered to stay through the night, it became clear that we should not go home. We called our dog sitter who knew the situation and had said she'd make herself available as needed. It was obvious my mother-in-law would not make it through the day. The night before, I had asked if anybody had come in to give Ann's mom her last rites, and the answer from one of the staff members was, "No. A request had been made, but no clergy member has shown up. We don't know why."

Not long after that, her mother woke up and appeared to be alert. I took it upon myself to ask her some questions about her faith. I asked if she believed in Jesus Christ and she said, "Yes." And I asked if she believed that she was a sinner and she said, "Yes." And then I asked if she knew that if she asked for forgiveness she would be forgiven for her sins. She said she wanted to be forgiven, saying, "Yes," once again.

At that point, she said she could see someone coming, but she didn't know who it was, and she couldn't tell if it was a man or a woman. She said, "They have long hair and a long white dress, but I don't know who it is. Too far away. But they're coming."

After saying this, she fell back to sleep, and we decided we had made the right decision to stay there. Three of Ann's four brothers and their wives—including John from Alaska—came into the room before their mom passed. John, the eldest brother, stood with an arm around his wife, Betty; while Bruce, the second eldest moved back and forth from bedside to chair as his wife Mary did her best to be consoling; and Barry, just two years older than Ann, and his wife Krisleen, stood resolutely by. Jim, the third eldest of the brothers, who had been there from the start, was trying hard to make it back with his wife Joan, because he'd had to return to work back in Ticonderoga. As we stood near the bedside, unbeknownst to the rest of us, Ann silently asked for a sign to show that her mother would be okay—that someone would be "on the other side" to greet her. Almost at the exact moment that her mother breathed her last breath, we were all amazed when a little wind chime that hung in the back corner of her room rang with one single note.

Hoarse with grief, Ann managed to say, "Did you hear that?" Everyone said that, yes, they heard the chime and she explained it happened immediately after she asked God for a sign—just seconds before their mother expelled her last breath. She said she had heard stories about family members greeting the newly deceased to the afterlife and she was wondering if Glenna or Margie, her mom's sisters, were there to greet her. Ann also prayed that her dad, a veteran from WWII, who passed a few years earlier, in 1999, would be there, too; but she knew how close her mom had always been to her sisters.

We all knew the windows were closed. We all realized there was no wind and the chimes were too high and too far away for any of us to have caused them to ring.

Ann was close to her Aunt Glenna, and I remembered how she had told me when we first met that she had heard Glenna's voice very clearly say, "Goodbye, Annie," one early morning. An hour later, she received a call from the hospital explaining that her Aunt had died. Just like her brother, Jim during their mother's last day, she had traveled back to her home, vowing to return to Glenna's bedside as soon as possible.

GOD WILL TALK TO YOU: "Ask and it will be given to you; seek and you will find; knock and the door will be opened to you." Matthew 7:7

DON's NOTES: The Bible promises that if you truly seek the Almighty God, you can know and experience Him in a personal way. But you must seek Him with all your heart. He created you for a specific purpose and it's likely that you will end up longing to do what God wants you to do.

CHAPTER 15

Godly Connections

One day I received a call from the Cape. The caller said my son looked awful, and ragged, and most likely was homeless. My heart sank. I hadn't heard from him for quite a while and knew it could be true. I tried to call my son and discovered his phone was not working. Soon I was packed and heading toward Cape Cod. I didn't know where to begin the search, but I knew I had to try to find him.

On the drive toward the Cape, I prayed and prayed, asking for the Lord's help. "God," I said. "I don't know where my son is. I have no idea how to find him. I need Your guidance and direction. I know You can lead me to him."

When I arrived, it was getting toward evening. The informant on the telephone said my son had been seen walking through a large mall, so I planned to check that out; but, then, I thought it was possible he was hanging around the Main Street area. On Main Street in Hyannis, I came upon members of a church who were passing out flyers, evangelizing and telling people how important it was to stop partying and becoming intoxicated—there was a better way: God's way.

One of the people handed me a flyer, but I didn't take the time to look at it. As we talked, I shoved it into my pocket. When he

DESTINATION D.C. A Modern-day Jonah?

started witnessing to me, I quickly explained I was a believer, too, and could witness lots of amazing things that he'd find were hard to believe. "But right now," I said, "I'm looking for my son. I was told he might be homeless, and I've got to find him." I soon went on my way and searched to no avail, until it was time to find a place to stay. Getting into bed, I remembered the next day was Sunday and it might be possible to find my son in church. He had previously mentioned one he had attended, but try as I might, I could not remember the name of it.

In the morning, I learned that God had directed me right from the start because when I took a moment to study the flyer from the evangelizing group, I realized they were members of the church my son had mentioned. *God truly is amazing,* I thought as I got dressed and prepared to attend their service. It was disappointing to realize he was not there, but at the church, I spoke to a woman who said she might be able to contact someone who could help. She said to wait a couple of days and then call her.

Who could just sit around, waiting? Not me. So, I drove the streets, walked the malls, and searched the stores, attempting to get a glimpse of my son. After two days, I placed the call to the woman and gained a glimmer of hope. She'd discovered the pastor of another church knew someone who had recently played softball with him. Calls were made, and as it turned out, one of the people I connected with said he knew a man who had been working with my son. "Very recently, but the guy's in Kansas."

Kansas? I was able to speak to him, though, and all I can say is, "Thank God for cell phones!" He was on his way back to the Cape and he knew exactly where my son was! He gave me the directions that led me right to the house where he was staying. My heart sank a bit a short time later as I studied the structure: it was under major construction; the walls were torn out and there was no heat, but at least I now knew my son had a roof over his head and he'd been working.

I was truly grateful for the information. I'd never have been able to find him on my own; he was about 20 miles from where I'd been searching. Thank God for guiding me to the helpful people and thank God for modern technology!

We spent a couple of days together and then it was time for me to return to Vermont. While my son's life was full of stress and loss, he did not want to leave the Cape at that time, and I had to abide by his wishes. The search had been exhausting, but well worth the effort.

Great news came later when my son agreed to come to Vermont for an extended visit. As I look back, I know God had brought us together at a time when he would be able to help with a major part of construction at The House of Angels, including the creation of a stone-lined drainage ditch and the round stone base that would hold a statue of the angel Gabriel.

The way we acquired that statue is another inspiring story!

GOD PLACES PEOPLE IN YOUR PATH FOR A REASON: "And we know that in all things God works for the good of those who love Him, who have been called according to His purpose." Romans 8:28

DON'S NOTE: God can help lead you to that which you seek as long as it is good and Godly and within His will. I found my son, and God saw to it that he came to me right at the perfect time to help with the construction of the House of Angels. The work I had to accomplish felt impossible to do alone. And God gave me even more assistance that you'll soon discover!

CHAPTER 16

Angels in the Sky

For several years from early spring to late fall—after spending eight hours on my full-time job—I worked up back at the House of Angels until dark. Sometimes into the dark. And, I also spent most weekends on it. It was hard work—clearing the brush, pulling the stumps, wrestling rocks of all sizes out of the dirt so about an acre of the once heavily-wooded area could eventually be sown with grass. And what a blessing it was to have my son stay with us that one summer. He was a great worker and a tremendous help.

One day at church, I was telling fellow parishioners about the House of Angels. I mentioned that I'd like to erect a statue of an angel up there some day. One of the women said she would like to donate money toward the purchase of one. Of course, she wanted to see the cross and the place where the angel would be placed and to pray for confirmation that she should donate her money for this cause. We arranged to have her come for a visit. It wasn't just her generosity, or the beautiful breezy day that would make her visit memorable, though. God revealed His approval with an unusual visual display!

When she arrived, our friend asked Ann to go up to the site and pray with her. She did not want to spend the money without God's confirmation. Ann was glad to comply. As they stood at the top of the hill facing the cross, they held hands and prayed. A split second after she said amen, Ann heard her guest gasp and exclaim, "My Lord! If that isn't confirmation, I don't know what is!"

Ann followed her gaze skyward where drifting clouds had formed the perfect shape of an angel. A few minutes later, they returned to the house, chattering excitedly about their experience; and the amazing thing is, while they were telling me about the angel in the cloud, Ann looked up and exclaimed, "There's another one. Look!" Two more angel-shaped clouds soared serenely across the sky. I thought they were holding their shape quite well, since clouds usually morph out of shape within a matter of seconds. Our generous friend exclaimed, "You look for a statue and tell me how much money you'll need for it."

My son's visit that summer was an example of God's perfect timing. We found a life-size statue of the Angel Gabriel, and soon the two of us were amassing a pile of stones from the property and mixing the cement for a base. It was wonderful to have his help. And you know what? When we found the angel and had created a stone base for it, our generous friend asked how much money we'd need. I said, "I think you should just give us what you feel you can afford, and that will be sufficient. We'll take care of the balance." I was amazed to discover the check she offered was only a couple of dollars less than the cost of the statue. Praise God!

My son helped with two other projects that summer—projects that I could not have accomplished alone. We built the stone walls that surround the raised patio-like area, spanning about 10-feet by 20-feet in front of the ledge. We also decided to create a drainage system to divert water that flows each year from snowmelt and heavy rainfall. Now, that was going to be one huge back-breaking project with nothing but a pickax and shovels to work with, but we believed we were both up to it. I had already worked on the overall site for 5 years or so and the area in front of the ledge badly needed that drainage system.

The day we decided to tackle the job, I said to myself, 'Please God, don't let this take 40 years like it did for Moses.' I mean, the amount of work to be done was nearly overwhelming and I figured it would take a lot more than a year to do it with hand tools.

DESTINATION D.C. A Modern-day Jonah?

Of course, God had it all worked out. About an hour after we determined how to start the project, my friend Girard Coursey, appeared, hauling a little Kubota with a bucket loader and backhoe. It was in great shape. He said it had just 55 running hours on the motor. Needless-to-say, our backs were saved and within two months we had created a great underground drainage system. I thank God for Gerry's generosity.

During those summer months, my son attended church with us. There was going to be a men's conference. The church offered some of the funding, so my son decided to go. He had a great experience, and while he was there, he purchased a gift for me. It was a key chain with an eagle on it along with verse 40:31 from the Book of Isaiah. I thought it was a great gift, but it became even more special, because a couple of hours after he gave me the key chain, I saw a bald eagle. A real one flying high in the sky. I mean, what are the chances that I'd see an eagle at that moment in an area where eagles were rarely seen? One thing I'm certain of? There were many times during my work on the House of Angels and throughout the Heal America Walk that I can only describe as "Godly encounters."

God surely puts us in the right place at the right time. That is a fact proven to me and Ann many times over. It happened once on the day of the celebration supper for a wedding we were invited to participate in. The groom-to-be had asked Ann to write a song for them and to sing it at the wedding. But, earlier in the day of the pre-nuptial supper, she went shopping in Rutland, and as she was heading for home, she saw a hot dog cart near a popular inn on the four-lane highway. At the time, she thought it was an odd place for a hot dog stand, but I think the oddest thing was she didn't really like hot dogs, yet she suddenly had a craving for one. So, she pulled over and placed her order for a dog. "With lots of ketchup and relish. And meat sauce." While the man was fixing her hotdog, she asked him why he set up his stand near a four-lane highway where traffic for the most part, sped by. He told her a big Christian event was going on at the inn next door and he expected—and got—a lot of business. He also said they'd been there for a couple of days already and he wasn't sure how much longer it would go on—but he did think it was the last night.

When Ann came home, she told me about the hot dog stand and how she had that sudden craving and low and behold, there was a faith-based event going on. She thought there was a reason for her encounter with the vendor and I agreed, especially since hot dogs don't appeal to her much anymore. We called the inn and asked about the group. They confirmed it was a Christian healing event and it was the last night. The activities were scheduled to start in the early evening hours, so we realized we could get there after we left the bridal supper.

There were about 300 to 400 people at the event. It soon became clear why we were there. One of the speakers announced that he wanted to pray for a specific healing and then asked all people with cancer to step forward. I turned to Ann and said, "I think I've been led here to pray for the cancer victims." Feeling skeptical, I said, "I don't know if they'll let me participate." Of course, she said to go for it; so, I found one of the organizers and explained how I was a cancer survivor and believed I was supposed to pray for others. I was readily welcomed to join in and spent the next two hours praying for people who had stepped forward. It was especially rewarding to see their positive responses to the opportunity to be prayed for by a cancer survivor. My story gave them hope.

I truly believe God's plan led me to that session. It was not within my comfort zone to speak in front of hundreds of people, but I believed I had to do it. Of course, I did! Who but God could orchestrate such an encounter, with a hot dog cart and a sudden, unusual craving? Yes, God does work in strange and unexpected ways!

POWER OF PRAYER: "Therefore confess your sins to each other and pray for each other so that you may be healed. The prayer of a righteous man is powerful and effective." James 5:16

DON'S NOTE: Talk about wonderful results! When our friend prayed for confirmation that she should help purchase a statue of an angel for the House of Angels, she received it—high in the sky. As we learn to pray and ask for God's advice, we must also learn to pay attention to the people and opportunities He places in our path. It was no coincidence that caused Ann to have an unusual craving for a hot dog near the mobile hot dog stand in Rutland. The conversation she had with the owner revealed the presence of the prayer and revival event that was happening nearby, where I was able to give my testimony and pray for cancer victims.

DESTINATION D.C. A Modern-day Jonah?

Don Duncan on his Heal America Walk. Photo by David McKeown, August 13, 2015, courtesy Republican Herald, Pottsville, PA.

CHAPTER 17

The Heal America Walk Begins!

One Sunday morning we woke up late. Too late, we thought, to get ready to attend church. After all, Jacob's Well was almost 50-minutes away; but the way things turned out, we found ourselves rushing out the door. We had turned on the television to watch Charles Stanley and he was saying how you must be obedient to do what God asks you to do—that you'll also wonder, if you had not been obedient, what the outcome might have been. Ann says that while I was out of earshot, she heard Dr. Stanley say you must take that walk of faith that God asked you to take. That was an amazing message since when we woke up, I told her that I felt as if my walk to Washington, D.C. should start soon, and she said she woke up with the same feeling. And so, after hearing Dr. Charles Stanley talk about obedience, we decided we had to get to church, even if it was too late to participate in the worship portion of the service.

At the church, to our amazement, when we opened the door to enter the sanctuary, we heard Pastor Cindylee say, "Don't be afraid to do what God asked you to do. Take that walk." This was around the first week in June. After the service, I was looking at a list of numbers that my Pastor friend Roger Whiting had given me, and the number 29 was the first number my eyes fell upon. Number 29 meant "Departure". I was sure that we had just experienced three incidents that told me to leave on the 29th. And it had to be June if I wanted to arrive in D.C. before the cold weather hit. After all, it was over 500 miles! These had to be Godly encounters: we don't often tune in to Dr. Charles Stanley on Sunday morning, we don't often arrive late and Cindylee doesn't always start the service with a special message. It all fell into place through God's guidance. I'm sure of it.

Godly encounters? There would be many on my Heal America Walk. Looking back, we should have known that He'd be in control; and yet, right up to the last day before I started out, Ann and I were incredibly busy with plans and preparations. As I finished packing my vehicle, I retrieved the cross George Crockwell, a fellow parishioner had built for me, and tried to remember if I could do anything to make it easier for Ann. After all, she'd be responsible for the household while holding down her full- and part-time jobs. I had just watered the gardens and cut the lawn and had put everything away that I usually use for the outdoor chores and told her to do the best she could—stressing that she shouldn't overdo it. I'd arranged to have Reggie Durrin, another friend from church, help with the mowing—the biggest chore as far as the property goes. I also assured her it would be okay if she fell behind with things. Mostly, I needed to remind myself not to worry. I simply had to be obedient and embark on the walk, no matter what.

Ann had already worked on a route. By photocopying pages from an Atlas and taping them together, she'd created a four-foot tall map containing the roads from Vermont to D.C. She had also made a few phone calls to places along the route to connect with churches and other groups to see if they would be willing to find people who would greet me. Before I knew it, night had fallen, and it was time to get some rest before the big day. June 29th. Tomorrow!

After all June 29, 2015, had been confirmed by the faith-based list of numbers to be the start date.

My friend Roger Whiting had interesting information about numbers, including a book entitled, "Biblical Mathematics," by Evangelist Ed. F. Vallowe. In his book, Vallowe reveals several reasons why the number 29 stands for Departure. And, if you look up

The Heal America Walk Begins!

the two numbers, 20 and 9, you see that 20 stands for Redemption, and nine represents the Fruit of the Spirit. Together, they reveal that the Christian who has been redeemed should bear fruit for the master—the fruit of the spirit.

I uttered a silent, "Thank You Jesus" the next morning and checked my list of supplies and instructions. It wasn't necessary, though, to have everything on the list for the first few days of the walk. I didn't expect to get too far because I hadn't done much walking since those visits to the gym the previous year when I'd exercised and worked to get into shape. But now it was time. No procrastination allowed. I picked up my cross and headed up back to the House of Angels. After a heart-felt prayer at the cross and a fervent request for God's guidance, I took a big breath and started down our dirt road, gave Ann a farewell kiss, then turned right onto Vermont Route 31, heading toward Granville, New York.

I made it to Main Street in the village. That was as far as I was going to go the first day. The next day the odometer revealed that I'd walked three miles to get there. That meant I'd walked another three miles to get back home, for a total of six miles. No cramps. No blisters. Not bad on the first day, for an old-timer like me, right? As I started out on the second day, I drove my vehicle six miles, knowing I had walked a total of that many miles the day before. From there, I started to walk again, then turned around at a certain spot, and walked back to my vehicle. On the third day, I used the same principle, realizing that on the second day I had walked a distance of four miles before turning back, for a total of eight miles. This system was explained to me by God so that I could have a vehicle and walk a full distance of over 500 miles. The system included times when I did not count some of the return walking so I could "save" mileage to make up for places where it is illegal to walk, like on highway stretches, and into Washington, D.C. Throughout the next two months, I kept a record of the miles I walked, making sure my end result would equal the mileage from the House of Angels to my designated end spot in Washington, D.C.

I needed to take it slow, build up my strength and sleep in my own comfortable bed for the first few nights. After all I was 65 years old and had health issues. I figured I could do this for 30 miles or so, then I'd start finding places where I'd sleep and/or eat that Ann had set up, or bed down in my vehicle. I was trying to save on expenses as much as possible because I knew it would cost quite a bit to complete the trip.

I also wanted to remain in the Granville area during those first few days, so I could attend the July concert in the park event. I expected it would draw a big crowd and I wanted to attend that gathering with my cross, hoping people would wonder about the cross and ask questions, including friends and people I did not know. I wanted to tell them about the interview I'd had on WCAX, Channel 3, if they hadn't seen it. But, until concert night, I continued to walk along Route 22 toward Salem, New York. I don't remember how many miles I had accomplished the next day or two, but I was sure each effort was more than the previous day. And boy did I appreciate the hot showers and good food at home.

The next day I reached Salem where I came across a man who had come to the House of Angels quite often. Of course, I told him why I was walking through the village with the cross. I smile now, remembering how he referred to the House of Angels as, "a piece of Heaven on Earth." I've often felt that way myself and I'm glad to have been able to connect with him before I reached the village limits. The next day when I resumed my walk, I hadn't gone too far when a woman pulled up. She got out of her car and, gesturing to my cross, asked where I was headed and what was I doing. Her interest made my travels through Salem memorable for a second day.

I told her my destination was Washington, D.C. and I was going for several reasons. "My main reason," I said, "is that I was told to do so by God. I also want to declare that I'm a Christian and I have a right to practice my religion, in public or otherwise." As she listened, I said I did not agree with many of the things happening in this country, like the racial division, the ethnic issues, the general unrest. I went on to explain the events in Ferguson, Missouri, were extremely troubling, especially since I did not think it was right for the president to tell the rioters to stand their ground. "It's like he was justifying illegal acts," I said, adding that the resulting public outcry for people to kill police officers was totally unacceptable.

"And then, to have the president of the United States suggest that we need a federal police force? I find it to be truly absurd. After all," I exclaimed, "this is not Nazi Germany!"

When she nodded in agreement, I added that I thought the country was going in the wrong direction—a bad direction, in most ways. "And look at the problems with illegal immigration," I said. "It's truly upsetting to think that people accept this illegal activity as being okay. "I have nothing against people coming here, trying to make a better life for themselves and their children. After all, my own grandfather came from Scotland. Legally. But we are a country of laws and they need to respect our laws. If they don't, then I can't help but wonder how else they'll show disrespect."

I paused for a moment then reminded her the most important reason I'm taking this walk is because God directed me to do so: "I'm simply being obedient," I stated. And then, I offered testimony, telling her about my two experiences with life threatening cancer and that I had received a healing gift. I also revealed many experiences connected to the House of Angels. That's when she told me she had a friend who was quite ill from cancer. She asked me to pray for her friend. And when I ended the prayer, she said her son was autistic. I told her about the time I had prayed for a boy with autism and how amazing it was to realize that about two weeks later, his doctors proclaimed they had never seen such a big improvement in an autistic child. I prayed for this woman's son, then, and after doing so I offered her two handkerchiefs, explaining what Christ had instructed His disciples to do in Acts. "It still works today," I said. "If we pray upon handkerchiefs and distribute them amongst the people who need a healing, it would be a blessing for them."

I also revealed, "God told me before I started this walk that I would be praying for people along the roadside and many of them would be healed." I also noted that it wasn't just handkerchiefs Christ had mentioned. "Prayers could be said upon aprons, too, but handkerchiefs are easy to carry and distribute."

As she departed, I wished God's blessing upon her and those she cared about, realizing this encounter had been a blessing for me, also. I continued along the road and soon found myself approaching

DESTINATION D.C. A Modern-day Jonah?

the home of a friend from church at Lake Lauderdale. I stopped to say hello, but no one was home, so I headed out, intent on reaching Jacob's Well, the church in Cambridge, New York that Ann and I have been attending. Our pastor, Reverend Timothy Bohley, who had been incredibly supportive of this walk, was there, along with a crew of people who were working on renovations. The entire church building, which they had recently purchased through an amazing Godly intervention was being renovated. I asked him if I could use the church driveway as my overnight stopover and of course he said yes. "You can return here as often as you need to, Don," he said.

I entered the church with a sense of excitement. And maybe even a bit of sadness. Here they were, my fellow church members and a few professional contractors, undertaking the exhaustive labor of renovating a major portion of the structure. I wanted to help, but I knew God had another mission for me. As I checked it out, I thought about Pastor Tim's story of how he and his wife and partner, Cindylee, had acquired the church. It involved a dream that Pastor Tim told me that he'd had.

He said, "When I went to bed that night, there was nothing out of the ordinary—just another night like so many others. Over the course of a few months, we had been praying about the big brick church that had been occupied by First Baptists for over 50 years. The Board of First Baptist, a group of praying women, had asked five or six ministries to meet with them and write a letter of purpose concerning the use of their facility.

"Our church, Jacob's Well, had been meeting in a rented facility that had been home to the ministry for over ten years. We wondered when that building came up for sale whether we should try to purchase it, but I kept getting a "check" in my spirit about it, so we did nothing, and now the First Baptist Church was closing and waiting for the Lord to speak concerning who might continue ministry in the church built as a Presbyterian Church back around 1847. Their heart and prayer focused on the hope that the church remain one that God be glorified in. Continually.

"But, getting back to the night of my dream—honestly, I cannot claim to be a person God gives prophetic dreams to. I always joked that I was a pizza dreamer. Too much pizza, too many dreams. But this night was to be different. As I was sleeping, I heard the Lord's voice. I can't say how I knew it was the Lord. I just did. I didn't see Him, I only heard Him. He said, "They're going to offer the church to someone else." I knew the someone else was one of the other ministries that had met with them and written letters of intent. He continued, "But they will quickly turn it down." I wondered why, but only murmured, "O.K" with a bit of a questioning tone."

Pastor Tim continued to explain, "I guess looking back on it, I kind of thought, *well then, why tell me?* I don't remember consciously thinking that, but it is the feeling I remember; and the Lord continued to speak to me again, saying, "Then, I want you to move forward." After the dream, I wondered why He didn't say something more in the way of, "Then, you take the church," or something along those lines. He said, "I want you to remember the dream!" I know that afterward I felt slightly amused at how well God knows us. I rarely remembered dreams. And then, very emphatically, He said it again: "I said, remember the dream!!" I responded, "Alright, Lord, I will."

Pastor Tim's account of his dream immediately reminds me of how many times the messages I've received had been repeated. It's also a reminder to remember that God is in charge and everything works out in His time. In other words, Pastor was telling us he'd have to wait.

As he continued with the rest of his story, Pastor Tim said, "A fairly short time passed, and I received a phone call from one of the Ladies on the Board of the First Baptist Church. After identifying herself, she said, "Pastor Tim, I called to let you know the Board has voted to give the church to the Bennington Baptist group." I told her, "Well, if that's what the Lord wants . . ." and let my voice fade away. Then she said, "Well, I don't know if that's what He wants, but that's what they voted." I thanked her, and we hung up.

"I remember sharing that with my wife, Cindylee, and the few others close to me that I had divulged the dream to. Then just a few days later, my cell phone rang as I stood in my kitchen. I looked at the number coming in and said to Cindylee, "Here we go." It was the same Lady from the church Board. She said, "Pastor Tim, the Baptist group has turned down the church. They said they are moving in a different direction." I almost laughed aloud, and I said to her, "So now what's the process." She said, "Well I want to know if you want to move forward."

"There it was. The exact phrase the Lord had used. Oh, what a wonderful all-knowing God we serve! Confident now, I said, "Absolutely." I know God was at work, but I asked if she would do me a favor. After telling her about my dream, I said, "Please don't tell the Board about my dream until after the vote." She had said they would take a second vote and asked me, "Why?" I explained that I only wanted the church if it was God's will and I did not want to sway the vote in any way. Only a few days had passed before I received the call that the Board had voted unanimously that the church should go to Jacob's Well for the huge sum of one hundred dollars.

"I was mowing my lawn when I stopped to take another call that almost caused me to fall off the mower. All I could think was, *how awesome is our God!* The miracle didn't stop with the confirmation that we would get the building! After occupying the church for about three months, I received a letter from a financial investment company telling us a woman whom we had ministered to approximately a decade before, had passed away and left the church her entire annuity. God provided a half a million dollars with which we could renovate the church! Praise His name!

"I must say, I'm waiting for the next dream, knowing that I can no longer claim to be just a pizza dreamer. Glory to His name, forevermore!"

After hearing Pastor Tim's story, knowing how God had brought our congregation to this church, made my tour of the renovation process so much more special. I was glad to see that Pastor Paul Stevens was there at the time—especially when he invited me to go to a lunch that was being offered by another church in town. After all, I'd already walked several miles and realized I should eat. I wasn't terribly hungry; the heat was probably suppressing my

The Heal America Walk Begins!

hunger, but as a diabetic, I knew I should get at least a little sustenance before continuing with the mileage for the day.

Things did not proceed as expected because at the luncheon, I had trouble swallowing. The food seemed to get stuck in my lower esophagus. I started to choke. Coughing didn't help. Liquid didn't help. I just couldn't get anything down and had become violently ill, so I decided to return home. When I got there, I was exhausted and knew I needed a day of rest. Then I remembered the next day was the Fourth of July and decided that not only did I need an extra day of rest, I wanted to spend this important holiday with Ann. After all, it was the celebration of this great nation that had been created by wise men who listened to their Lord. Despite the delay it caused during the first leg of my Heal America Walk, I believe it was a good decision and we had a great time.

On July 5th, feeling rested and refreshed, I resumed the walk from where I'd left off in Cambridge, and headed straight for Hoosick Falls. I returned to Jacob's Well that night and discovered a real blessing the next day. Donna Fisher, a woman from our church whose husband tapes the services for a local cable television station, had seen me on Route 22, the previous day and she explained that as she passed me, she felt the Lord told her if I make it all the way to Washington, D.C., I'll be greatly rewarded. This brought tears to my eyes. She asked why I'd become so emotional and I explained that I had received the same message just a few days before, and I believed her story confirmed it would prove to be true.

While I was walking through the village of Hoosick Falls, I thought about the delays and realized several days had already passed and I'd only gotten about 40 miles into the walk. *At this rate,* I thought, *I might not make it in time.* But then, I realized I should not be concerned. The Lord will take care of it all and I will arrive in D.C. just in time. My puny human brain was having trouble with that confident reaction. I couldn't help but wonder: *Just in time? For what?* I simply did not have a clue, but what I did know—and still believe—was . . . it would be in God's time. I was just grateful the Lord had given me the ability to embark on this Heal America

Walk. And to get even this far, considering my physical challenges, was already an inspiring feat.

I had passed through Hoosick Falls and was heading toward Petersburg, when Pastor Paul, caught up to me to see how I was doing. He then said he had to return to Jacob's Well to finish some things. "I'll come back later," he said, "before you get settled for the night."

By early afternoon, despite the sweltering heat of the sun, I made a fair amount of progress. Anyway, a car came along and pulled off the road in front of me. A woman got out. She had a lot of questions and seemed to be intrigued with the fact that I was walking with a cross. She wanted to know where I was going. Where I came from and why was I walking along the side of the road with the wooden cross. I answered her questions, and as it often happens, I asked, "Are you a person of faith?" It's one of my favorite questions because no matter what the answer is, it can lead to wherever you want to go. If they say no, it gives you an opportunity to witness; if they say yes, it makes it even easier to talk and share beliefs. At any rate, this woman was ready to talk. And she was ready to help.

"I just finished grocery shopping," she said, "and I wondered if you need a drink or something to eat. I have juice, and milk and water, and I also have meat and bread, so I could make you a sandwich."

"No thanks," I said. "I have water. I'm okay, but I appreciate your offer and I'm glad you stopped." Then I asked her, "Do you go to a church in the area?" She said she used to, but it had closed, and she was between churches at the time. At that point, Pastor Paul parked behind her vehicle. She quickly said good bye, and I wished her well, feeling grateful for her encouragement and interest.

It was good to see my friend again, but I wasn't ready to stop walking, so we agreed to meet a bit later and he said he'd go up the road a few miles to find a good place to stop and read. Later in the afternoon we got a bite to eat before heading back to Cambridge. *Oh no*, I thought when I turned my key. "Why's my check engine light on?"

I'd already been delayed by the illness, so this setback was frustrating; but I resolved to get through it and not let it stop me.

We both drove to Bennington, Vermont, about a half hour away, where a mechanic said I needed a new part and since it was late Saturday, he wouldn't be able to fix it until sometime the following week. "We're pretty busy," he said. I decided I was not going to wait; he might not be able to get to it until Tuesday or even later, so I decided to get the part, go home and fix it myself. I absolutely did not want to wait until Tuesday, Wednesday or even later in the week. This was just one of many occasions when I believe God was pulling the strings and each delay ended up putting me where I needed to be when I needed to be there. I'm not a mechanic and never will be one, but I believed that the part was not hard to install.

Of course, it was harder than I thought: I dropped a small piece of the first one into the engine and couldn't retrieve it, so I had to race back to the store to purchase another one. But, while I was at home, I was able to mow the lawn and do a few other things I did not want Ann to have to do. After all, she had just finished her air shift at the radio station when she found me working at home.

Despite my inexperience and the troubles with my clumsy fingers, I was able to fix the car, do the chores and hit the road again early on Monday. At the spot where I needed to resume the walk, I reflected on the encounter with the woman who offered the food and drink. She was the second person I'd given a prayer cloth to. It was for her mother's friend who had cancer. And so, it was with happy thoughts that I headed toward Cherry Plains where Ann's cousin, Malinda Goodermote and her husband, Doug lived. She and Doug were going to let me park for a night or two at their farm. The sun continued to beat relentlessly, and I was glad to reach their farm . . . and their shower. I also felt blessed to learn they were planning to attend a special worship session at their church that night, and I was invited! I thoroughly enjoyed the evening, realizing if I had not had the delays of the previous days, I might have missed it. Memories of my stay at the Goodermote farm solidified my beliefs about farmers and how they can be considered the backbone of this country. They have a special perspective on life and how God's creation works.

Like God's plan, they plant a seed, watch it grow, and help to nourish it until it bears fruit.

DESTINATION D.C. A Modern-day Jonah?

The next morning, I came upon a store where a young counter girl had come to the side of the road to ask what I was doing. After a quick account about my Heal America Walk, she said her mother was suffering with cancer and was living in an old run-down trailer. So, of course I told her about the House of Angels and my ministry of healing. She happily accepted a handkerchief and a prayer for her mom. She also said she was a bit confused about things going on in her own life, including her relationship with her boyfriend. I was only too happy to tell her to look to the Lord for guidance. "His word can lead you in all aspects of your life," I said. "You should really ask for the Lord's guidance."

I believe it's important to note right here that I stopped in at that store a few years later and learned that the counter girl's mother was healed. While I was there, the door bells jingled, and Doug walked in. She told him, "This man must have some special power with prayer!" She explained that after I gave her the handkerchief, she and her mother held it and prayed over it for over an hour and she was healed. Then she repeated her story about how things had gone better in her life, too. The knowing smile on Doug Goodermote's face told me he wasn't surprised. We both knew it wasn't my power—it was God's power working through me.

Getting back to the walk: The store had great food, so fortified with a breakfast sandwich and coffee, I resumed my walk, anxious to put more miles behind me, feeling well able to do just that. It was still early enough to avoid the heat, so I decided it might be good to increase my effort by walking faster and farther before the sun hit the hardest. By using this new plan, I covered more miles than usual before turning back. That's when I realized my blood sugar level was becoming a problem. I took one candy, then another and still didn't feel much better and to make matters worse, I had three or four more miles to go to get back to my car. I was beginning to worry about ending up on the ground. While I knew Pastor Paul and Dottie were planning to catch up with me at some time that day, I did not know when or where, or if they'd make it at all; and more importantly, I realized if I collapsed on the side of the road, they might not be able to see me. With God's help, I kept trudging on.

They arrived just in time. Quickly realizing my situation, they brought me back to the store where I had eaten the breakfast sandwich. We placed our orders and I was soon ready to resume walking. I put in a few more miles and then gratefully returned to Malinda and Doug's property for the night. To this day, I remain grateful for their hospitality, their meals, their shower, and of course, their Godly wisdom!

I resumed my walk the next morning. In Lebanon I had my first bad encounter with a dog, having to keep him at bay with the cross! At first the owner thought I was provoking her pet, but after she realized I was just trying to stop him from biting me, she yanked him away. Thankful to still have my legs and pant cuffs intact, I proceeded on; but not long after the dog incident, I heard thunder in the distance. "Time to call my friends," I said to no one. "I don't want to end up with wet sneakers." Walking hundreds of miles in wet shoes? Not a good idea. Especially for a diabetic.

Cell phones can be great. And sometimes they're not. This was one of those not-great moments. I couldn't reach Pastor Paul or Dottie. I guess you could say at that moment, my cell was about as useful as the two cans and string my brother and I used when we were kids. I did manage to connect with Roger, my pastor friend from Granville. Roger had expressed an interest in walking with me. He had some issues with his legs because of a knee operation, but he was still willing to join me for a little while. After all, the walk wasn't just about distance—it was also about witnessing. He caught up with me in Lebanon and as I think back on this whole adventure, I believe he played an intricate role in it. He was the one who gave me the "new beginnings cross" two years before I started out, which helped to confirm that the walk was a "new beginning" to further strengthen my faith and obedience. The cross is made with cording tied into a specific number of knots. He was also the one who gave me a list that explains the meanings of the numbers as they pertain to the Jewish faith. That list helped to determine when this walk was supposed to start.

The writing Roger provided says numbers have meaning in the ancient science of Gematria that gives a number value to each symbol in both the Hebrew and Greek languages. According to Roger's information, the science of Gematria was created to insure the correct copying of the Scriptures and predates the Arabic symbols we use for the English language.

The top section of the new beginnings cross that Roger makes, has eight knots because the number eight signifies a new beginning. The bottom section has twelve knots, and this relates to the Governmental Perfection of the New Jerusalem which is the Bride of Christ. The top and bottom knots in the cross total twenty, the number that represents Redemption. The cross bar has a total of six knots, representing the failure of mankind, with three knots on each arm—three representing Resurrection. The cross has a total of 26 knots, representing the Gospel of Christ. The write up goes on to say that since man has fallen, God provides a new beginning through Resurrection, giving man power through Jesus Christ to become the Bride of Christ. That is the Gospel (good news) of Jesus Christ. Praise Him!

As we sat and talked, Roger told me about a sermon he had delivered not too long before the beginning of my walk. His sermon explained how Christ had died and had purchased Redemption and Resurrection and suggested the Lord Jesus Christ never said we must leave our physical body to be Resurrected. We can receive the gift He gave to us while we still are here on Earth.

I asked myself how can that be? But it wasn't long before I realized he was correct. According to evangelical pastors, we are mortal creatures who lead dead, decaying lives until we are born again. To be born again, we must profess our belief in the good news Jesus brought to us: that we can be resurrected into a new, fresh life and the filth and stench of sin will be gone—if we continue in a Christ-like walk. I was amazed at the simplicity of it. And the truth of it. His explanation reminded me about my feeling of being resurrected to a new healthier life on Easter Sunday.

The Heal America Walk Begins!

You too, can be resurrected today if you stand before the Lord and receive His gift of forgiveness. You too can rise to claim your place in heaven and eternity. Of course, there is a difference between Christ and you. He had no sin even though He had a body of flesh while He walked upon the earth. You, on the other hand, must struggle with sin and temptation which continue to creep into your earthly being. And that's what is so amazing: You can embrace your own resurrection while you are here on Earth. Think about it: Jesus did not say to wait for forgiveness after we die — He wants us to ask for forgiveness while we are here on Earth. He also said that by His stripes we are healed. I'd always thought that the mention of His stripes pertained to being cleansed of our sin, but could it be that He also meant we can receive healing of the body? Didn't Dean Braxton return from heaven with a fully healed body filled with vitality? Perhaps we should pray for healing as often as we pray for forgiveness.

After my inciteful friend drove away, I resumed my walk, filled with emotion, determined to make headway toward the Berkshire Spur Truck Stop. My feet did not take me all the way to the truck stop; I decided to drive there for the night and then drive back to resume the walk. It felt good to get a soothing, muscle-relaxing shower. The day included a very strenuous trudge up a steep mountainous road. I returned to the truck stop for a second night; and while I did not think it would be prudent to spend $18 every night, I did decide it was worth it to spend the money on showers during this difficult leg of the trip.

As I thought about the past couple of days, I remembered the large amount of litter along the roadside. I realized there was a greater number of angry people in the litter-strewn area — people who would shake their fists and shout angry words as they drove by; and later, when I came to an area that had very little litter, people were friendlier. When I told Ann about this revelation, we both wondered if anyone had ever done a study about the relationship between anger and roadside litter and if there's a correlation between these circumstances and faith . . . or the lack of it.

Just south of Hillsboro I noticed a man and a woman who were pressure washing the exterior walls of Johanna's Motel. Their parking lot was empty, so I figured they weren't very busy. I wondered if it would be possible to offer $20 to just take a shower. The woman, named Angie Wilkinson, was the owner and manager and after I told her about my walk and explained that I couldn't afford her rate of $75 a night, she offered me a room.

"I'm sorry, I just can't afford it," I said. "I have so far to go and have to be very careful with my money."

"No," she said. "You don't understand—you won't have to pay. You can stay for free tonight."

I don't know if my sweaty scent wafted to her nose and prompted her to rush this odorous guy into a shower or what; but I took her up on the offer, overwhelmed with gratitude and tickled that the motel bore the same name as my youngest step-daughter. It was still early in the day, so I thanked her, then said I'd be going a few more miles before returning to the motel. I'd only gone another quarter of a mile or so when I began to admire the surrounding countryside. *What a beautiful country we live in,* I thought. There were handsome homes and bounteous crops growing in the fields. I recognized corn fields, but something else was also growing there. After deciding it must be soybeans, my attention was directed upwards.

A buzzard was circling high above me. That scary bird followed me for quite a while and I finally lifted my cross and waved it, declaring, "This isn't a perch, you know!" Then I took a sniff, wondering if I smelled like roadkill. "Hey, ugly bird. I'm not dead. I'm still walking," I proclaimed, before wondering just how bad I must have smelled back at the motel. Maybe the manager was tempted to spray me with her pressure washer before allowing me to enter one of her rooms.

It was wonderful to have the room and a chance to get cleaned up and I thanked Angie for being so generous. Then I asked her, "Are you a woman of faith?" She said no, but she also said she had an open mind. "I think it makes a difference to be open and accepting," she said. "And I'm a good person!" I told her how important I thought it was to have faith and to believe in the Lord.

"The Jehovah Witnesses sometimes stop to talk to me," she declared.

"I'm non-denominational," I responded. "Christ did not ask us to go out and start denominations. He instructed us to be as He was."

"What church do you go to?" she asked.

"I attend a church in Cambridge, New York. Jacob's Well Family Worship Center. It's an outreach of the Living Waters Evangelistic Ministries." The Founder is Reverend Timothy A. Bohley, and the co-founder is his wife, Reverend Cindylee Bohley.

"I know that church!" she exclaimed. "I've enjoyed watching them on television."

I was pleased to hear she had tuned in to listen to some of our pastor's sermons. Pastor Timothy Bohley can be seen on local cable TV. His church services entitled, "The Sword and the Spirit" can usually be seen on CAT TV in Bennington, Vermont (although the schedule does change frequently) and in New York State the services can be viewed on Spectrum TV on channel 1301. Pastor Bohley can also be seen on You Tube under jacobswellfellowship. The church also has a FaceBook page—you can check them out and like them at Jacob's Well. He can also be heard on a 15-minute Bible teaching radio broadcast, also called, "The Sword and The Spirit," at 2:40 PM Tuesdays at 91.9 FM. I think he takes seriously, the scripture, Mark 16: 15,16 that says, "Go into all the world and preach the good news to all creation. Whoever believes and is baptized will be saved, but whoever does not believe will be condemned."

The next morning, I stopped to thank her again and she offered the use of the room for another night if I needed it. As I resumed my walk, I looked around and peered up at the sky, thinking, *No buzzards! I guess I don't reek enough. At least not yet.*

When I reached the Hillsboro, New York area, I tried to get in touch with Paul and Dottie Stevens. It took several tries that day, and when I finally reached them, we agreed I'd come to a point that was too far for them to continue to check on me. I assured them I would be fine and thanked them for their efforts. I also expressed my belief they had been a great blessing the day they found me with the low blood sugar. I prayed it would not happen again and vowed to be more careful. I was now on my own without regular assistance.

At one point I came upon a food truck and decided to stop for a bite to eat. At a nearby picnic table, I struck up a conversation with a couple who wondered why I was carrying a cross. He said he was a deacon in their church, and we had a pleasant conversation. As I recall the day, it increases the gratefulness I feel for the friendship and support I received throughout the walk and it reinforces my belief in the basic goodness of so many of the people in this country. After the pleasant couple and I went our separate ways, I called Ann. She said Copake wasn't too far down the road and we decided she should try to connect with someone there: perhaps a church, a truck stop, or some organization. When she called back a while later, she said she couldn't connect with anyone. *Oh well,* I thought. The lure of the shower and motel room was too much to resist, so I decided to take Angie up on her offer of a second free night at Johanna's Motel. At that point I realized Johanna's Motel was in the town of Copake and when I arrived, Angie seemed pleased to see me again. I thanked her, assuring her this would be the last time. The blessing of her generosity overwhelmed me, and afterwards, memories of the previous years before this walk flittered across my mind's eye. I started to think about the House of Angels and all the blessings connected to it. I have so many memories of healings and God-driven encounters:

OVERCOMING OBSTACLES: "Cast all your anxiety on Him because He cares for you." I Peter 5:7

DON'S NOTE: Anxiety? I certainly was feeling it, wondering if this walk would ever get going. I mean, during the first few days, my car broke down, I got sick while eating at a public luncheon, then a day or two later my blood sugar got so low, I thought I'd drop, exhausted, on the side of the road. But, remembering all the obstacles Jesus faced during his short life here on Earth helped me to find the strength and perseverance to continue. Like the lesson in the story of the tortoise and the hare, I realized it didn't matter how much time it took. It mattered that I continued until I reached my destination. After all, God was in control!

The Heal America Walk Begins!

A partial view of Christ's House of Angels. Cement lion sculpted by Ann Rich Duncan. See Website www.christ'shouseofangels.com

CHAPTER 18

A Guiding Light

Throughout the years as I worked on the landscaping and maintenance of the House of Angels, I've met several memorable visitors, but one year, Ann and I decided to attract more people by organizing a Christian concert. The site was looking great and it was a shame more visitors had not had a chance to enjoy it; and those who knew about it were asking if we held events there.

"Let's go for it," Ann said one day. "We could have several groups here, singing and worshipping throughout the day. Maybe three or four groups." I was already out straight, working eight grueling hours for my employer five days a week, then maintaining and improving the grounds each weeknight and during most of the weekend hours. Ann said she could organize it. "After all," she said, "I organized all sorts of events when I worked as a hospital's PR person."

We did not host just three or four worship groups; she scheduled eleven! Some were singles. Some performed duets. And many of our performers had multiple members. They ranged from the daughter of a well-known former pastor, to an accordion player, some church worship teams, and Christian entertainers who played on a regular basis throughout the region. One of the groups—The Angel Band—had a generator and generously donated their time and sound equipment, offering to come early to set it up. We will forever be grateful to Darryl and Brenda VanLeuven for their hard work and all the time they spent helping us make it a successful event. In all, there were about 70 entertainers and there were about 200 visitors who came and went throughout the day.

A few years later, we organized a Christmas caroling event. And while she was decorating the sanctuary for the big day, Ann avoided a painful encounter and experienced a beautiful miracle instead.

Of course, preparations for the event meant a lot of work for me. Before I knew it, I was up back, preparing the site. I crafted a metal fire pit and made sure the grounds were as cleared up as possible. And Ann got to work too, by gathering grapevines for an oversized wreath to hang on the cross, and I mean oversized—it measured over three feet in diameter. She also set up three five-foot garden teepees that she spray-painted white and decorated with ornaments and vines. We purchased a few Christmas trees and a few were donated for the event, along with hundreds of ornaments that people contributed. Some of those ornaments were made by a local family who painted popsicle sticks with bright colors and fastened them together to create little wooden crosses. They looked great on the trees. Soon, the site was transformed into a Christmas caroler's dream and we had eight Christmas trees and several bags of ornaments that we gave to families in need after the event.

That night, we gathered around the fire and enjoyed the beauty that surrounded us. Although I'm still not big on caroling, I do agree it seemed wonderful to be able to give people a touch of joy during the holiday season—with the event and with the donation of the trees and ornaments.

Here's what happened when Ann went foraging through the woods for the grapevines. It was a chilly day in early December, but not frigid, so she did not feel the need to pull on snow pants or leg warmers. She walked a short way up our dirt road then veered into the woods. Eventually she came upon several thick vines that hung from tall trees. Perfect for a large wreath, they were fastened tight about 20 feet above the ground and it was a struggle, but she managed to pull two large ones free from the trees. Each vine was thick and measured several yards in length. They reminded her of the vines she and her brothers used to swing from, like Tarzan, as children. She immediately wound them into a large, heavy wreath shape that would be the perfect size to hang from our 20-foot cross. *Great,* she thought, *it's already a wreath!* But then it was time to lug the heavy circle home. And I mean heavy!

She was so happy with the results of her efforts, she did not pay much attention to her surroundings. The large circle of vines blocked her view of the path and pushed away the vegetation she was walking through, and she eventually found herself in the middle of a thicket of blackberry bushes. Suddenly, with every movement, angry thorns threatened to snag her legs. Fearful of painful scratches, she tried to escape, but couldn't. I know how she felt; I've had encounters with blackberry bushes. Their perilous thorns can cause extremely painful wounds.

As I think about it, I'm reminded of just how much pain Jesus must have felt when the crown of thorns was jammed down onto his head. It is so sad to realize how cruel mankind can be.

But, getting back to Ann's plight, she did finally decide to stop to say a prayer and ask for guidance. As you might guess, the guidance came. When she opened her eyes and looked around, she spied a bright sunbeam stretching out slightly to the right, through a stand of soft green ferns. She says the beam of light looked like one you might expect to see shining from heaven. It led her totally out of that thick prickly patch of blackberry bushes, straight to our dirt road, just a hundred feet or so from the house.

That caroling event holds a special place in her heart, because she was surprised to see an old friend had come. She had known Erna Atkinson since they were about five years old and had not seen her more than two or three times over the past few decades. The two stayed in touch after our night of caroling, often emailing and talking on the phone, until we received a sad call, informing us that Erna had unexpectedly passed away in her sleep.

We know she's in a better place.

Ann's blackberry sunbeam was just one of the times she was guided from above in connection to a creative project. The House of Angels now has a 500-pound cement lion that she created with chicken wire, foam and several bags of cement. It took the better part of a summer to make it. And lots of prayer! Whenever Ann just started work on the life-sized creature, intent on using her own talent, she'd have to undo what she'd done—and that's a chore when you're working with cement! But it didn't take long for her to realize she needed to say a prayer, asking for guidance from above, before adding each layer of the special cement mixture. The same thing happened with our sign—a six-foot oval attached to the top of a stone wall that I built. For several weeks, I would come home from work to see her floundering with disappointment over her rendition of the ledge and cross, not to mention the cloud-filled sky. She'd end the day by grabbing a tube of white paint to cover what she called "the atrocity," insisting the project was "too big" for her to do. I'd insisted that she be the artist to create our sign after seeing a painting she'd done of three angels, entitled "Dance of the Saved."

She'd taken up painting again after promising Gloria Vanderbilt that she'd try her hand at acrylics. Ann had interviewed Ms. Vanderbilt on the radio when the creative icon's own work was being featured at a gallery in Manchester, VT. Ann had commented that years ago she had to stop painting because of a painful reaction to the fumes from oil paints and chemicals used to clean the brushes; and back then, she did not like acrylics. Ms. Vanderbilt made her promise to try acrylics again, saying they are much better to work with these days.

Getting back to Ann's attempt to paint our sign, one night she woke up around 1:30 AM and had a wonderful revelation! She said a prayer, asking for guidance, and wouldn't you know it? She got right to work and had ninety percent of our beautiful sign completed within an hour! It includes a gorgeous blue sky with three angels floating in the clouds above a rocky ledge that holds a cross. A talented friend and author who does pinstriping on vehicles added the lettering to what became a magnificent piece of artwork!

DESTINATION D.C. A Modern-day Jonah?

OVERCOMING FEAR: "For I am the Lord, your God, who takes hold of your right hand and says to you, 'Do not fear; I will help you'." Isaiah 41:13

DON'S NOTE: Ann's predicament in the blackberry bushes ended without injury because she looked to the Lord for help. The ray of sunshine she saw that revealed the right path to take was miraculous. It could also be a metaphor for life: ask God and He will guide you out of troubling situations! And, her success with the sign and the lion? It's all about the power of prayer!

CHAPTER 19

Visitors and Answers

One visitor came to the House of Angels to find peace in her grief. She said her father had recently been killed when he was struck by a tree he was cutting down. She went on to say her mother had fallen into a deep depression and was less and less inclined to leave her home. When we talked about having her mother come to the House of Angels, I was surprised to hear she did not live far from us; but as close as they were, I had not heard about her husband's accident. Well, my visitor said she did not think her mother would come, but she agreed to ask her.

Not long after that, I was cutting brush along the side of the road leading to the worship area when a car came along. My grieving visitor's mother had agreed to come! They stopped to say good bye and I don't know why it happened, but I knew I was moved to say that God might have had a reason—not known to us—to take her husband at that time. I've mentioned the belief to many people that we do not die even one second before or after we are supposed to. We are called home at the exact time it was meant to be.

They said they could not stay long to talk—they had to leave because the rest of the family was coming for a birthday party and they had to be there to greet them. They also said they would like to bring the whole family up to see the House of Angels. I did not think the whole family would agree to come but of course I said they'd be welcome. As it turned out, they did all come, and I was able to pray with them and once again, offer my sympathy for their loss.

About two weeks later, the mother and daughter returned. I offered to go up back with them and we sat on a bench at the top of the hill that offers a great view of the cross. After a few minutes, I said, "Something tells me you're wearing your husband's hat." She confirmed it was his. I think we were both surprised I had known this—there wasn't anything special about the hat—it was a baseball cap like many worn by men and women. But the next thing she said surprised me even more.

"Remember when you said perhaps my husband was killed at that time for a reason? I think you were right. During his autopsy, they discovered much to our surprise that he was full of cancer and most likely would have suffered a great deal, if he had lived much longer."

This knowledge reinforced my belief that sometimes, if we don't keep our eyes upon the mercy of the Lord, it can be hard to recognize it. Knowing this does not cause us to have less grief when we lose a loved one, but it can show us there's a purpose for things we don't understand, especially when we think there should have been a different outcome. It reminds me of a song I heard years ago with a line about thanking God for unanswered prayers. I've learned through the years how true it is that we should thank our Lord for many unanswered prayers. After all, some things I prayed for in the past would not have been for my own good, or for the good of the world. That song was titled, "Unanswered Prayers." Released in 1990. Sung by Garth Brooks.

One prayer was answered in an amazing way. If the experience filled its own chapter, I might call it "A Special Appearance," because, according to one pastor, I made a special appearance. And I wasn't even there!

It started when Pastor Tim at Jacob's Well asked his congregation to pray for the pastor of a Jacob's Well affiliate. Pastor Don was seriously ill. While he was a former military man and certainly was not elderly, he was bedridden and so weak he could no longer

Visitors And Answers

lead his congregation. The illness had tormented him for a few years; but had never been as serious or draining as it had become. Everyone was worried. There even was talk that he might not survive. And so, in response to Pastor Tim's request, I walked up to the cross at the House of Angels and prayed.

I prayed intensely for Pastor Don's healing. You could say I was pleading with God to heal our friend. After all, he was a great, Godly man and a dynamic, gifted preacher. I spoke from the heart, stressing that Pastor Don could do so much good by continuing to serve his Lord. The amazing part of this story occurred well over a year later.

Pastor Don did receive a healing and eventually, I saw him at our church. It was good timing because I wanted to have a chance to preach at his church. I said, "I'd love to preach to your parishioners, Pastor; but it's been quite a while since I did my Heal America Walk, so I'd like to talk about something else. Should I call to let you know what the topic will be and to arrange a day to speak?" He said he knew it would be from the heart and he believed I had a heart for God, so I'd be welcome to speak at any time—and he said he did not need to know the topic.

To make a long story short, we set a date and I gave a sermon at Pastor Don's church. After my talk, we shared a meal and he thanked me for visiting him in his bedroom when he was so sick.

"I'm sorry," I said, "but I didn't visit you. I should have, but never did."

"Of course, you did," he insisted. "You were in my bedroom. I remember it distinctly."

Again, I said I had not been there. "I've never even been in your house," I said. At that point he called to his wife, Pattie. "Hon," he said. "You remember Don's visit, don't you? He came to see me when I was so sick. He was right in our bedroom."

She said, "No. Don's never been to our house." Seeing her husband's puzzled expression, she said it again, "Really! He's never been in our house!"

Pastor Don finally accepted what we said, and he also thanked me for the handkerchief I'd prayed over and had sent to him. He said he had kept it at his bedside throughout his ordeal with the sickness; but he insisted my appearance at his home was as real to him as it was at this moment when I was standing with him. I know unusual things have happened during prayer time at the House of Angels—or, perhaps I should say blessed things. The only explanation I have is that my prayer for Pastor Don was so intense, we somehow connected on a spiritual level.

Ann does say that some of the experiences we've had are stranger than fiction. For instance, one day on the way home from work on a stifling summer day, after being totally exhausted and feeling dehydrated from working construction in a very, very hot building, I was thinking about jobs I'd had in the past. I'd had some sales jobs and to be honest I enjoyed sales.

But there was one sales job I hadn't even applied for. I had a chance to work with someone who sold food products to people in their homes. I don't remember now why I did not take the job, especially since I had a background in food. Thoughts about this job just floated into my head as I drove toward home, and I wasn't sure why. But it soon became clear. About ten minutes after I got home a food truck pulled into our driveway.

My eyes widened, and I said to Ann, "Hey, there's a food truck out there. I was just thinking about one of those businesses on my way home. It was a job I almost applied for, but in the end, I didn't." Before opening the door to greet the guy, I peeked out the window one more time. The name on the truck was different; it wasn't the same business. Or so I thought. Turns out, it was the same company from years ago, but it had changed hands and currently had a different name. The sales guy was pleasant, and we talked for about twenty minutes. After viewing a lot of great cuts of meat in his refrigerated truck, I had to say no, I just didn't have the money or space for a purchase; but while I was returning to the house, something made me stop. I turned back to the truck and when he rolled down the window, I said, "I know this is a strange question, but do you have cancer?"

"Yes," he said, and that's when I explained about our worship area up back and how occasionally I just knew things without knowing why. I asked if I could pray for him and he said yes. I prayed, and he went on his way. I saw him a couple of times after that and he told me he was doing alright. There came a time when I did not see him anymore. Perhaps he succumbed to the cancer. Perhaps he got better and found a different job. I try to remind myself I don't have to know everything about the fate of everyone we pray for—sometimes we just need to keep the faith and leave it up to Jesus Christ, the Almighty Savior.

Every now and then someone will show up at the House of Angels and they'll say something like, "I don't know why I'm here." That was the case once when Ann was home alone. She loves to do crafting and this day, there was something she needed from our storage trailer out back. Now, she can be quite a procrastinator and didn't want to search through the stacks of boxes in that darkened trailer, but something compelled her go out to do it. That's when she saw a telephone truck parked on the roadside at the top of our driveway.

A man was standing outside the truck, and when he saw Ann he said, "I don't really know what I'm doing here. I see you have a phone box connected to the ground and there's a new telephone pole on the north end over there. I know the pole doesn't have anything to do with this box, but for some reason I felt like I needed to stop and look at it." He shrugged, then said, "Well, I'll be going shortly."

"Okay, then," Ann said and headed back toward the house; but part way down the drive, something told her to go back and tell the young man about our cross and worship area.

"Really?" he said. "Can I see it?"

"Of course. You can drive your truck right up to the top where the road circles around. You can't miss the cross; it's twenty feet tall, up on a ledge."

He eased his truck up the roadway into the woods and Ann returned to her project. After a few minutes, she looked out the window and saw the truck was parked in the driveway. The man was sitting in the driver's seat, looking very sad.

She decided to check on him. "Are you okay?" she asked.

DESTINATION D.C. A Modern-day Jonah?

With tear-filled eyes, he said, "My brother. He's dying. But I should be the one to die."

"Why?" she asked gently. "Why do you think you should die?"

"I was in a motorcycle accident. They didn't think I'd survive my injuries. I was close to death, but somehow, I survived. And now, my brother has cancer and he probably won't make it." He had been staring at his hands while he spoke, but then he looked up with a guilty scowl, "My brother has a wife and two kids. He needs to be there for them. I'm single. Nobody needs me." The hand that suddenly gripped the steering wheel was wet with shed tears.

"I'll bet somebody does. Need you, I mean. And, I bet your brother needs you now. You know, we never realize the impact we have on people, just in our everyday lives." With a hint of hope in his voice, he said, "Well, on my way back down from your site, I was thinking how after I recovered from my accident, I gave someone a ride when he needed one. He was really down and out if you know what I mean, and I was thinking maybe something bad would have happened to him if I left him on the side of the road. And, there was another time when I was driving around a corner and saw a woman in a wheelchair that was tipped over and her stuff was spilled all over the road. I helped her get back up and mobile." He was silent for a beat, then muttered, "but I just don't know. My brother's kids need their dad."

"Well, that woman in the wheelchair could have been hit by a less observant person, you know, and who knows the consequences if she had been killed." Then she added, "We're all here for a purpose. That's what I believe."

He nodded, and Ann sensed that he was kind of appreciative, but still skeptical. She knew he was feeling survivor's guilt, but before she could say anything else, he said, "Well, you've got a great place here. I think my supervisor would like to see it: maybe I could bring her?"

"Any time," Ann replied. "My husband's been working on it for a few years now, and it's here for anyone who needs it. He had cancer twice and he was miraculously healed."

"Really? Well, okay, I'll tell her about it." He started to close his window, then said, "Thanks—maybe there's hope for my brother."

Visitors And Answers

Ann said her own eyes were a little teary as the telephone man drove back onto the road. The visit must have had an impact on him, because he did tell his supervisor about the House of Angels and they both came the following week. That's when we learned he was not from this area. He lived about a hundred miles away and had been sent here for a temporary assignment. An assignment arranged by God, perhaps?

God certainly does arrange things in fascinating ways. For instance, while I was in the beginning stages of developing the House of Angels, Ann interviewed a man on the radio who was a true believer. He had a sister who had suffered with cancer for several years and he was quite interested in visiting the House of Angels. He asked if I would pray for his sister. Of course, I said I would, and before we knew it, he had purchased a bench with her name engraved on a name plate. About a week later a car pulled into our driveway. I greeted the driver and asked if I could help. He said, "Well, I'm here to talk with you. My brother-in-law wants me to bring my wife here so you can pray for her."

I said, "That's great. You can bring her anytime." Then, he said to me, "Well, she's a believer, but I'm not."

"That's okay," I said. "You are still welcome. Bring her and be with her." We arranged to have them come about a week later; and when they arrived, we headed up to the worship area where I led his wife to the bench that her brother had purchased. I sat with her and we talked as her husband stood a few feet away. As we sat there, I told her about some of the healings that had taken place, including my own healing. Then, I asked if I might pray for her. When she agreed, I knelt at her feet and her husband listened as he remained standing nearby. When I finished the prayer and stood up, she asked, "What is that music?"

Her husband approached us and looked at me with a puzzled expression. I shrugged my shoulders and he said to her, "We don't hear it."

DESTINATION D.C. A Modern-day Jonah?

She looked at us both and asked, "You don't hear that? It's the most beautiful singing I've ever heard!"

He stared at me. I shrugged my shoulders and he said once again, "We don't hear it," but he assured her, that he was sure she did.

As we headed back to the car, he loudly proclaimed, "I don't believe that!"

I said, "I do," and immediately thought, *here's a non-believer, one of the people that I pray to Jesus about.* I said, "I ask Jesus to be here for people. And for those who don't believe? I ask that their hearts would be filled with the love of Jesus. And for those who are believers? I ask that their hearts would be overflowing with the love of Christ. I also ask for the angels to be here," thinking she had heard angels singing.

He replied, "No, not that. While you were praying, two deer walked just ten feet away from us."

I soon reasoned that they had no fear in the presence of God.

Some weeks passed and I heard that his wife was in the hospital and would soon pass away. I asked if I might visit her and I was told, "Of course."

She did pass a few days later, but something happened a few months later that made my heart glad.

It was at our annual Easter service, and it was a very cold one—so cold we were standing in the snow—and yet, this man, this non-believer, came to our service with his grown children. It seemed to me that what I had stated to him about Jesus filling hearts with His love, had happened.

He came to our Easter service the following year; but moved soon after to one of the southern states.

Isn't it incredible how God works?

You see, this man had been a deer hunter and probably spent many hours hunting, just hoping to see a deer. He knew deer don't just walk past you without fear. God had appealed to him in a way that he could relate to! That experience inspired Ann to render a water color painting depicting angels peeking through the trees at a couple of deer on a snow-covered ground. It was one of her most popular paintings.

GOD'S TIMING: "Now it is God who has made us for this very purpose and has given us the Spirit as a deposit, guaranteeing what is to come. Therefore, we are always confident and know that as long as we are at home in the body we are away from the Lord. We live by faith, not by sight. We are confident, I say, and would prefer to be away from the body and at home with the Lord." 2 Corinthians 5:5-8

DON'S NOTES: It's often hard to understand God's plan for us, but it is easier to face the loss of a loved one when we hold tight to the knowledge that God knows what is best for us. If he knew the Lord, I know the man who was found to be full of cancer after his accidental death has gone home to a better place. And when we think of the telephone man, we pray that through his unexpected visit to the House of Angels he became enlightened and got a glimpse of how God works.

CHAPTER 20
Blisters and Miracles

Thoughts of the House of Angels ended abruptly one morning during the early stages of my Heal America Walk. It was my last free overnight stay at Johanna's Motel in Copake, and I discovered a clear blister on one of my eyes. *What is this?* I wondered. I blinked and leaned closer to the mirror. I was not happy to think it might hinder the walk and I muttered, "How am I going to get to D.C. if the Devil continues to throw obstacles in my way?" Then I took a deep cleansing breath, determined the evil one was not going to keep me from completing my mission. "I won't have you diminish my love or my quest for Christ," I declared. "He'll give me the ability to deal with this." I decided to return to a diner I had recently stopped at, hoping to find someone wearing glasses. If they were local, I could ask for directions to their eye doctor.

When I arrived at the diner, a man was leaving, and I happily observed he was wearing glasses! He directed me to an ophthalmologist that was not too far away, so I climbed into my van and zoomed in that direction.

As pastors often say, God takes what was meant to be bad and uses it for good. And here is a perfect example. The ophthalmologist I was seeking was away on vacation, but another one was right across the street. It was a female doctor. She looked at the blister with some special lenses. It only took a few minutes, but during this time, I explained that I had been walking in the sun for several days on my Heal America Walk and had discovered the blister earlier this morning. Our conversation quickly turned toward religion and I asked if she was a woman of faith. She said, "I am, but I am Jewish, and my husband is Christian."

"That's interesting," I responded. "So, do you go to church or to the synagogue?"

"I go to both. One week to the synagogue, the next week, to the church."

At that point, I described several of the things that had been happening on my walk. Her eyes widened with each new story, but eventually she had to leave the room. When she came back, she said, "There's a broken blood vessel in your eye. It's nothing to worry about and it will take care of itself."

Praise Jesus, I thought. I don't know what I would have done if she told me I'd have to avoid sunlight or that I should not continue with the walk. Once again, God has proven He is a great and gracious God.

I never did see that ophthalmologist again, but I can't help but wonder if maybe—just maybe—she attended a few more Christian services than usual since my visit. I hoped it would be the case as I returned to the Hillsboro area to resume the walk. On the way, I had to pass Johanna's Motel in Copake and I just couldn't continue without stopping to offer another thank you. As I pulled into the parking lot, I recalled one of our conversations when Angie, the owner said she had been very sick and was often in a lot of pain, but the doctors could not figure out what was wrong. I kept the visit brief and prayed for her once again, then proceeded to the spot where I would be able to resume my walk.

It was gratifying to experience people's positive reactions: horns honked in approval of the cross; people slowed to roll down their windows and bid me, "God bless." It happened often enough to help buoy my spirits despite the unpleasant heat and humidity. And those supportive reactions always overshadowed the times when people shook their fists with disapproval. Along this portion of the route, neither Ann nor I could find any place to park

DESTINATION D.C. A Modern-day Jonah?

overnight that offered a shower without having to do a lot of backtracking, so I opted to park near a stream where I could wash up.

The next time I spoke to Ann, she said I'd probably reach Pine Plains the following day. "That's good," she said. "It's where you'll be able to stay with that family I told you about. They're looking forward to your arrival."

On my way to the house in Pine Plains, my heart felt light with the knowledge that I was still walking and was not stopped by the things the Devil had thrown into my path. My thoughts once again wandered back to the earliest days at the House of Angels and the healings that took place. And of course, the healing services I was involved with. I had stated that Christian churches should not be separated by denomination and we should all believe in God the Father, Jesus Christ and the Holy Spirit. And as a local pastor and I talked, I expressed my conviction that we should all be united as believers in Christ and should go strictly by teachings of the Bible. He agreed, so, we decided to invite other churches in the area to participate. I also expressed my desire to have it become a monthly event.

Our first healing service was a success. And the ones to follow also yielded positive results. Tumors disappeared or shrunk considerably, while various other health issues were resolved. For the first time in four years, since she began having rotator cuff issues with her shoulders, Ann was able to lift her arms high above her head. I remember one service when a couple came forward, asking for prayer because they said they were having troubles in their marriage. I assumed they were fighting, and I started to pray for them, asking for a healing within their marriage. It was a couple I'd never seen prior to that night and I did not see them for quite some time after the service. But I did hear they had received a blessing from the service and eventually learned they had previously not been able to start a family. They had gone to specialists who said it was very unlikely for them to be able to conceive. But God knew about their issue, and He answered those prayers during our healing service! To the day, nine months later, they became the proud parents of twins!

Even with the confirmations and healings that had taken place, there still were a lot of things I did not understand during those early years. Like speaking in tongues. It was strange, like listening to a foreign language that isn't of this planet. Yet, it is Biblical—the Bible does speak about the gift of and the interpretation of tongues. Usually, when a person speaks in tongues, someone else will receive a revelation and interpret the message. It was a strange experience for me because sometimes I would be sitting there, receiving a message and then someone would speak in tongues and I could just feel that I'd received the interpretation before they uttered a sound. Of course, it did not always happen, but it did occur quite often. And even with the ability to interpret the message—if that's what I was doing—I still did not have a good understanding of that gift. So, after it occurred a few times during our church services, I asked the pastor about it. Unfortunately, I still had questions after his attempt to explain it.

To this day, I do not understand or even agree with some of the things people say about speaking in tongues: I've not seen any passages in the Bible that say every believer will be able to do it. In I Corinthians 12, it states that speaking in tongues is one of the gifts of the spirit, but it clearly states we don't all receive all of the gifts. For instance, not everyone receives the gift of healing. Or the gift of teaching.

I've been told I should practice, but I don't believe it makes sense to practice. After all, I've never had to practice receiving a gift. One of our visitors at the House of Angels suggested I try it.

"Go ahead," he said. "Try speaking in tongues."

"But it wouldn't feel natural," I said.

"Try it anyhow. You never know."

So, to appease him, I mumbled a few sounds. He listened, then said, "Why don't you try it again, but this time, add a few more vowels."

I thought, *I don't think so*. It shouldn't be so difficult to receive a gift. And, I just didn't believe you had to speak in tongues to be in right standing with God. My opinion? If it was to happen, it would. And if it was not supposed to happen, it wouldn't.

Speaking of gifts, I had a disappointing experience one time during the early years of the development of the House of Angels. It was as if one preacher was intentionally trying to stop me from witnessing to another person about the healings. Not long after that, I was mulling over the experience while burning brush. To think this person had tried to stop me from witnessing was upsetting. Very upsetting. And as I raked hot coals toward the middle of the brush fire, so it wouldn't spread too far, I thought, *why would someone stop a person from witnessing to another about the success of a prayer for healing? It must be a sin.* And so, I asked, "Christ—is that a sin?" While bending over to pick up a bundle of brush to toss into the fire, I heard, "Ecclesiastes 5:16."

I immediately stopped and went to the house to get my Bible. It was a King James version of Thomas Nelson Bibles, printed by a Division of Thomas Nelson, Inc., copyright 2003. And when I opened it to Ecclesiastes 5:16, it said, "And this also is a sore evil." To me, this answered my question, confirming it was a sin, and it emphasized the depth of it by describing it as a 'sore evil'. While it used the word evil, I interpreted evil to mean sin. And Ecclesiastes went on to say it's like 'laboring for the wind'. In other words, by stopping someone else from spreading the news that God is at work today, this person's own efforts on God's behalf come to nothing.

This memory reminds me of the state of our nation and the need for my Heal America Walk. Too many non-believers have ascended to positions of leadership and are turning us away from our Creator. Too many people follow those officials without questioning their wisdom. And as a result, too many have been led to mistrust our heritage, our values . . . our faith.

GOD IS WITH US AND WORKING FOR US TODAY: "And I heard a loud voice from the throne saying, "Now, the dwelling of God is with men, and He will live with them. They will be His people, and God himself will be with them and be their God." Revelation 21:3

DON'S NOTE: God still works in our lives today. Healings still occur. God's miracles did not end with the Biblical era. I want everyone on earth to understand the message: "He was. He is. And He will come again." And I want to shout it to the entire world!

CHAPTER 21
A Glowing Report

"Well, as I drove past you, there was a light that surrounded you. It was like a glowing light. It was amazing!" That statement from a stranger blew my mind. It happened in Pine Plains, New York.

When I arrived in Pine Plains, I decided to immediately find the home of the people who had agreed to put me up for the night. I found it without much trouble and after introducing myself to the woman of the house, I asked if her son was still interested in walking with me for a short distance. He was not there at that time, so I decided to set out to get a few more miles in. I pulled the cross off the top of the car and headed out. Trouble is, the sky looked onerous and I was sure it would soon be raining. Always hesitant to get my sneakers wet, I stopped at one of the village stores for a coffee and to study the sky, deciding to take a chance and walk about a hundred yards before realizing the rain was imminent. I decided to head back for a second cup of coffee and watch the sky, really wanting to get in a few miles before returning to that new host family.

The sky was sunny and bright in the other direction, so I thought I'd take a chance and head toward the sunshine. After a few minutes, I came across a man who was weed whacking. When he saw me, he turned off his machine and I said, "Hi!" With a friendly nod of the head he said he'd seen me walking through town. And that's when the conversation got interesting. Very interesting.

"I'm surprised anyone saw me," I said, thinking I'd only gone a few hundred feet before stopping to consider the weather.

"I saw you, that's for sure, and it was quite amazing."

"What do you mean?" I asked.

"Well, as I drove past you, there was a light that surrounded you. It was like a glowing light. Quite stunning!" I have since heard that a whole-body image of radiance is sometimes called an 'aureole', or 'glory' that radiates from all around the body. My heart skips a beat when I think that one of these radiant lights had been seen around me!

We continued to talk, and he said he was not well; he might have to have an operation. The doctor had told him it was diverticulitis. Since we'd already been talking for quite a while, I asked him if he had time to hear my witness about another case of diverticulitis. He said he did.

"Well," I said. "I'd gone to a hospital to see my mother and discovered that a relative who was one of her best friends had also been admitted. She was suffering from diverticulitis and the tests revealed a hole in her colon. I could see she was quite upset because she'd have to use a colostomy bag for several months until she healed. I asked if I might pray for her and she said yes. A day or two later she was in a much better mood and said they took her down for more X-rays the day after I prayed for her to determine what exactly needed to be done; but she said shortly after the X-rays were taken and she was still laying on a gurney waiting to hear the results, she noticed a gathering of doctors. First one was there. Then another arrived, and another, and they were talking in low voices across the room.

"Several doctors joined them, and they kept turning to look at me," she said, "so I finally asked them what was going on and if anything was wrong." She said they wouldn't answer her, at least not right away; but a short time later, they said the problem was gone.

"What do you mean, gone?" she asked. One of the doctors finally said, "The hole the X-rays had revealed in your colon? It isn't there. It's gone!"

The doctors told her the X-ray technician must have done something wrong, but I think there was another explanation. The Great Physician, the Great I Am, healed her. She was released from the hospital, free to go home. Not long after that her own doctor said he absolutely knew she'd had diverticulosis for a while, which is what the condition is when it's not inflamed. He had been treating her for it for quite a long time, but he also confirmed that it had become seriously inflamed, enough to warrant an operation, yet according to the latest tests, it was totally gone. Then he blurted out, "A hole from Diverticulitis doesn't just disappear—it never goes away—how can that be?" He offered to take another look, but she declined. She said she'd take his word for it. The last time I spoke to her, which was about four years later, she said she still did not have any symptoms of diverticulitis.

After I told my story, the man who'd seen the light surrounding me, just stood there, staring; so, I broke the silence by asking if he would let me pray for him.

"Yes," he said softly. "That would be great." So, I prayed for him over one of the handkerchiefs and left it with him after explaining its meaning.

I don't remember how much farther I walked that day, but it felt good to be able to return to the home of the family that had agreed to take me in. When I got there, they had a surprise: they were going to take me to a play. I wasn't too keen on plays, but I decided it would be better than spending the evening in my vehicle. As it turned out, it was a musical about Rip Van Winkle and I really enjoyed it. I was also pleased to learn that they were a church-going family and they invited me to attend services with them the next morning. I'll always be grateful for their hospitality.

THANKFULNESS: "Give thanks to the Lord, call on His name; make known among the nations what He has done. Sing to Him, sing praise to Him; tell of all His wonderful acts." I Chronicles 16:8-9

DON'S NOTE: It was so amazing that my mother's cousin received a full healing from her diverticulitis. I want to let the whole world know what God has done. As I tell everyone I emphasize that the results of my prayers come straight from God. It's His power, not mine. At times I feel unworthy of this gift. And then to hear that a glow was surrounding me one day during my walk? I have no words to describe the great encouragement I received from that witness.

CHAPTER 22

A Spiritual Lift

Almost every day of the Heal America Walk felt like a holy day. My awareness of God's presence remained from morning to night. The intensity of the spirit was incredible, like I was in a big enclosure—just me with the Lord. I'm not saying He isn't there 24 hours a day every day, but throughout this experience, it felt so obvious—so intense! I wished it would go on forever, and I wanted so much to share it with others. What a great, awesome, wonderful world this would be if everyone could feel this way!

I'd made it to the other side of the Hudson River, arriving in Kingston where I used some of the miles I had saved up. You're probably wondering what I mean by using saved up miles? Well, God had worked out the mechanics of this trip back in June when I was finalizing the plans for this walk, so my needs, like medication and provision would be taken care of. As I explained earlier, God's plan was to have me walk from my vehicle for a certain distance, then walk back to the vehicle where I'd set the odometer to zero. Then, when I drove forward to the point where I had stopped walking, I could see how many miles I had walked. For instance, if the odometer registered three miles at the point where I stopped to head back to the car, it meant I had walked a total of six miles—three forward and three back. Then I could move the vehicle three miles further from that stopping point, before beginning the next day's walk. But sometimes, I'd "bank" the miles and not drive beyond the stopping point so I'd be able to drive through places where it was illegal to walk, without "losing" total foot mileage. Some of those extra miles also came in handy when I entered a city or large town where there were parking meters. It would be very costly to keep moving from meter to meter.

In the Kingston area, I came to a point when I felt downright grungy — in desperate need of a shower. Eventually I noticed a man working in a yard and stopped to ask if he knew where I could take a swim. He said he was just working there and was not familiar with the neighborhood; but he did live in the Kingston area. By the end of our conversation he gave me his number, so I could contact him for help if I found myself lost or in need at the end of the day.

I was in need, alright, and soon I was following directions to his apartment. Despite some trouble finding his address, it was well worth it to get a shower. He also provided a meal. We talked for a while before I bid him goodbye and God bless and returned to where I'd stopped walking before finding a place to park for the night — with a clean body and a full stomach!

At this point, Ann and I both realized I was no longer following the route she had plotted out, but it seemed to be working well. I decided God was truly taking the lead. With the belief that His hand was guiding me, I looked heavenward and agreed to go wherever He led me. Ann agreed to this change in plan and waited each day for me to call to let her know where I was and what route I believed I'd be traveling upon. Then, she called churches or other organizations in the upcoming towns, hoping to reach someone who would assist with my needs.

One of these contacts was the female pastor of a church. She said she would like to meet me and suggested that I pull into the church parking lot. We were only going to talk for a few minutes, but as I gave my witness, her enthusiasm grew and soon she was asking me to pray for people in her congregation. She also asked if I'd stay and attend her services the following Sunday, but I had to say no . . . I had to continue the walk. But I did agree to pray over handkerchiefs for two specific people and to say a special prayer for the entire congregation.

A Spiritual Lift

I remember it was terribly hot. I was extremely uncomfortable throughout that night. Sweltering was an understatement for the daytime hours, but it did cool down quite a bit most nights—but not that night! There wasn't a smidgeon of cooler air.

The next day, I resumed my walk, trekking at a good pace despite the sweltering conditions. Along the way, a man pulled his car to a stop on the other side of the highway and held a drink out of his window. He'd already taken a swig or two, but said, "I thought you might need a drink, even if I'd already had some of it." With an apologetic look, he added, "I left most of it for you." I didn't want to offend him, so although my fanny pack was full, I accepted the drink. Then he thrust two bouquets of flowers out the window. "Take these, too," he said.

"I don't know what to do with them," I said. But once again I did not want to offend him, so I accepted the flowers. After extending my thanks, I continued down the street, trying to balance the two big bouquets, the extra drink and my wooden cross. With a light-hearted chuckle, I thought *maybe I can take up juggling and make some money on the side. Probably not,* I acknowledged, as I grappled with one of the bouquets that threatened to fall to the ground. Then I hoped he would be rewarded for his kindness.

I did soon figure out what to do with the bouquets. I gave them to two women who worked in a convenience store. They seemed glad to receive the unexpected gifts and I'm sure it was a blessing to them. Most women appreciate flowers, right?

That evening, after finding a place to park and eat and sleep, I called Ann, knowing she'd soon be leaving for her third-shift job. I wanted to report on how the day had gone and tell her that I missed her. But I also missed Ginger, Gabriel and Yeow—our two dogs and cat. As I waited for her to answer the phone, I thought, *here I am, 65 years old and I'm feeling like a homesick kid.* After we spoke, I tried to settle down to get some sleep. But, man, it was another hot night. As I shifted around, trying to get comfortable, I glanced out the window. The stars were shining bright. The beautiful night sky brought on a smile.

I thought, *what a heavenly sight those stars are,* and I wondered how often people bother to take the time to look up. *Not*

DESTINATION D.C. A Modern-day Jonah?

often enough, most likely. So many, so busy, rushing to do what they think they need to do to get where they think they need to go—trying to be the people they think they need to be. A sudden burst of sadness overcame me as I realized that too often Ann and I also rush through our days. I vowed to try harder to be the person God created me to be and to encourage Ann to do the same.

The next day gusts of wind tried to flip my hat each time a vehicle whizzed past—especially from those 18-wheelers—and I was reminded of the previous night's musings. Sometimes it seemed like the drivers weren't paying attention to what they were doing. I suddenly felt blessed, knowing as I walked each day, I could take the time to look, to truly see and marvel at God's creations.

Traffic was heavy that day and I thought about the reactions I'd witnessed. Some people expressed their disapproval of me and my cross by aiming their car toward me as they zoomed close by. I guess they thought they were funny. Others expressed their approval by honking and waving. The positive reactions seemed to outnumber the disapprovals by about two to one, if not more and it seemed the approvals became more prevalent the farther South I traveled; but I also realized about 50-percent of the people on the road just looked the other way. Some, who did not like the idea of me (or probably anyone) walking along the road with a Christian cross chose to stop and confront me. Then again, there are those who stopped—if even momentarily—to offer their blessings with enthusiasm. One time, I felt so happy when two men came up in their truck, and one of them rolled down his window to say, "Jesus saves. Bless you brother." On the other side of the coin, one man pulled his truck to a stop and shouted, "What the hell's wrong with you?" At first, I didn't know what to say, but as he slowly pulled away, I yelled as loud as I could, "I love Jesus," and continued down the road, doing what I usually do: carrying the cross with one hand and having it rest against my shoulder, and pointing up toward the sky when a vehicle passed. As I did this, I'd pray, "Let them come to a place in life where they'll receive the Holy Spirit" if they have not yet done so.

Thoughts of the negative encounters get me to thinking how Jesus must have felt when He was being persecuted. What I was doing was a walk in the park, compared to what Jesus had experienced. Each time I think about it, I just have to say, "Thank you Jesus for coming to us and for Your suffering on this Earth, especially the suffering You undertook upon that cross to save us."

I continued to walk until late afternoon and at one point the traffic suddenly increased. A lot. I mean, bumper-to-bumper traffic, going steadily along. I guessed they were going about 40 miles an hour and were probably heading home from work. I proceeded, basically going against the traffic as I walked along the shoulder of the road. The path was about the width of one car. A dangerous spot for sure, especially when one of the cars slowed down to make a turn. Trouble is, one of the drivers behind him did not have time to slow down, so he veered to the shoulder, heading straight toward me because there was no where he could go to avoid a collision. I realized he had not seen me in time either, so I jumped over the rail just as his car whizzed into my little pathway. I saw him kind of shrug as if to say, "I'm sorry, fella, there wasn't anything else I could do without causing an accident!" I knew it was true, and my heart pounded as I watched the traffic continue as if nothing had happened. I looked toward the sky, then and said, "Thank You, God, for saving me once again!"

That experience caused me to reflect on another unfortunate incident that had occurred before this. I had come across a very charitable man who offered to let me park in his yard and even got pizza for the both of us. After being blessed by this man's generosity, I got an early start the next morning, only to discover my gas gage was registering way too low. I quickly concluded that at some point the day before, someone had siphoned off a significant portion of my gas, so, I stopped to fill up. I believe it happened while I'd been parked in a secluded spot when the tank was nowhere near empty. I thank God for seeing to it that I noticed the lack of gas and would not become stranded in some isolated area. But, I had even more reason to thank my Creator, because after I found a new place to park and resume my walk, I came across another stranger who handed me some money. It was almost exactly what I spent to replace the missing gas! Thank You, God! With a smile I decided that two generous events certainly cancelled out the theft.

Further proof of His presence occurred about three weeks into my walk, when I was almost crushed with fatigue. I was so tired, I started

DESTINATION D.C. A Modern-day Jonah?

to grumble and complain, wondering if I was crazy to be on this Heal America Walk. "Am I crazy, God? Or did You actually tell me to do this?" Of course, deep down, I knew He had directed me and was orchestrating the whole thing. Still, my puny human brain thought it would be helpful and uplifting if God would give me a sign to confirm that He did truly want me to continue. "Give me a sign," I asked, immediately thinking it would be great if it came in the form of a dove.

You might ask, "Why a dove?"

Well, for years now, I've associated the presence of one dove as being a sign of the spirit, while two doves indicate the father and the son. And the presence of three doves? They represent the trinity: Father, Son and Holy Spirit. And if you were to ask, what if there's a whole flock of doves? I'd say, "It's the Father, the Son, the Holy Spirit, and the whole congregation!"

God was faithful with a reply! And He demonstrated a sense of humor, too. Within fifty feet of my request, I came upon a sign that said, "Minister Flats."

"Oh, that's funny," I said. "Are You telling me the air is out of my tires or the wind has gone out of my sails?" I chuckled as I proceeded further along, only to be stopped with awestruck wonder: one dove suddenly fluttered down about fifteen feet in front of me!

Throughout the Heal America Walk, I usually called Ann during the early morning hours when I figured she'd still be up, having arrived home around 7 AM from her job. Or I called her close to 9 PM to catch her before she'd be leaving for her work shift. This time? While I rarely tried to call her at other times of day to avoid interrupting her naps or her rush to finish daily chores before heading to work or bed, I felt compelled to call right away. I wanted to tell her about the Minister Flats sign and the dove. I thought it was incredible and knew she'd find it captivating. So, I crossed the road to take advantage of a shady spot. As we were talking, a white van pulled to a stop beside me. It had just two front windows on the driver's and passenger's sides. The driver didn't say anything. And, curiously, he kept one hand on the steering wheel while the other remained out of sight, down at his side. He simply stared at me. The silence was unsettling.

This guy isn't going to do me any good, I thought. *And I'm in the middle of nowhere without anyone around to help.* But I figured I did have a witness, sort of. So, I turned to reveal that my cell phone was at my ear and I was having a conversation. That's when the silent-guy-in-the-white-van sped away. I believed that God was with me—after all He had shown me the dove—and He'd probably given me the idea to call home at such an unusual time.

When my walk ended that day, I decided to call Pastor Tim, thinking he'd get a kick out of hearing what happened. And he did. But as we continued to talk, I began to express my concerns about the trip, explaining that I still didn't know what was going to happen at the end of this walk. Would the sky open up? Would the earth quake? These were questions I'd often ask myself when I felt the need to understand why I was on this journey. Of course, I was walking from Vermont to Washington, D.C. because God told me to do it. But for what purpose? Neither of us had an answer, but we both believed God was in charge and He would reveal His purpose. Eventually.

One thing I was sure of as I settled down for the night? God's hand of protection had been upon me. I pictured in my mind's eye the unsettling scene when the man-in-the-white-van drove up and stared with that unfriendly glare. And while his left hand remained on the steering wheel, I could not forget how his right arm was hanging down, out of sight. I imagined he was tightly gripping a gun. I also imagined that when he realized I was on my cell phone, he figured I could have been describing him and his vehicle, so, there'd be a witness. Sort of.

He quickly drove away.

One day, I came upon a hot dog vendor, set-up in a pull-off area on the side of the road. It was close to 12-Noon. He said the dogs weren't quite ready and offered me a water.

"Sure," I said. "I have one on me, but I can always use more water, thanks. And, I'll just wait 'till your dogs are ready." We talked as he went about his business, and he told me about another hot dog vendor down the road. He suggested I give that guy a try if I came upon him. A few minutes later I paid for my hot dog and while I was eating, another customer pulled up. *Hmmm*, I thought. *Maybe I'll say hello.* Like a magnet, his friendly demeanor drew me to him. I was sure he'd seen my cross, so I didn't think it would surprise him too much if I asked if he was a man of faith. He said, "Yes, I'm Catholic," so I said, "Well, I'm non-denominational. I don't believe we need different denominations. I see no place in the Bible that says to start different ones. It says to go out and be Christ-like." He was quick to agree. Then, I pointed at the skin on our arms and said I was lighter than this when I left home in Vermont and I'll be darker when I get to D.C. I also said, "I know that to many people, skin color matters, but it shouldn't! And I can tell it doesn't matter to you. We're all the same in the ways that truly matter because we all need purpose; we need self-worth; we need provision; and we need love."

Then I pointed to the sky and told him it all comes from God above. "It's all for each one of us," I added, "no matter what the color of our skin is." At that point, I said I needed to get going or I'd never reach D.C. Suddenly, he stretched out his hand and said, "Here. Take this." He gently folded my fingers over an offering of money, and added, "To help with your trip."

As the hours came and went that day, I added more miles to my trek and a few more conversations. Before I knew it, I had to find a place to park for the night. It was hot and humid and after a minimal amount of sleep, I decided to get an early start, wanting to put miles in before the heat of the sun became unbearable. After all, I was getting a daily reminder that this was a record-breaking scorcher of a summer in the northeast.

A few miles down the road, I came upon a small town. As I proceeded along the sidewalk, I noticed a woman who was throwing her arms around and looking behind her. She seemed to be tormented, and as I got closer, I could hear her curse with insane profanity, telling someone to get away from her. "Leave me alone," she shouted to no one. All I could think was, the poor woman was possessed. I stopped and prayed fervently for her and later wished I had tried to lay hands upon her as I prayed. It broke my heart to see a woman like that who was obviously living a torturous existence. I believed she was truly under the crushing dominion of the Devil. So often during my trip I felt the glorious presence of the Lord, but this encounter was a stark reminder that evil exists and seems to be more prevalent and has a greater influence on this world than I care to think.

Even so, each day of the Heal America Walk felt like a blessing. Some more eventful than others. On some days? I'd walk a great distance without incident. Other days? Not very far. Sometimes the oppressive heat held me back, and sometimes, I'd encounter people and have lengthy discussions. I believed God put people in my path for a reason. He had a plan for every day, and I was not going to rush it. He would show me the way, and get me to Washington, D. C. on just the right day.

PRIORITIES: "The most important one," answered Jesus, "is this: 'Hear, o Israel, the Lord our God, the Lord is one. Love the Lord your God with all your heart and with all your soul and with all your mind and with all your strength.' The second is this: 'Love your neighbor as yourself. There is no commandment greater than these.'" Mark 12:29-31

DON'S NOTE: I believe God protected me several times. He used people in my path to provide provision and to provide reminders—like the heart-wrenching encounter with that poor demented woman—of the necessity to be strong among disbelievers and to feel compassion for those less fortunate. And, He revealed a sense of humor! The joy I felt in God's presence helped to instill within me a deep sense of the priority of keeping Him the focus of my life and to help others to feel this same joy.

CHAPTER 23

Detour to Rejection

As I scanned the map one day, I could see that I'd be coming to Wurtsburo, a place that had a direct route to New York City. I decided to give Ann a call and get her impression on whether I should go into the city. We had talked about taking this detour to try and get attention from the major news media.

Each morning when my conversations with Ann ended, I'd look for something to eat and then continue walking until it was time to find a place to spend the night. And throughout the walk, I'd look forward to the next day, knowing I would once again be filled with the presence of God. Each morning, I'd also take my medication—a chore that I did not like. Diabetes is not an easy condition to live with; and, I was often on the lookout for ice because the medication had to stay within a certain range of temperatures.

On the way to Wurtsboro, I remembered to keep a lookout for the next hot dog stand. I did find it, about 25 miles beyond the other stand and I quickly realized the dogs here were just as good as I was told. Good thing, too, because on top of loving hot dogs, I also really needed a meal. I put my cross down in the grass and approached the stand to place my order. I'd eaten about half of the hot dog when a state cruiser pulled up and parked behind the cart. I thought, *he must be hungry, too,* and I figured he probably knew these were great hot dogs. But I soon realized he didn't want a hot dog. He headed straight for me.

"You're the one I'm looking for," he said.

"Why is that?" I asked, not having a clue, unless I'd been walking on a road that didn't allow pedestrians; but I was certain I was on a secondary road. "Wait a minute," I said. "Let me get my weapon." I bent down and picked up my cross. "Okay," I said, "what do you want with me?"

"We got a report from a woman about a man in a green vest, carrying a cross along the side of the road."

"I think this is a secondary road," I replied, "and I have a right to walk on it."

He agreed. "Yes, you do, but everybody seems to have a cross of their own to bear. Can I see your I.D.?"

I reached for my wallet and said, "I'd be kind of foolish if I was in trouble with the law, and made myself conspicuous by walking down the road carrying a cross and wearing a bright reflective green vest, don't you think?"

"You'd be surprised what people do."

After he entered my information into the system, he said there were no warrants, messages or warnings about me.

I replied, "Nobody wants me, huh?" He chuckled, and I asked, "What was she objecting to—the color of my vest? Or the cross?"

At this point, I was sitting in his patrol car and we began to talk about my walk and why I was doing it. I explained that I was sick and tired of the things that are wrong in this country and throughout the world, including the persecution of Christians. "It seems as though every time you turn around, Christians are losing their rights to worship, but everyone else seems to gain more rights. And I'm tired of the racism in this country." I said, "I'm not prejudiced."

But then, I corrected myself. "Well, I guess I am prejudiced. I don't like bad people. You know, there are good and bad people in all groups. We have good doctors and bad doctors and good teachers and bad teachers. There are good white people and there are good people of color. Most of the time when I talk to people, I hold out my arm and direct their attention to my tan. Then I tell them I was a lot whiter when I started out and I'll be darker when

I get to D.C. But the color of my skin doesn't define the kind of person I am. The way I see it? We all have the same needs. And it all comes from one place—God."

Once again, I explained that I was non-denominational; the Bible does not tell us to find different ways to worship, and it doesn't tell us to divide ourselves into different denominations.

With a nod of the head, he said, "You're right."

At that point, I thanked him for his service. He responded by saying there is no place in the Constitution that says we have a separation of church and state. That concept was taken out of context from a letter Thomas Jefferson wrote. As a matter of fact, as president, his thoughts about church and state were made clear in numerous declarations—including letters to clergy and in his second inaugural address—for he clearly confirmed his belief about the constitutional inability of the federal government to regulate, restrict or interfere with religious expression. He merely wanted to be sure we did not have a "Church of the United States of America" that would be similar to the "Church of England," where people are forced to be members.

I said people twist the separation of church and state into what they want it to mean. And of course, the people I was talking about do not want to see Christianity flourish in this country. When the trooper agreed with me, I added, "It has become the will of so many to accept everything except the will of God. Too many people only want to do what pleases them and they don't care about God's rules."

When you think about it, isn't that how mankind has always behaved? For thousands of years? They think they can rule God's creation, and they think its man's fault that the world changes. I believe as far as global warming goes, we should respect this earth and try our best to do what we can to preserve any part of it. But it's my understanding that volcanos and natural disasters have contributed much more to the changes in this earth than man ever could have done. For instance, there are reputable scientists who say the eruption of Mount St. Helen in May of 1980, put more carbon in the air than all the pollution man has created since the rise of the industrial revolution. That volcanic eruption devastated nearly 230 square miles, hurling fiery rock and dust to a height of 60-thousand feet into the atmosphere while the mountain lost 13-hundred feet of altitude. And even more astounding? The force of it was said by many scientists to be 16-hundred times the size of the atomic bomb dropped on Hiroshima—and the snow and rock that accumulated within the crater formed by the volcanic blast created the youngest glacier on the earth. Not to mention that the ash in the atmosphere drifted across the United States in three days and encircled the entire earth in 15 days. And there are 1,500 potentially active volcanoes in existence now and 169 of them are in the United States.

The eruption of the Tambora volcano in Indonesia in 1815, was so disruptive to the earth, it lowered global temperatures by about 3 degrees Celsius and caused parts of Europe and North America to declare that the following year was "the year without a summer," because of the blast. And the eruption of Mount Pinatubo in the Philippines in 1991 caused cooler temperatures around the world because the resulting droplets of sulfuric acid blocked sunlight from reaching the earth.

So, why is it that our children are being taught that we have caused the climactic changes? Of course, scientists have made great progress regarding the discovery of so much on this earth; but, let's give credit where credit is due. I believe that most of the time the scientists are just trying to find out how God put it all together as they try to understand how all the things in this world work. And on the same subject, I don't understand how some religious leaders can jump on the band-wagon and agree with them about climate change and global warming. Don't they know that God's creation has been changing since the beginning of the earth's creation? If man is the power, why doesn't he make himself smarter, stronger and better in all ways? Why is it so hard for us to accept our limitations and accept that we were made in the correct form that God wanted?

Again, and again, I ask myself, *why is it so hard for world leaders, cultists and some religious leaders to accept that their power does not come from themselves*? What a great and glorious world this would be if leaders around the world ruled with love and in God's way. They would be more highly exalted by their people if they did so; and wouldn't it be great if we could unite and be able to look to God for all things: wisdom, provision and contentment—just as our founding fathers did?

DESTINATION D.C. A Modern-day Jonah?

I wonder if because many men and women have followed certain rules for decades, they are reluctant to accept the fact that they and their families were wrong for so many years. It is so sad for us believers to realize that perhaps pride makes it hard for them to accept the need to develop a personal relationship with and belief in Jesus Christ. Probably the biggest problem in this world is pride.

After our discussion and my little speech, I thanked the police officer for his service, then got out of the cruiser, quickly making my way to the hot dog stand to place another order.

As I began to eat my second dog, the vendor asked if he could take a picture of me with the cross. I agreed, and after he took the shot, he posted it to his website, proclaiming he had "Heavenly Hot Dogs." I thought with a grin, *I sure hope I didn't walk all this way just to promote this man's business!* "Of course, not," I told myself, as I picked up my cross. "There's a deeper meaning to what I'm doing—a blessed one put forth by God."

What lay ahead of me besides hot asphalt, I did not know; but I was soon going to find more disappointment in mankind, and I would also be finding things to delight in.

I had told the hot dog vendor I was looking for someone who could cut my cross apart because as it was constructed, I couldn't break it down—in case I wanted to carry it on a bus. You see, Ann and I had agreed that it might be a good idea for me to veer off my route to go to New York City, and I knew the cross was too big for public transportation.

Eventually I was delighted to come upon a large river. It was at least 50 feet wide and I decided it would be an excellent place to return to at the end of the day. A great place to cool off, wash up and get a shampoo. It felt so good to cool off and get cleaned up.

When I returned to my car, I noticed a man working with a saw at the house across the road. Perhaps he could help with the redesign of my cross. Trouble is, he could not understand English. He appeared to be Oriental. While I was trying to talk to him, another man came out of the house. He was American, and I asked if one of them might be able to make my cross collapsible. Then I gave a quick explanation of who I was and what I was doing. I asked if he was a person of faith. By this time, his wife had come out to see what was going on. She was Oriental. They said they were not Christians, they were Buddhists, and they'd be happy to help me if they could; but they didn't have any of the hardware or other things needed.

One thing led to another, and I asked about their faith and if there was a temple in the area. The husband said there were a few and many of the Buddhists in the area had come from China to escape persecution and possibly even death. When I asked about the persecution, he sent his wife inside to get a brochure, and he described the brutality the Chinese government inflicted upon people who practiced their religion. He said they were members of a new Buddhist order. Called Falun Dafa, it was an advanced system for improving mind and body, rooted in thousands of years of traditional Chinese culture. The Falun Dafa's teachings encompass the values of truthfulness, compassion and tolerance and include four gentle exercises and a sitting meditation.

Falun Dafa became popular across China in the 1990's, and by 1999, the members had grown in number to about a hundred million. Plus, he said there were many others in 70 different countries practicing their faith. The Chinese Communist Party determined the religion to be a threat to the regime, and since 2015, in China, people who practice Falun Dafa face imprisonment, torture or even death. He also said investigations have revealed that more than 60,000 of them have been killed so their vital organs could be sold for profit.

"Why haven't we heard about this," I asked.

"The Communist Party has gone to great measures to hide it from the public. They have imprisoned people who tried to get the word out, and they've assaulted many of those who acted as informants for foreign journalists. Yes," he nodded sadly, "they've gone to great lengths to cover it up."

Makes you feel blessed to be living here in America, doesn't it?

After saying goodbye to these good people, I returned to the park and ride area where I was planning to stay for the night. It wasn't too noisy, but every now and then a bus would pull up to unload people who were picking up their own vehicles and, most likely heading home after a day's work in the city.

The next morning, I woke up to discover I'd lost the cross I had been wearing. As one of the crosses Roger made, it meant a lot

DESTINATION D.C. A Modern-day Jonah?

to me. I was sure I had picked up everything the day before when I was down at the river, but I quickly returned to the bathing site, hoping to find it. The ground was strewn with sticks and branches and leaves, but I easily found my lost cross.

Soon, I was walking again, and hadn't gone very far when a vehicle pulled up on the other side of the road. The driver crossed over to talk to me. My immediate impression? He was curious, and somehow a bit hopeful. So, I told him what I was doing and why, and ended the explanation with a few questions of my own. He said that, yes, he was a man of faith. He was a Christian, but he didn't go to church all the time. He then explained that his wife had left him, and he had custody of their three sons. He also said he was on his way to an appointment and the three boys were in the car, so he had to leave; but he wanted me to go to their home later and pray for all of them, including his estranged wife. After I agreed to do this, he gave me the directions and we arranged to meet.

After racking up enough miles for the day, I drove to his house. We conversed for a little while and then I prayed for them. I asked if he knew anyone who would be able to help to alter my cross so I could carry it on a bus. He said his father was a woodworker and had lots of tools and he offered to call him right then and there. His dad said he'd be glad to help, and I soon found myself being led to him. Sure enough, he was able to customize the cross to my specifications. All I could think was, "Thank You God for bringing us together!"

We exchanged phone numbers and I thanked them, adding that their friendship and assistance was a great blessing. After we said our goodbyes, I drove back to take advantage of the refreshing cool water of the river; then I had dinner and gave Ann a call to let her know I was planning to catch the bus the next morning. I also said while I was reluctant to spend the money, I decided I should stay at a motel that was a short distance from the park and ride. I thought it would be much better if I was able to shower the next morning and get dressed to make myself presentable before heading to the city. And, truth be told? I did not relish the idea of getting up before sunrise to bathe in a cold river.

When I entered the motel, I spoke to the man at the desk and soon I was asking, "Are you a man of faith?"

"Well, not anymore," he said, explaining that his father had died awhile back and when he was in the funeral home and asked the priest where he thought his father was, the priest admitted he did not know.

Although I was longing for the nice soft bed that was waiting for me at a rate of about $15 an hour, I had to continue the conversation. About two and a half hours later, we said our goodnights and I'd lost a big chunk of sleep time: but, I guess, in retrospect, it was worth it because I believe I successfully brought the desk clerk to a point where he might attempt to re-establish his faith in God. With a mental shrug, I realized I hadn't been getting much sleep anyway, so what was one more night?

Before I left the motel, the desk clerk gave me some cardboard to wrap and protect my newly transformed cross during the trip. A short time later, the cross was safely stored under the bus, and I was on my way to New York City. The ride gave me plenty of time to think. I wondered *what's going to happen when I arrive? Will my walk attract attention from the media and help to convince people to pray for the health of this country?*

I want so much for this country to turn back to God and recognize that He is the one who made this country so great. After all, our founding fathers looked to Him for guidance and they demonstrated wisdom beyond that of any other country's leaders. And, God had told me to walk to the capital and declare Him to be the power, the blessing and the grace that made this country great. The first thing to do in New York was to find a place where I could reconstruct my cross. Then, I set out for a major conservative news station, thinking they'd be interested in a faith-based journey like the Heal America Walk. Or not.

"Not," was the definitive word for my experience. When I arrived at their broadcast building, I was told I couldn't stand where I was standing. After I explained that I believed I was on a public sidewalk and had a right to stand there, I was once again told I had to move away.

"Why? Why can't I stand here?"

"You have a sign, sir, and they're not allowed."

"A sign?"

DESTINATION D.C. A Modern-day Jonah?

They said my cross was a sign because it had lettering on it. So, I moved about 25 or 30 yards away, toward an intersecting street where a patrol car was parked. The policeman was leaning against his car and I asked if it was okay to carry my wooden cross. He said he would not bother me; and I looked around, wondering what to do next. I soon spied the front entrance. It was about fifty feet wide and fifty feet deep. I thought maybe I could go in and talk to the receptionist. I approached the entrance, intending to leave the cross at the door while I went in to speak to someone.

Unfortunately, before I could proceed very far, two men came out. They were huge: 6 and a half to 7 feet tall. "Where do you think you're going?" they asked. I told them I wanted to go in to speak to the receptionist and they informed me that it would not be happening. They also said I had to get off the property. When I asked why, since there were many other people walking across the same area, I was told I could not have a sign.

At least they asked me what I was doing, so I had a chance to tell them. "I'm 65 years old and I'm on a walk from Vermont to Washington, D.C.—protesting things like prejudice in this country against people of color and against Christians, and I believe we need to change." I also explained we need to go back to our roots, where our forefathers started this country. "They looked to God for blessing and guidance," I said.

I also explained we didn't need to be putting the police in danger by questioning everything they did and not giving them the respect that most of them deserve. "We don't need federal police, either," I said. I was glad to realize that at least these guys were listening, even if they didn't let me enter the property. So, I continued, proclaiming to them that this country is much too complacent with the blessing and grace that God has given us. "We need to once again be compliant in His word. We need to turn back to God. The only blood that has ever been shed that did any good for mankind was the blood of Christ. "And that," I stressed, "was a great blessing."

The two giants listened as I continued to state my belief about denominations, adding that we have become a nation that puts God behind us, and puts our wants and our pleasures ahead of Him. I concluded my little speech by saying, "He asked us to go out and

Detour To Rejection

be Christ-like, and we need to return to that and to the values of our forefathers who were wise because of their faith."

"Well, that's a good message and I agree with you," one of them said, practically folding himself in half to meet my eyes. "But you still can't go inside."

Disappointment was probably etching lines on my face as I realized I should return to Grand Central; but first, I headed toward Times Square. I'm not sure how it started, but I entered a discussion with a woman who was promoting bus tours. I sensed a kind heart as I learned that she lived in the city throughout most of her life. She had a son and asked if I would pray for him, explaining the city was a hard place to raise a boy. "A very hard place," she stressed, "with all the crime, especially the drugs."

At one point she suggested a bus tour to ground zero. "The former site of the twin towers is now a tourist destination," she said. It sounded interesting. After all, I had considered taking the time to visit the area, especially since there's a little chapel there that George Washington had entered so he could pray after giving his inaugural address. Pastor Tim's wife, Cindylee had suggested that I visit that chapel which had been mentioned in Jonathan Cahn's book, *The Harbinger*. It was also one of the five things that seemed to be confirmations, encouraging me to take the walk. But, after hearing the details of the trip, and discovering how expensive it was, I thought, *once again man has found a way to detract from important issues and make another dollar.* So, I said, "No thanks. I'll just grab a bite to eat at one of the carts on the street before I get back to the bus station."

"I'd advise against that," she warned. "Let me show you a good place to eat, Don," she said. "It's not too far away."

"Sounds good," I said.

I offered to buy something for her to eat and she declined the offer of food, but she did accept a drink. I bought a drink for her and a sandwich for myself; and after we finished, I prayed for her and her son and was on my way to the bus station.

At Grand Central, I discovered a practice that was slightly amusing, but annoying at the same time. Someone came along with a stack of newspapers and began to lay them on the floor behind the last person

DESTINATION D.C. A Modern-day Jonah?

in line, creating biodegradable stepping stones, each representing a person who had not yet made it to the line. It didn't take long for the bus to arrive and I got on board, thanking God that I had secured my own place in line before the "paper layer" showed up.

During the bus trip, I had an interesting conversation with a fellow passenger. After the usual introductions and sharing of personal information, the discussion somehow turned toward contrails—you know, those smoky lines that airplanes leave in the sky. He said some of the planes were dropping chemicals as they went across the country and it was affecting people. The funny thing was, at my suggestion years before my walk, Ann used contrails as part of the plot in her thriller, *The SEED*.

The discussion made the time fly and I soon found myself back at my vehicle. After a quick trip for a bite to eat, I hunkered down for the night. Happy to be out of the city, I spent a reasonably comfortable night. Early the next morning, I got up, pulled my meds out of a pool of cold water, and headed out for breakfast. And more ice.

POWER OF GOD: "... so that your faith might not rest on men's wisdom, but on God's power". I Corinthians 2:5.

DON'S NOTE: I think this verse and events like the volcanic blasts and the power so many men mistakenly feel they have, says it all!

CHAPTER 24
Miracles and Memories

After my trip to the city, a couple of uneventful days passed before I met a friendly family in a campground. They were from New York City, and most of them did not speak English. The oldest son, though, became a translator between me and the father. I asked if there was a place to swim or get cleaned up. They said the campground had showers, and then the father asked his son to find out what I was doing with the cross.

I told them about my walk and explained some of my beliefs about race and prejudice and how we should all just consider ourselves to be members of the human race. I mentioned the blood of Jesus was the only blood that was shed that made a difference for mankind. I also, of course, told them I did not believe there was a need for different religious denominations.

The father told his son to thank me for my faith-based message. He said he had never heard such things being put that way before, including the fact about the blood of Jesus. He also held out his hand to offer a few dollars in support of my walk; and after proclaiming God's blessing on them, I headed toward the campground manager's office to ask if there was a place where I could just park and get cleaned up. The guy manning the office said there were campsites available for rent and showers were included. Well, the price was too steep, so I asked if I could just pay for a shower. He said, "No," but he did say I could swim in the river. Trouble soon reared its head. The ground was too hard on my feet, so I decided to buy a pair of flip flops at a nearby shopping mall.

On the way back to the river, my cell phone rang. It was already quite hot, so I ducked into a shady spot to talk. It was the man with the boys, whose father had fixed my cross. And what a great message he had! He was calling with a special thank you. He said he believed my prayer of protection had saved them from a terrible injury! They were sitting at his kitchen table when a rock flew through the double-pane window, whizzing past them. He said, "It came so close to us, at such a velocity, I can't believe none of us was seriously hurt. I believe your prayer protected us, Don. Thank you so much!" I said I was truly glad that no one was hurt and confirmed that prayer was a powerful thing. Then I wished him and his family a Godly day.

Now, I know there are a lot of people who would say it was just a coincidence. I mean, rocks fly through windows all the time, right? Not really! I know that a rock spit out by a lawnmower can do some damage, but to have the velocity to crash through a double-pane window and whiz several feet beyond? I'm not so sure about that. I think if I believe it was a coincidence that the rock missed them after I prayed for their protection, then perhaps all of the experiences I'm writing about in this book are coincidences, too—and I certainly don't believe that!

Soon after that discussion, I found myself at a little stream that I'd have to cross to get to the river. I walked upstream a bit, looking for a narrow area that would be easy to cross. The water was ankle deep, but the power of the current pulled a flipflop off and I felt helpless as I saw my hope of cooling off being carried far out of reach. I knew it would be foolish to continue without protection, so I turned around, and struggled back to the bank. When I limped onto dry land, I scanned the path leading back to the car. *Not good!* It was rocky and rough, and my foot was already on fire. Then, I noticed some stairs built into the hillside. *That's good*, I thought. *It'll be somewhat smoother. No pebbles or sharp stones!* As I hobbled to the stairway, my foot throbbing with each step, I got an idea: *my towel!*

I sat on the bottom step and folded the towel in order to create a looplike sling that could pad my foot. When I stood up and slid my foot into the loop, I could pull the ends of the towel upwards to help take the pressure off my foot. Not exactly the ideal way to walk to the car, but it beat being stranded at the bottom of the stairs. Not exactly graceful, either, but each wobbly step avoided a lot of pain. As I mentioned, my feet had given me a lot of trouble for years, with deep cracks, dry skin and terrible burning sensations. When they hurt, they really, really hurt! But at that moment? I felt like singing, "Hallelujah!" Especially when I got to the top of the stairs. Trouble is, the struggle was only half over. I had to hobble, step, hobble, step across another 50 yards or so to reach my vehicle.

It was incredibly disappointing to have missed my swim in the river. I was desperate enough to pay for a camping area to take a shower, so I gathered up my soap and shampoo and razor and a few other items and proceeded toward the shower building. Although it was only about 20 feet away, I couldn't help but scan the sky for buzzards before heading toward the shower building, now feeling like I could relate to Ann's reaction to spiders and the "spidy" places that she avoids.

I knew the guy manning the place had left, so I just took the shower, intending to return to pay for the camp area as soon as possible.

After the shower, I got a bite to eat, then headed to where I'd spend the night. Before settling down, I made a few telephone calls. The first person on my list was Angie, the wonderful woman who had given me the room in the motel.

"How are you doing?" I asked. "I'm doing well now," she said. "but I had to hire someone to help with the rooms. I was in a lot of pain and had to go to the hospital." Not happy to hear that, I prayed for her. She thanked me, and knowing she was busy, I hurriedly said, "Bless you," and added that I'd visit with her at another time.

I'd been calling a woman in Granville every now and then, to pray for her mother. Her mom had been having problems for a while, even before I left home, and I wanted to stay in touch and let them know I was still praying for her. With that call behind me, I decided to contact Pastor Tim. As the head pastor of Jacob's Well, and founder of the Living Waters Evangelistic Ministries, he had ordained me as a minister. When he suggested that I be ordained, I thought it would be great. I knew I'd been ordained by Christ, but I understood that on this earth it's important to be associated with a reliable Christian organization. His wife, Cindylee was the co-founder.

I respected Pastor Tim's opinion and appreciated his support and was always glad to connect with him. We spoke for a little while, and on a humorous note, it seems that every time I called, he was out mowing his lawn. He joked about losing weight just by what the mosquitoes were eating. I laughed, saying, "I guess if you're out destroying their homes, they'll retaliate!" We chatted for a while and I filled him in on the events of the last couple of days. As usual, he prayed for my journey and safe travels. As I clicked off, I thought I'd better give Ann a call and let her know that I'm having trouble with my foot.

I could envision her nodding her head with understanding as I repeated one of my favorite lines, "I guess since I've made it this far, I'm sure God will see me through what He's given me to do."

It has been a challenge. I mean, between the trouble I had getting started and all the little things along the way such as getting sick, having the trouble with my eye and the breakdown with the vehicle, and the latest episode with my foot, it sometimes feels like there's always going to be struggles. She asked if I was going to be okay and I assured her I would be. After all, I believed I wasn't alone—God was with me—and I knew that He doesn't promise an easy life; He promises to help you through the rough times.

Many of the people I'd met said they felt an awareness of the presence of God. He surely was guiding this journey. Except for the angry drivers who cursed me on the roadside, most people seemed to understand the need for my message. They all were frightened about the path this country was on and have been frustrated about the violence and puzzling political situations that keep popping up. Most of them expressed an understanding that things simply were not right with the government and they all agreed we should turn back to God and not be complacent in His Grace.

When I woke up the next morning, I was obligated to return to the campsite to pay what I owed them. When I found the manager,

Miracles And Memories

he said to forget about it. He was so impressed with my honesty, he was happy to help me out.

I was about to resume my walk and was pulling the cross off the top of the car when I began to think about a 16-year-old boy I had met at a state trooper's barracks back when I started walking on Route 209. I had stopped there to ask for information about the route I was taking. The boy was just sitting, looking quite sad. I told the police I was a minister and was walking to Washington, D.C. After telling them about my walk, I explained that I'd been telling the police all along the way I did not believe we need a federal police force like the president had mentioned. I stressed that I believe there are good cops and there are bad cops, adding, "I know that most of you just want to do your job and most of you are good cops." They understood, and I could tell the boy was listening. It wasn't long before I had an opportunity to ask him why he was there.

"I was caught driving without a license," he said. "My friend had been drinking and I thought it would be better if I drove instead." I had to agree that if it had been the only choice, I might have decided to do the same thing. But then I said, "Maybe you could have found another way to get to where you were going. Sometimes we make mistakes, even when we think we're doing the right thing. But the law is the law, and we must follow it."

At one point, the boy reached up and removed two chains from his neck. "I found them, and I was planning to keep them, but I think maybe I should give them to you." He handed them to me and said, "I think you'll like these." When I saw they each bore a Christian cross I asked, "Why would you give them to me? I think you should hang on to them and we should pray that you'll find the Lord's guidance in your life."

"Yeah. I guess I'd like that," he replied. And so, we prayed. When I told Ann about that boy and his necklaces, she thought I had done the right thing and that perhaps they would remind him of that day and the messages I had given him.

I was soon on my way and you know what? It must have been for at least the next 75 miles after that, that every state trooper passing by would give me a wave or turn the lights on the top of his cruiser to pay homage to what I was doing. Anyway, thoughts

DESTINATION D.C. A Modern-day Jonah?

of the boy and his necklaces helped to keep my mind off my foot which had become extremely painful. I was determined to walk no matter what, and I believed with all my heart that I had to make it to the capital. Later that day I came upon a young girl working at a vegetable stand. She appeared to be in her late teens. During our conversation, she said she had a boyfriend. I asked if he was a Christian. She said yes, but she also told me that she was not.

"He treats you well, doesn't he," I asked.

"Yes, he does. Why do you ask?"

"Well, I just want to call your attention to the fact that if he truly is a Christian, it's his faith that will keep you happy with him." Of course, I said I hoped she would soon start attending church with him. Then she said she had started to go, but she didn't attend church with him every week and her parents didn't go, so she never really knew what church was all about. While we were speaking, I noticed a young man had parked his vehicle and was waiting nearby. I wasn't sure if it was a customer, someone who had come to take her place, or if it was her boyfriend.

Eventually I asked, "Are you her boyfriend?" He said yes and when he confirmed that he did go to church, I asked him to keep taking her to the services. Then I wished them God's blessing and proceeded down the road.

GOD'S PROTECTION/CONFIRMATION: "The LORD is my shepherd, I shall not be in want. He makes me lie down in green pastures, He leads me beside quiet waters, He restores my soul. He guides me in paths of righteousness for His name's sake. Even though I walk through the valley of the shadow of death, I will fear no evil, for You are with me; Your rod and Your staff, they comfort me." Psalm 23:1-4

DON'S NOTES: What an honor it was to pray for that man and his sons. His faith and gracious attitude are a great example of how a family should operate. I'm not surprised God had protected them from the rock that hurtled through their window. I hope I got through to that young girl at the fruit stand. It's a simple message we should all ask: "Do you want to be happy in life? Be a true Christian and be with one. Then God will lead you on the right path."

CHAPTER 25

Troubles on the Road

I still believed God was directing the route to be taken each day. Sometimes I'd end up in scarcely populated areas. At one point I was going down the east side of the Delaware Gap toward Blairstown. There wasn't much to see along that road, but I needed ice, so I was happy to come upon a little store and decided to stop and get something to eat while I picked up a bag of ice to keep my medications cool. While I was paying for it, I noticed they had pizza. It looked good, so I decided it would be a fine place to come back to after I packed my current purchase into the ice chest in the car.

The young woman at the counter asked what I had been doing, and if I was just traveling through the area. I explained that I was on a Heal America Walk and told her about it. Then, of course, I asked if she was a woman of faith. She said she used to be. "Sort of."

"What do you mean, 'sort of,'" I asked.

"Well, my parents are probably quite disappointed in me. He's a pastor and of course they're both religious. I used to go to church all the time, but now I hardly ever go."

"Well," I responded. "I guess you do have some understanding about Jesus Christ, and you must still have some faith."

"Yes, but I have time when I get older, to do the faith thing," she said.

I shuddered inwardly and quickly said she was making a big mistake that many people make. I explained, "You don't really know how much longer you have in this life. None of us do." I couldn't help but think about the young girl from my gym, who was planning to join the military, then died in an awful car crash. And then this young clerk said she didn't really know if what she was taught was true or not. It seemed to be true, she said, but she also stressed that she wasn't sure.

I said, "Let me tell you this. I don't know how old you are, but I'm going to assume you're about 21." She confirmed my guess, so I continued. "Let me give you something to think about. Do you know that every seven years you have died?"

"What do you mean," she asked. Judging by her facial expressions, I wasn't sure if she was skeptical and wondered what kind of nut she was talking to, or if she was horrified at the thought.

"Every seven years or so, every cell in your body has died and been replaced. The human body is described in the Bible as a vessel—in other words, I believe it's a container that houses your soul which I think of as your spiritual nature; your heart which represents the love and emotions you feel; and your mind—the knowledge you acquire." I looked her in the eye to be sure she was paying attention. She was, so, I continued: "Your soul is still present in your new physical body. And your memories are still there, too while your love for others is not lost or replaced or diminished— even though your body has been replaced. Fully replaced." I hoped I was getting through to her with the notion that a person's soul is an important part of them . . . and that to be healthy and strong, it must be fed in a spiritual way.

"Gee," she said. "That's something to think about. I guess I should consider going back to church." Then she gave an honest shrug and declared, "Well, at least I'll think about it more."

While I ate a slice of pizza, I noticed a couple of men seated at one of the tables. One was saying he never remembered when it was so hot and so humid, and it was obvious that he was old enough to have witnessed many seasons. I agreed. It was so humid my clothes felt as if I had been walking through water and my hair was slick and sweaty. Even so, I knew I had to continue my journey.

I left the store and picked up my cross. Oh! One thing I haven't mentioned was that a couple of days earlier the cross that had been cut down to fit on the bus was damaged. It broke at the cross arm and I couldn't find a way to fix it that would survive the continual use, so I started out that morning thinking I would just walk without it. I hadn't gone too far when I realized nobody knew me from Adam, nor did my presence make anyone realize they need to be looking to Christ. You see, every day I would walk along holding the cross with one hand and would point to the heavens with my other hand. I did that for most of each day throughout the walk, and my prayer in the morning was that if those who passed me did not have the spirit, they would become seekers who would receive the Holy Spirit in the near future after passing me by. And for the ones who did have the spirit, it would be a reminder for them to be looking to Christ that day.

With those thoughts swirling around in my head, I decided I simply could not walk without a cross. So, I realized I'd have to make another one. That meant, I'd have to purchase lumber, a brush, dark stain, and some screws. I knew I should not walk without a cross. The men at the hardware store were helpful; when I bought a board, they cut it to the lengths required to make a new cross.

After finding a lot to park in, I stayed through the night; and by 4:30 the next morning I was searching for my screwdriver—soon building a new cross beneath the parking lot lighting. By the time I had put it together I was hungry; and as a diabetic, I knew I should get a bite to eat before applying the stain to the cross.

After breakfast, I pulled off the road at the entrance to a rail trail. You might ask what a rail trail is. It's where a train used to run, but they removed the tracks and turned it into a trail for hiking and biking. As I got ready to stain the cross, a biker came along. He shot a quizzical glance my way, and I knew he was wondering why I was staining a big wooden cross on the side of a rail trail. He didn't stop to ask; he just kept peddling along. It seems to be a shame that he did not show any interest, but you never know the outcome of an encounter—even a wordless encounter. Perhaps he would mention it and be enlightened by someone?

The stain dried quickly despite the humidity, so in no time I was ready to resume my walk; but boy was my leg hurting! I was thinking it was shin splints, so I called Ann and asked her to look for a way to relieve the pain from shin splints. My left leg was hurting so bad, I didn't know if I was going to be able to walk any further that day. I'd probably only accomplished a mile in the last hour. Not a very good progress report!

When she called, Ann told me about some exercises that might help—if the problem was shin splints. I tried the exercises for about 30 minutes, and they seemed to relieve some of the pain; but when I tried to walk, it was just too much to bear. I started to ask people I came across if they knew where there was a place like a park and ride, or something similar where I could park for the night. Then I saw an 18-wheeler and asked the driver. He said there was a truck stop at the end of the road that allowed cars to park overnight. He also said they had showers and a diner. *Perfect!*

I decided the best thing to do was to rest my leg and foot and realized the ability to stay at the truck stop would be a blessing. I called home and asked for the telephone number of my podiatrist, Martin G. Carmody, DPM. I didn't call him that day. I just rested and showered, but the next morning when I woke up, my ankle was the size of a softball and my leg was at least half again as big as its normal size. I asked Ann to call Dr. Carmody. He said to try icing my ankle a few times a day. Despite the pain, I decided to try to walk.

It was not easy. I had gone only a few miles when I had to stop and sit on a guardrail. I knew if I tried to walk too fast or too far, I'd be in trouble. Eventually, a man stopped to see if I needed help. After receiving assurances that I'd be okay, he drove away.

I kept on walking toward Blairstown, trying to do the best I could. Near the town line, a woman and her husband pulled over. "Bless you," they said; and, gesturing toward my cross, they asked, "What's this all about?"

I told them about the Heal America Walk, and I also mentioned I'd had the opportunity to pray for many people along the way. Then they asked if I would pray for their two daughters—two young Chinese girls they'd adopted. The girls were having a difficult time adapting to their new language and surroundings; and so, I began to pray with them. Before we finished praying, a truck pulled to a stop.

It was the Mayor of Blairstown! He had heard about my walk and the cross and said he wanted to welcome me to his town. We spoke for a little while and then he said he had to run along to complete his errands. I thanked him for the friendly welcome and proceeded with my walk, thinking it had been good to have spent that time talking and resting. Despite the throbbing pain, I pushed myself to go a couple more miles. When I decided to stop for the day, a woman and her son pulled up.

"What have we here?" she asked, so once again I described the Heal America Walk and said I had started from my home in Vermont. I told her about a lot of my experiences throughout the journey; and before I knew it, she was rubbing my leg. It was so swollen, it was obvious for her to see how painful it was. After ending my stories about the walk, I said I'd be spending another night at the truck stop, and she invited me to their home for dinner. "It's only about a quarter of a mile up the road," she said.

"I'd love to," I said, my mouth watering at the thought of sharing a home-cooked meal. So, after I returned to the truck stop and got a shower, I followed the directions to her house. She fixed a great dinner for me, her husband and their two sons. They were all anxious to hear about my trip and we enjoyed a great evening. Nights like that still fill me with warm feelings about the wonderful people I've met during the walk. It's so amazing to have been able to serve God in this way and to meet so many people like this family.

They invited me to come back for dinner the next day, offering also to let me take a shower. I was only too happy to say yes! *No buzzards will be following me while I'm in this area,* I thought with a slim grin. That next evening became even more special because before I left, they asked me to pray for them. All four of them! They had health issues and they wanted me to pray for healing. Of course, I said yes, and before leaving, I gave each of them a handkerchief.

They invited me for a third visit, but I had to decline—I had to meet up with a friend in Ocean Grove, New Jersey.

I explained, "Just before starting this trip, I purchased the vehicle I'm using, and I still have the temporary license plates. They're almost ready to expire, so I've got to connect with my friend Roger, who's bringing the permanent plates to Ocean Grove where I can install them."

DON'T WAIT TO PRACTICE YOUR FAITH: "Listen, I tell you a mystery: We will not all sleep, but we will all be changed—in a flash, in the twinkling of an eye, at the last trumpet. For the trumpet will sound, the dead will be raised imperishable, and we will be changed. For the perishable must clothe itself with the imperishable, and the mortal with immortality." 1 Corinthians 15:51-53

DON'S NOTE: The Bible clearly states that no man knows when the end of life as we know it will come. But we must believe in Jesus Christ and acknowledge the fact that He is our Savior before the trumpet call. I pray for all those who do not believe this or understand it.

CHAPTER 26
Meeting Rabbi Jonathan Cahn!

Thanks to Roger, I got the new plates and installed them on the car. I must admit my leg was still throbbing, and I was worried about being laid up and losing a lot of time; but as I started to leave the area, I remembered that Rabbi Jonathan Cahn's church was not too far from the route I'd be traveling on and decided a slight detour would be a good thing. I truly wanted to attend one of his services if it was at all possible. And, of course, I was hoping to meet him and explain how his book, *The Harbinger*, had played such an important role in confirming what God had told me to do. I believe *The Harbinger* also provided much reassurance that the walk, indeed, was God ordained. Many of the scenes in *The Harbinger* coincided with experiences that I've had. Although we fully intended to read it, we had not taken the time to acquire the book; but God saw to it that one would fall into our hands! Ann's eldest brother, John—the treasure hunter who inspired the main character in her novels and children's books—sent it to us.

The receipt of that book was truly a sign from heaven. You see, we had often agreed that we should read faith-based books together; but somehow, we never got around to it. Life just seemed to get in the way. But, when *The Harbinger* arrived, we decided we just had to make the time. Each morning Ann would read a chapter or two

DESTINATION D.C. A Modern-day Jonah?

out loud. And, I must admit, listening to that book was an incredibly emotional experience. So many passages and events lined up with our life and our experiences since we moved to Vermont! Ann often had to stop reading, because I was so choked up by the scenes, my reaction affected her, and she became too moved to continue reading.

Without a doubt, *The Harbinger* helped to confirm to me that I just had to embark upon what would be the Heal America Walk. So, it was not surprising that during the journey, things worked out to allow me to take the time to visit his church. What a magnificent memory! The Jerusalem Center in Wayne, New Jersey is an impressive structure, with a white and gold facade, and two fearless lions roaring above the front entrance.

When I first arrived at The Jerusalem Center it was not a day when they conducted their services. I joked to Ann on the phone that the Devil was not going to stop me from meeting Rabbi Cahn. I resolutely returned the next day and was pleased to meet some ushers who appeared to hold positions of authority. One of them was quite interested in what I was doing. He said he would be sure to get together with me after the service and help provide an opportunity to talk to the Rabbi. That was positively encouraging! And, I was hoping that Rabbi Cahn would sign my copy of *The Harbinger*. After all, it contained five points that strongly served as confirmation that I should embark on my Heal America Walk. I genuinely wanted him to know about it!

As promised, I did get to meet with him right after the church service. But I had to get in line. It was a lengthy line, yet, despite my throbbing leg, I did not mind the wait. And then, when I said I'd like to purchase his other book, *The Shemitah*, and have that one signed as well, I had to go to another table to purchase it, then return to the line at his table for the signing. *No matter,* I thought. *It's worth the time!*

After he signed the second book, I explained how things in *The Harbinger* related to the message I received from God to walk to Washington. I also acknowledged the importance of his explanation of how our forefathers had looked to God for direction in creating the Constitution and how this nation was so blessed because so many of our leaders continued to look to God for wisdom. Then I told him my pastor's wife had suggested I might want to visit the chapel his book referred to that was next to ground zero. It was the chapel where George Washington prayed after his first inaugural address. Then I explained how I just knew before it was mentioned in *The Harbinger*, his character would be led to Washington, D.C. Thoughts of that place reminded me of all the similarities *The Harbinger* revealed between the fall of the temple in Jerusalem and the fall of our towers on 9-11.

There were so many things in *The Harbinger* that influenced my decision to walk to D.C. and coincided with what I was doing: like how he wrote that a man was supposed to put a Bible in his breast pocket, and I was told by God to bind a Bible to my chest. Also, the character in *The Harbinger* was told it was because he was a writer when he asked why he had been chosen to embark on the adventure that was guided by a prophet. It felt humbling to realize also that I was directed to testify about my faith and this faith-based walk and that I had started to write a book about my faith approximately six months before God directed me to take the walk. While talking to Mr. Cahn, I also explained that my wife was a talented writer who could assist with it. After all, her books have been endorsed by educators, from grade school teachers to college professors. Then I told him about a trip to Washington, D.C. that Ann and I had taken a year before *The Harbinger* was published.

Ann had been in touch with a group she saw on television called Moms for America. They were concerned with the way our children were being taught about American history, with God being taken out of our schools, and how our founding fathers were not given the respect they deserved within those studies. Ann contacted the head of the organization and told her about her Johnny Vic adventure books, stressing the fact that they included positive messages about our country and our Christian foundation. After sending one of the books to this woman, Ann was invited to sell her series at their event at the Washington Marriott, following Glenn Beck's Restoring Honor Rally on August 28, in 2010. Michelle Malkin, the conservative author and TV commentator, was the keynote speaker at the Moms for America event.

In preparation for the Restoring Honor Rally, knowing that hundreds of thousands of people were expected to attend, I felt directed to

DESTINATION D.C. A Modern-day Jonah?

write a piece called, "The Constitution and God's Hand." It focused on how blessed our nation was because our forefathers relied on God to create and lead this country and included passages from Lamentations that speak of the sins of and exile of Jerusalem. As I mentioned these analogous truths to Rabbi Cahn, I expressed the excitement my wife and I experienced when we realized just how similar these messages were to many of the passages we found in *The Harbinger*!

I've included "The Constitution and God's Hand" at the end of this chapter.

After our discussion ended and he signed my books, I said I hoped we could meet again in the future and Brother Cahn said he would not be surprised if he did see me again. I said I wouldn't be surprised either, knowing it was not a coincidence that his book had found its way to my home.

As I was leaving The Jerusalem Center, the usher who had connected me to Rabbi Cahn walked me to my car and asked for a healing prayer from me. He explained that he and his wife were both suffering from health issues and they had no insurance. They were praying for God's help, but they understood the wisdom of asking other believers to pray for them as well. I gladly consented and as he returned to the church, I carefully sealed the two signed books into a plastic bag without even reading what Jonathan Cahn had written. I was so happy to have had the chance to talk with him, I was determined to protect the books and not allow them to be left out to be harmed. Only later, much later, after I completed my walk and returned home, would I discover how significant the messages he penned to me would be!

That visit was important for another reason. As you know, I had been suffering with the torturous swelling of my leg, so when I was at Rabbi Cahn's church service, I limped forward when they offered to pray for individuals in need of healing or some other form of God's blessing. Hours later, I returned to the truck stop, ate dinner, iced my leg, then settled in for a night of rest.

As you might guess, my ankle was almost back to its normal size the next morning! With a grateful heart, I realized God was working to see me through what He has given me to do!

Meeting Rabbi Jonathan Cahn!

THE CONSTITUTION & GOD'S HAND
Compiled by Don Duncan, 2010

Our forefathers came together to form the groundwork of a new nation, known to us as the United States Constitution. Though they were men of knowledge, they were also the recipients of wisdom (all wisdom is of God). They knew that as mere men they were not capable of the task before them; so, they turned to the wisdom and morals of The Lord.

Oh, how far we have come as a nation! How blessed we have been! Growing faster, and more prosperous, than any other nation in such a short period of time. But it seems now, that we are spiraling, faster and faster out of that blessing.

Let the Constitution of this nation be as it was meant to be ... only to be updated with faith-based principles. Not through human knowledge that always ends in disaster. May we not repeat or experience the fall of Jerusalem. May we not be driven to our knees to lament what has happened to this nation because we fell from God's Grace.

All who pursue her have overtaken her in the midst of her distress. After affliction and harsh labor, Judah has gone into exile. She dwells among the nations; she finds no resting place. Lamentations: 1:3

Her foes have become her masters her enemies are at ease. The Lord has brought her grief because of her many sins. Her children have gone into exile, captive before the foe. Lamentations 1:5

Jerusalem has sinned greatly and so has become unclean. All who honored her despise her, for they have seen her nakedness; she herself groans and turns away. Lamentations 1:8

Her filthiness clung to her skirts, she did not consider her future. Her fall was astounding; there was none to comfort her. "Look, O Lord, on my affliction, for the enemy has triumphed." Lamentations 1:9

The enemy laid hands on all her treasures; she saw pagan nations enter her sanctuary—those YOU had forbidden to enter YOUR assembly. Lamentations 1:10

Christ's House of Angels.com
4738 Vermont Route 31, Poultney, VT 05764
Founders: Minister Donald Duncan, Ann Duncan

PRAYER HEALS: "Is any one of you sick? He should call the elders of the church to pray over him and anoint him with oil in the name of the Lord. And the prayer offered in faith will make the sick person well; the Lord will raise him up. If he has sinned, he will be forgiven."

James 5:14-15

DON'S NOTES: I felt blessed to be able to meet Rabbi Jonathan Cahn and to have the chance to tell him that his book, *The Harbinger*, played an important role in confirming the message I'd received from God to take the walk. And I am so grateful that the prayers of his congregation were so effective.

CHAPTER 27

The Redneck Reverend

In the café at the truck stop, I asked for directions and was told to ask one of the men working in the yard. They said, "He's the one who can give you the best directions." And they were right.

"Sure, I'll probably be able to help," he said when I found him. "Where you headed?"

"I need 2 East. Toward Stroudsburg."

He rubbed his head and squinted, searching his memory for the right directions. "Sure," he said. "Here's a way to get there." It didn't take long and when I confirmed that I'd be able to follow the course he laid out, he nodded with satisfaction. But then, I just had to ask, "Are you a Christian—are you born again?"

"Well, if you mean, do I believe in Jesus Christ, the answer is yes, I do, so I am a Christian. In fact, I refer to myself as a Redneck Reverend." His face broke into a wide smile, quickly crinkling into a serious countenance of wrinkles. That's when he said he knew he was a sinner, but his next admission was surprising. "I used to be in a cult," he said. "I worshipped demons. The Devil, too." Then, with a final apologetic shrug of honesty, he confirmed, "I was *so* into the occult."

He looked down at his feet, his demeanor signaling that he was waiting for my reaction. I could tell he had an even more important revelation, so I encouraged him to continue. With a glimmer of tears, he finally said, "Then one day I was just standing there when I felt a presence, so I turned to look and right next to me was a demon. A real demon! I was scared to death and turned away. My heart was pounding, and I could barely speak, but somehow the words came out. I said, 'If you're real, I'm sure Jesus Christ is real, too'. And just mentioning the Savior's name gave me the courage to turn back, and when I did, the demon was gone! It just disappeared!"

That's when this Redneck Reverend looked me straight in the eye and proclaimed, "I've been a Christian and have been learning about Christianity ever since I saw that thing." Then he squared his shoulders and insisted, "When I saw the demon I wasn't drinking. I wasn't on drugs. I tell you I know what it was, and I know it was there as real as anything can be." During our discussion, he quoted several Bible verses and I could tell that he was a serious believer. I believed him, convinced that he was not a kook.

This amazing man said he knew what was coming and he did not believe in violence but was convinced he would someday die in battle. He declared: "I won't take the mark of the beast and I won't bow down to Satan, and I don't call him Lucifer—he is not the bearer of light." He then said he was lucky he had not already been killed by the Illuminati. He said many other people might not know that they exist, but he was sure they do. To most people it's a fictitious organization that only the "nutty conspiracy theorists" believe in.

I do not know much about the Illuminati. I've only heard about them in movies as an organization of the global elite who try to create a malevolent world government. I guess the word malevolent says it all, and I can't help but wonder if the fact that he'd seen the beast has made this Redneck Reverend feel targeted.

I asked if he was going to be there later, because if I came back, I'd like to talk to him more. I told him I wish I could bring him back home where he could provide his witness to churches in my area. "It's the usual thing, to have someone witness to the workings of Christ and God the Father with a focus on love and heaven," I said. "But your experience is on the other side of the coin. People need to know that Satan and demons are out there. They do exist. We just don't have enough people speak of it, and by ignoring this truth, we tend to forget the work of the Devil and the power he has over so many people in this world."

That was a powerful discussion, and I wanted to hear more, but it did not come about. I knew he had to continue his work and I had to continue my walk. I am so glad I had that encounter. I am so glad I can record it in this book. And, once again, I was reminded: God's blessing was with me on the trip and He was bringing me face to face with special people like the Redneck Reverend who is ready to be a warrior for God. Speaking of warriors, Richard Setzer is an associate pastor at Jacob's Well who served our country faithfully in Iraq. While serving overseas, he worked with fellow soldiers to pen a moving message entitled, "I Am a Christian Soldier." It can be found at the end of this chapter.

Although my leg felt so much better after receiving the prayers at The Jerusalem Center, my ankle was still bandaged and I had resolved to take it slow; so, I decided to walk just a little to see how my leg would hold up. After managing to gain a couple of miles, I returned to the vehicle to rest and remove the bandage. Then I struck out again. I guess this time I'd gone too far because I had to stop for a while. A car pulled up and when the driver asked if I needed help, I said I didn't think he could transport the cross. He looked at it, glanced at his car, then nodded resolutely and said, "We can do it."

He had me stick the cross out the window with the base passing over my lap to nestle between us in the front seat. Back at my car, I thanked him profusely, knowing it would have been a big struggle without his help. He said, "No. Don't thank me. I want to thank you for doing what you're doing! God bless you!"

I gave a big, "God bless you," right back at him!

A short time later, Ann found a church in East Stroudsburg that would provide a place to shower and to park for the night. When I arrived, there were meters in front of the church. I only had a couple of quarters to plop into it and went inside to search for the contact person. She said she could issue a parking permit. "Just put this in your window and no one will bother you," she explained. And then she asked about my walk.

Once I started to witness to her, she plied me with questions. Each question led to more witness. Before I knew it, a couple of hours had passed, and I realized I had to add a few more miles to the day's walk. Once I completed my walk for the day and had showered, I decided to do my laundry. At the local laundromat, I started a conversation with a young woman who suddenly realized she hadn't put her quarters into the dryer—a half hour after she had loaded it!

"It could happen to anyone," I said and then, as we talked, I discovered she was not a person of faith, and did not attend church; but she revealed that she thought perhaps she might start going to church before too long because her boyfriend attended church regularly. "He's a Jehovah Witness," she explained.

"Well," I said. "I don't mean to cause a problem between you and your boyfriend, but as for the Jehovah Witnesses? I see them as a cult. They don't believe that Jesus Christ is deity. No matter what they say, if you study their true doctrine, they just believe Christ was a human prophet who did good things."

"Well," she said. "He has a Bible—they use them at their church."

I said, "Let me go to my car and get you one of the Bibles I have, and you can see if there are differences. Their Bible is not like the regular Bible that most Christians use. There are different variations of the Bible, but most of them agree on the major things that were in the original Scriptures. For instance, most Bibles proclaim Jesus Christ to be the Lord and Savior, and they say there is the one true God who is the father of Jesus Christ. And besides that, there's the Holy Spirit."

I quickly headed toward my car and returned with a Bible for her. I finished folding my laundry and was about to leave when I asked her to please check on the different churches that are out there, and to really look at the Bible I gave her and see for herself how it differs from her boyfriend's Bible.

"And, most important of all," I said with urgency, "You should not make any quick decisions." After administering that last piece of advice, I headed out to get a bite to eat and to return to the church where I'd be parking and sleeping overnight.

When I think about that young woman, I can't help but feel heavyhearted for all the lost souls that inhabit this earth and are misled. I also thanked God for the closeness I felt toward Him. It saddens me to know I fall short of His will so often myself. During those times, I pray for forgiveness and thank Him for His love and His mercy. I just feel so honored and yet so undeserving of His love and His faith in me as He continues to lead me on this remarkable journey. I so wish that someday I'll be in heaven and I'll be able to say I made a difference in people's lives. Perhaps I'll see that young woman from the laundromat . . . and her young man, too!

I was up and walking early the next morning when I got a phone call. Talk about good news! Remember the woman near one of the truck-stops who invited me to eat with her, her husband and their two sons? Well, they all had been suffering with health issues for a while and had all gone to see their doctors after I had prayed for them. She was calling to say that for the first time in quite a while they all had received good reports! She said her doctor was surprised and pleased. She thanked me once again for my prayers and I thanked her for telling me the good news; but I also stated very clearly—it was not any power that I possessed—their healing came from God! It's always nice to get a report about prayers that have been answered.

It's encouraging to hear about the blessings people receive through the power of prayer. Praise God! I give Christ the credit for healing because indirectly or directly, it comes from Him. I do realize that my prayer is a healing prayer and only through God have I been given the authority to effectively pray for the healing of someone.

I Am a Christian Soldier
by Pastor Richard (Rick) Setzer
2 BCT, 28th ID, 1/172 ARBN, Ar-Ramadi Iraq 2005-2006

I am a Christian soldier, a prayer warrior, of the army of my God. The Lord Jesus Christ is my Commanding Officer. The Holy Bible is my code of conduct. Faith, Prayer and the Word are my weapons of warfare.

I have been taught by the Holy Spirit, trained by experience, tried by adversity, and tested by fire.

I am a volunteer in this army, and I am enlisted for eternity. I will either retire in this army at the Rapture or die in this Army; but I will not get out, sell out, be talked out. I am faithful, capable, and dependable. If my God needs me, I am there.

I am a Christian soldier, a prayer warrior. I am not a baby. I do not need to be pampered, petted, primed up, pumped up, picked up, or pepped up.

I am a Christian soldier, a prayer warrior. No one has to call me, remind me, write me, visit me, entice me, or lure me.

I am a Christian soldier, a prayer warrior. I am not a wimp. I am in place, saluting my King, obeying His orders, praising His name, and building His Kingdom!

I am a Christian soldier, a prayer warrior. No one has to send me flowers, gifts, food, cards, candy, or give me handouts. I do not need to be coddled, cradled, cared for, or catered to.

I am committed. I cannot have my feelings hurt bad enough to turn me around. I cannot be discouraged enough to turn me aside. I cannot lose enough to cause me to quit.

When Jesus called me into this army, I had nothing. If I end with nothing, I will still come out even. I will win. My God will supply all my needs. I am more than a conqueror. I will always triumph. I can do all things through Christ.

I am a Christian soldier, a prayer warrior. Devils cannot defeat me. People cannot disillusion me. Weather cannot weary me. Sickness cannot stop me. Battles cannot beat me. Money cannot buy me. Governments cannot silence me, and hell cannot handle me.

I am a Christian soldier, a prayer warrior. Even death cannot destroy me. For when my Commander calls me from this battlefield, He will promote me to a captain and then bring me back to rule this world with Him.

I am a Christian soldier, a prayer warrior, in the army, and I'm marching, claiming victory. I will not give up. I will not turn around.

I am a Christian soldier, a prayer warrior, marching Heaven-bound. Here I stand! Will you stand with me? HALLELUJAH!!"

ANOTHER CONFIRMATION: The "Redneck Reverend" was serious about the existence of evil. The Bible refers to Satan frequently. You can see this in Luke 10:18, and in Matthew 4:10. He's also referred to as the Devil in Matthew 4:1, and as a man in Isaiah 14:16, while Isaiah 14:19 says he's like a rejected branch or a corpse trampled underfoot—to name only a few examples.

DON'S NOTE: I was so happy to receive a phone call shortly after I spoke to the Redneck Reverend from the family of 4 I had prayed for, saying they all had received good reports and felt grateful for my prayers. As I mentioned, I am always quick to remind people that it is not through any power that I have—it's always through the power of Jesus, in whose name I pray or through the authority given to me by Jesus. It is an authority that has been given to many, many Christians!

CHAPTER 28
A Tough Witness

Soon after I received the good news of answered prayers, I came upon some interesting wooden creations along the side of the road. The best way I can describe them is to say they were incredibly well-done artistic wooden pieces. I decided to check them out. Couldn't help but wonder who lived there and if they had made them.

When I reached the front door, a man was on his way out. He said he could not talk for long, but he did ask what I was up to with the cross. After he listened to a brief explanation, he went on his way and the fellow who had made the wood pieces invited me inside to see more. He had all sorts of interesting sculptural pieces, along with practical items like bureaus and tables—all made with incredible craftmanship. Of course, the conversation drifted toward the subject of faith.

"No," he said. "I'm not a man of faith, but many of my friends are. I just don't believe in that." He seemed to be very definite regarding his beliefs—although, it might be more accurate to say lack of belief. Even so, I wondered if I could get him to talk about it. So, I asked him why he did not believe in God.

He said he had a bachelor's degree in one subject and a doctorate in another, and he saw the world in a scientific way. "I just don't believe in faith at all," he repeated. In response, I gave him a synopsis of how we die every seven years because our body totally replaces all of its cells every seven years, and that fact sort of lines up with the Biblical description identifying our bodies as containers, or vessels. Yet we still maintain the same memories, feelings of love, and such."

He quickly countered, "I've been to school and I've had a great education and know that what you are saying just isn't so. There is part of our bone marrow that is never replaced during our lifetime."

I said, "Well, I don't know about that, but you're just talking about one tiny part of the body. If you're right, I still hope you'll look at the other facts and consider something other than what you learned in school."

"Most of my friends are Christian," he said for a second time, "and I often have this discussion with them."

"So, you think you are totally unerring, and all of your friends are wrong?"

He didn't seem to have an answer for that. Even so, we talked for about an hour and a half, until I was about blue in the face, and finally said, "I have to head out—I have a long way to go yet." Before saying goodbye, I told him there's a verse in the Bible that tells us, "Do not cast pearls before swine."

"What does that mean?" he asked.

I explained, "You do not see the beauty in what I'm trying to show you, nor the value. We do have free will, to believe or not to believe. And the fact is, true Christian teachings tell us that faith should not be forced upon anyone."

As I remember this encounter, I'm thinking, may God bless this man. I'm praying that he does eventually see the light.

Around 7 o'clock that evening, I stopped walking, figuring I had done enough for the day. I was happy to realize my foot and leg had almost been restored and I was very happy with my progress at that point. I had found a place to shower and a bed to sleep in for the night. It was a men's shelter in Lehighton.

After spending the night, I asked for directions. Perhaps I should say, I tried to get directions, because when I got closer to the center of

A Tough Witness

town, Route 209 became very confusing. It was as if it went in two directions, one on either side of town. After becoming thoroughly confused, I located the Chamber of Commerce where I could get a map of the area. At the Chamber, I noticed there was a TV station there as well. It was a small office used by two reporters from the local cable station. *A good chance to let people in the region hear about the Heal America Walk, I thought. And to get the message out that I wanted to encourage people to donate money to an orphanage in Peru.* After I asked for coverage, a young woman said they'd be able to do a short story if I waited for a little while.

"Great!" I said. "By the way, I've been carrying a cross throughout the walk and would like to be holding it during the interview."

She was okay with it, so I said I'd be right back and headed out to get it. On the way to my vehicle, a woman came running down the sidewalk. Before I knew it, she was pulling me into a big hug.

"Thank you! Thank you for what you're doing," she exclaimed. "I heard you tell the TV crew about your walk and I wanted to tell you about my son."

"Sure," I said as I glanced toward the young man who was with her.

"Oh," she said when she saw me looking at him. "I've taken this young man in and I truly love him as if he were my own son: but I want to tell you about my son who has died." And then she explained how they had been living in a building that contained black mold. To make a long story short, she and her son moved away from their moldy home, but apparently it had been too late. He had become seriously ill and developed emotional and mental issues. She said his condition was caused by the mold, and it had become so unbearable he had taken his own life.

After hearing her sorrowful story and consoling her as best I could, I returned to where I'd be interviewed. Before the taping started, they spent a few minutes with prep for the interview, asking basic questions about what I was doing; and they wanted to know what I'd like to focus on. First, I asked the young TV interviewer if she was a believer. She said she was not, but she revealed that she was a seeker.

DESTINATION D.C. A Modern-day Jonah?

Great! I thought, happy to have the chance to witness. I told her I had been healed from two life-threatening cancers. Each one miraculously, and I knew each time it was a blessing from God. I had already told her I currently have diabetes, so she asked, "So, if God healed your cancer, why didn't He heal your diabetes?"

"Well," I said. I don't know why, but He must have His reasons." I went on to explain, "If God didn't heal the person who wrote most of the New Testament of his infliction and had instead, proclaimed that His grace was sufficient for him, I guess I'll stand on that statement and believe God's grace is sufficient for me, also." I was, of course, referring to the passage in 2 Corinthians 12:9, when Paul explained he had asked God to remove the thorn from his side. Biblical scholars teach that Paul's "thorn" was symbolic of an affliction that was interpreted as being as painful as a thorn.

After the interview, I was on my way again. It was another scorcher. I'd figured out which route to take despite the puzzling maze created by Route 209. I only walked about three miles before deciding to return to my vehicle. And right about there, I saw a gun shop. The parking lot was empty, and the man inside the shop didn't look too busy, so I figured I'd ask if it would be okay to park there while I walked for the next three or four hours. Of course, I asked if he was Christian. He said he was not, but his mother was born-again. Although he was not a believer, he was open to some discussion on the matter, so we talked for about 15 or 20 minutes, and he said I'd given him a lot to think about. Before I left, I asked him how the gun business was going. "I've met a lot of people since I left Vermont who were afraid of what was going on in this country," I said.

"They must see that something is coming," he declared with a knowing nod, "because business is great."

PEARLS BEFORE SWINE: I can't say anything more about my experience with the wood worker except to quote the passage I spoke about. In that passage, Jesus stated, "Do not give dogs what is sacred; do not throw your pearls to pigs. If you do, they may trample them under their feet, and then turn and tear you to pieces. *Matthew 7:6*

CHAPTER 29
A Magnificent View

In Tamaqua, I asked if there was a shopping center nearby. I was hoping to get permission to park there. "It's on top of the mountain; a steep drive," a friendly person said, so I headed upwards, soon thinking, *they weren't kidding when they said steep*. I mean, it was so steep I was beginning to wonder if a shopping center really was there; but my car finally did chug into the parking lot. It looked as if they'd chopped off the tip of the mountain and plopped the store on top. And, wow. What a view!

I felt blessed. They said I'd be more than welcome to park there. And so, with the happy knowledge I had a place to stay for the night—a place with an immense vista, at that—I drove back to where I had stopped walking and continued my trek for the rest of the day. As I think about that beautiful parking spot at a shopping center, I can't help but realize my shopping trips often turn into opportunities for testimonials. One encounter I believe was orchestrated by God occurred long before I started this Heal America Walk. It happened in a supermarket back home that I shop at only occasionally. I was in the produce aisle, near a stand of flowers when I met a woman. After we commented on the fruit and flowers on display, I sensed she had health issues and asked if she was a believer. Seeing her quizzical reaction, I explained I sometimes

DESTINATION D.C. A Modern-day Jonah?

sense things about people, and I was wondering about her health. She said she was having problems with her bowels. Of course, we talked about the possibility of a colonoscopy; but I also said she should look to Christ for guidance. She acknowledged she was a woman of faith but did not attend church. I stressed the importance of faith and that being committed to a church is the best way to strengthen one's faith and have fellowship.

Sometime after that encounter, we met again in the aisle of a supermarket and she said she had gone for a colonoscopy and they did find some issues that most likely would have become a serious threat to her health if left untreated. Thank the Lord, the problems were dealt with before that could happen. Every now and then we run into each other and she'll ask, "Why are you here? Did God send you?" I guess she recognized the importance of our first discussion. *Perhaps*, I thought, *I'll experience a similar encounter here, in Tamaqua*. Well, I did! Sort of. But it wasn't at the shopping center. It was at the laundromat.

After a day of walking, I had other things to do, like fill up my gas tank and get some dinner. And then, there was the issue of laundry—I couldn't put it off any longer. And that's where I encountered another chance to witness. A mother and daughter were there with young children. The older woman was visiting her daughter-in-law and, of course, her grandchildren. She was from New York City.

After they loaded the washing machines, the grandmother headed out for subs. When she returned, she offered me some of hers and I said, "Thanks, but I've already eaten". Of course, this was an opening for conversation, which eventually led me to learn that she was a Muslim. We talked between washer/dryer cycles and folding. So, I had the chance to tell her a little about Jesus Christ. By the time I had folded my laundry, I realized it was 11 PM and I was exhausted, ready to pack everything up and climb into the car to head out; but something was niggling at me. *I should give her a Bible*, I thought, then quickly dismissed the idea.

"I'm too tired," I grumbled. "I need to get some sleep." So, I drove a few feet. Then stopped. My conscience wouldn't give up. Like a mosquito in the dark of night that you can't seem to swat

A Magnificent View

away, the thought kept buzzing in my brain: "I really should give her a Bible, and maybe some other Christian literature." *But I'm not sure if her family would like for her to receive Christian information,* my weary side whined, so. I slid the car into motion, determined to head toward bed, only to screech to a stop once again. I knew what I had to do. I just wouldn't feel right unless I offered the woman a Bible; so, I wearily returned to the laundromat.

I was relieved to see that she was still there. "I would like to give these to you, if you'll take them," I said.

She asked, "What are they?"

"It's some information about my faith. A sound-track to listen to, and a Bible. Would you like them?"

She said, "I would be happy to receive them. My bus leaves for the city tomorrow, and it's a long trip. It will give me something to read while I'm traveling."

To this day, I'm hoping she read what I gave her and has learned more about Jesus and Christianity. Perhaps she and her family will become believers!

CHRISTIAN RESPONSIBILITY: "He said to them, "Go into all the world and preach the good news to all creation. Whoever believes and is baptized will be saved, but whoever does not believe will be condemned." Mark 16: 15-16.

DON'S NOTE: It gives me great peace and frees me from worrying about my dogs and cats and if I'll see them in Heaven! When the above passage refers to all creation, I believe it includes animals. I have seen the question in the Bible saying, 'why would God abandon such great works (referring to animals) and leave them to perish?' It also reminds me of the message that Dean Braxton reports to his audience when he talks about his experience. He had been pronounced clinically dead for an hour and forty-five minutes, and then came back to life. And, he saw pets were in heaven.

CHAPTER 30

The Missionary

Often as I walked, I thought about home and my church family. I missed them terribly. One memory that came rushing back one day was a special encounter I had with an evangelist named Mark Swiger, quite a while before I began the Heal America Walk. It started with Pamela Bolton, Pastor of the Out of the Box Worship Center in Whitehall, New York. Pam is a pastor affiliated with the Living Waters Evangelistic Ministries, who arranged to have Dr. Swiger speak at several locations throughout the area. Pam and her husband, Bill, have organized several similar events. Ann and I decided to attend Dr. Swiger's talk at Jacob's Well.

We listened as he described that while he was a pastor, here in the United States, he was directed by God to become an evangelist in India. He explained how it required a lot of resources and several steps for him to become an evangelist in a country like India. He worked hard to become accredited for it and in time, he began his ministry in that faraway land. Once he was established, he appealed to large crowds that numbered into the tens of thousands. He said he had prayed for the healing of many people and many were, indeed, healed. His influence drew innumerable people of India to the Christian faith.

At first this evangelist received little resistance from the government, but his growing influence on the people apparently became recognized as a threat. He said officials increasingly gave him problems and he was finally asked to leave the country. Reluctantly, he returned to the United States, not sure of the path that Christ had suddenly allowed to be put before him. Eventually, he decided to talk about the many healings he'd witnessed in that faraway land and to profess to the miraculous way Christ still worked.

So, we first saw him at Jacob's Well in Cambridge, New York. And after he had spoken about his work in India, he asked people to come forward to receive prayer for healing. Now, there are times when I go forward and other times when I do not. I did not go up for prayer that evening. You might ask why I didn't go forward at that time, and my answer would be the spirit just wasn't leading me to take that step. The evening passed quickly and soon Ann and I were on our way home.

We talked about the experience and Ann reminded me that this man would be speaking the following night at a church that was much closer to our home—only a fifteen-minute drive away. Well, the next day I busied myself with yard work, but as the day wore on, the thought that I should receive prayer from him started niggling at me. It became an internal battle. On the one hand, I told myself there was too much work to do and I should not take the time to go to the talk; but the later it got, the more I'd feel that tug at my heart. Ann had decided to stay home, but she encouraged me to go, even if it was late and I'd probably miss the introductions and some of the opening worship time. As it turned out, I am so glad I went! Although the talk was very similar to what he had said at our church, the overall experience was wonderful, and I've just got to tell you what happened.

When I first entered the church, I saw a couple and their little girl, who was about 10 or 12 years old. I recognized them as having been at Jacob's Well the night before; but as I entered this church, I felt very strongly the little girl had been given a healing gift and she would eventually use that gift to serve the Lord. I approached the pastor of the church and explained how I felt this little girl was going to have a healing ministry at some point in her life.

DESTINATION D.C. A Modern-day Jonah?

"That's strange," the pastor said. "Just this morning I was discussing that very thing with her parents. Perhaps you should go and talk to her mother."

At the first opportunity, I introduced myself to the family and told them about my thoughts about their daughter. The little girl's mom said, "Isn't that funny—she isn't our daughter by birth—we adopted her; but before the adoption, I received a vision foretelling that we would adopt a little girl who would have a healing ability!"

After that remarkable conversation, I turned my attention to the speaker. As he had the night before, he called people forward for prayer and for healing. This time I got in line and as I waited, I started to talk with a woman who was standing in front of me. She said she was immensely grateful for the healing she had received, and that God had blessed her with a tremendous amount of mercy and grace. I asked her what she was referring to and she said, "I had Multiple Sclerosis and now I'm healed."

She said she had been so debilitated with M-S she was in a wheelchair and had been admitted to a nursing home. What a blessing! Praise Jesus! I mean, how can you do anything other than praise God when you're confronted with such a miracle?

Just minutes later, while I was still waiting for my turn at the platform, I noticed the evangelist's wife and decided to speak with her. I claimed the seat next to her and introduced myself. Soon it was put on my mind that her husband—the evangelist who was praying for others—needed a healing; so, I asked her, "Does your husband need prayer for healing? Is he sick?"

She said he had some needs and that's as far as she went with an explanation. I soon returned to my place in line and went forward to ask for prayer for myself. But I was quite curious and concerned about this wonderful man's needs, so I returned to the seat next to his wife. As we continued our conversation, I noticed her husband had finished the prayer session and was speaking to a man whom I later learned was from Jamaica. They were too far away for me to hear what they were saying; but I turned back to his wife and suggested that perhaps we should pray for her husband. There were other pastors in the church that night and soon we all gathered together to pray for this remarkable man. A short time passed after we finished praying for him when he declared, "I have never had such a feeling come over me. I don't know what to make of it."

When I found myself alone with him, I said, "I want you to know something. I don't think the reason you're back here in the United States is because the Indian government wanted you out of their country. I've had a premonition that God wanted you back in this country to do a work for Him here." After my bold statement, he said, "Isn't that strange . . . the fellow I was just talking to (meaning the man from Jamaica) had just told me the very same thing."

We just looked at each other for a few seconds, then I asked, "By the way, what did you mean when you were praying for me and you said you were going to pass the baton you were carrying over to me, and that I was going to run a great race for the Lord and I would do a great work in His name? Can you explain it more?"

"I don't know," he replied. "I don't understand myself what that meant. If I passed the baton to you, then what will I do? Will I be taken out of the race?"

I'm still not sure what it all meant. It happened before the "Heal America Walk" and I have not had the opportunity to speak to him again, although Ann had called him to let him know I was on the walk. One thing I do believe? We are all a part of God's plan, and it all will be revealed in His time.

Another great speaker that Pam and Bill brought to local churches was Dean Braxton, a man with a story about heaven. It's well documented that Dean was clinically dead for one hour and forty-five minutes. Excerpts from his medical history and medical records include: Profound Septic Shock, Prolonged Cardiac Arrest, CPR for one hour and 45 minutes, Post-prolonged CPR and Post Cardiac Arrest, just to mention a few. During that time, he visited heaven. It's true! Over a dozen people testified in Dean Braxton's book, *In Heaven! Experiencing the Throne of God*, that Dean's descriptions of Heaven and his insights into the afterlife have made believers out of them. He's also the author of, *Deep Worship in Heaven*. If you find a chance to listen to him speak, you'll also become a believer. Dean Braxton's enthusiasm and aura of truth explode with the intensity of no other story Ann and I have ever heard!

CONFIRMATIONS: Do not let any unwholesome talk come out of your mouths, but only what is helpful for building others up according to their needs, that it may benefit those who listen. Ephesians 4:29
"Therefore, my brothers, be all the more eager to make your calling and election sure. For if you do these things, you will never fall. And you will receive a rich welcome into the eternal kingdom of our Lord and Savior Jesus Christ." 2Peter 1:10-11

DON'S NOTE: The above passage from Ephesians seems so appropriate when I realize how we confirmed the vision regarding that mother's adopted daughter. And, the success of the evangelist's efforts in India show very clearly that he did "do diligence to his calling". Thoughts of the connections and confirmations that I experienced because I gave in to the tugging at my heart to attend that second testimonial session still add to and confirm my faith.

CHAPTER 31

The Grace of God

Early one morning before starting my walk, I became exceedingly fearful with worry that I may have sinned. I knew I would be forgiven. Had no doubt about that, but what about my mission? The walk? Would God still give me the power I needed from Him to complete the Heal America Walk? This concern filled my heart with unbearable sorrow, but I simply had to try to please God, so I repented and asked for His forgiveness and continued down Route 209. For the next two miles or so, my heart nearly broken, I kept thinking there was no way I could complete this Heal America Walk without God's power! No way! But then I did realize He put this mission before me after forgiving all my past sins.

Still filled with troublesome thoughts, I came across an indoor flea market. *Gee*, I thought. *I wish Ann was here. She loves flea markets.* Knowing she'd love to hear about it, I reasoned, *well, perhaps I'll stop on the way back, if only for her sake.* A tiny smile forced its way onto my face despite the sadness that filled my heart, because I knew my wife would chuckle at that thought. She knows I love flea markets just as much as she does.

I made good time that day. Filled with determination to please God, I covered about 12 or 15 miles. Being on the shaded side of the road helped; and, in addition to that good fortune, my leg and

DESTINATION D.C. A Modern-day Jonah?

foot were healed. I wasn't experiencing any pain! And so, I headed back toward the car and the flea market in a much better mood.

A grin spread right up to my eyes when I got there, thinking, *I should stop in to see what's here. For Ann's sake, of course.* At the doorway a woman approached. She had seen me walking with the cross and she wanted to tell me how wonderful she thought it was.

"I think it's so great to see you doing that," she said. "And you just have to let me bring you over and introduce you to one of the men inside. I just know he's going to be excited to meet you!"

I figured he must be big on Christianity, so I let her lead the way.

It wasn't long before he was also introducing me to people at the flea market. And once they learned about my walk, I explained how I had received a healing gift after being healed myself. Soon, my new friend was introducing me to a husband and wife, and his own wife, and a mother and daughter. They were all in need of healing and wanted me to pray for them. So, before I left the marketplace, I prayed for all six of them. Then, my flea market friend gave me Christian hats, T-shirts, and boxes of crosses to give to others. He was so generous we reached a point where I had to tell him I just couldn't carry even one more thing. After a heartfelt thank you, I headed back to my car, figuring I'd stay at the same spot one more night before moving forward.

The next morning, I received a call from Josh, a friend who loved the House of Angels. I always enjoy hearing from him and don't get to see him very often. He lives in the Utica, New York area—quite a trek from Vermont! We must have talked for an hour. During the discussion I learned that his wife Laurie had fallen while she was in York, Pennsylvania. After extensive medical treatment, she had been admitted to a rehabilitative nursing home. I don't remember which one of us brought up the subject of prayer, but I offered to veer off my walk to go and pray for her. We talked some more, and he said he'd let me know when it would be a good time. I said I'd give him another call soon to see if she was ready and willing to have me visit. At one point he asked if I was going to church while I was on the walk. I said yes, and thought I'd like to attend a service in the area I was currently in, but I did not know where to go. However, I did explain that God never fails to send me to the right church with the right message. Josh gave me a little information before we said goodbye, and then he said, "Remember, it's not the beginning of the journey, nor is it the end of the journey that counts—it's everything in between." I know Josh was right. There was so much amazing "in between stuff" on this journey that it left me feeling exalted and privileged . . . yet I continued to feel totally unworthy.

I stopped to get a breakfast grinder and the place was pretty much empty, except for one couple; but as I began to eat, recognition clicked. It was my generous friend from the flea market! As he and his wife ordered their food and got their coffee, I realized he didn't recognize me yet. After all, I didn't have my cross or the wide-brim straw hat. It didn't take long, though, before he realized who I was, and I heard him exclaim to his wife, "Hey look—that's Don, the guy with the cross. He's sitting at our favorite table!" He came over and sat down, telling me he and his wife always come here on Sunday before going to church.

"You're going to church?" I asked with an air of expectancy.

"Yes, we try to go every Sunday."

"Where do you go?"

He said they went to one church most of the time, but they also went to another one every now and then. So I asked if I could go with them today, saying, "I don't know any churches around here and I was just thinking I should attend a service somewhere."

"Of course!" he replied. "We'd be happy to have you join us." So, I went with them, and we agreed that after the service we would meet up later at the flea market. As it was with most Sundays, I thought I would take it easy and I looked forward to the opportunity to enjoy the company of my new friends—and to reflect on the things that occurred during the week, including the blessings of God.

I recalled how concerned I had been as to whether I was still worthy in God's eyes to complete His mission. It was a moment when I confirmed to myself that I did not want to fall out of the grace of the Lord. Not after all this effort! Not ever! I love the Lord! And then, I remembered how I was treated like royalty, receiving gift after gift, not to mention the kindness, and I began to realize that previously, as I walked, there were many people who would honk and wave, but there were many who did not and, instead, had displayed their anger. But as my thoughts drifted through yesterday's experiences, I realized there never had been a day like that, where in a short distance of a quarter of a mile or less, about 47 out of 50 cars honked their horns and waived—some even rolled down their windows to say, "God bless you. Thank you for what you are doing."

It's God, I thought with a thrilling revelation! *He's revealing to me that I'm still worthy within His eyes and He is pleased with me! That's why I was lavished with gifts and so many people were showing their approval.* Overcome with the joy of the Lord, I started to weep. The presence of His love and assurance, the feeling that He approved, was simply overwhelming. Even as I think of it today, a tear comes to my eye and my chin quivers as I struggle to speak. The emotion was that strong—overflowing from the joy I felt through the overwhelming love of God.

My flea market friend and his wife, and a couple of their friends and I, got together later for dinner. At the end of the night he asked if I would like to meet up in the morning for breakfast. Of course, I said, "Yes."

Connecting with these wonderful people helped me to realize that Josh was right about how much the "in-between stuff" matters. I mean, God had given me the opportunity to attend Rabbi Jonathan Cahn's church and to receive a healing; and to hear messages from people I prayed for who reported their healings! For a short time, my thoughts meandered back to the day I went to Jonathan Cahn's church in Wayne, New Jersey, when I had so much trouble with my foot and leg. When they were praying for me, one of the men confirmed that I have the strength and the protection from God to do the greatest thing I have ever done or ever will do. I didn't know if his message was true or not; but now that this walk is over, and time has gone by, I believe it just might be true. And, little did I know at the time the Rabbi signed my books, he would be giving me cryptic messages from God's word that would help explain this walk!

I called Josh to ask if it would be a good time to come down and pray for his wife. He said it would be a great time and he thought

The Grace Of God

the prayer cloth would work. She was still receiving rehab in the nursing home in York.

It would be almost a hundred miles each way for me to go, but I was only too glad to do it.

Before I left for York, I made plans to see my flea market friend's son, a veteran who did a lot of interesting films on the area he lived in. I was hoping his father had told him about me and that he might do a short report on my walk. He did film a short segment, but I believe it did not come out for quite a while. Anyway, after we filmed the interview, I headed toward York to meet Josh and Laurie at the nursing home. When I arrived, it was almost time for dinner, and he ordered an extra meal so I could eat with them. We visited for an hour or two, then I prayed for her, left a handkerchief and headed back to get on track.

FEAR OF FAILURE: "But He said to me, "My grace is sufficient for you, for my power is made perfect in weakness." Therefore, I will boast all the more gladly about my weaknesses, so that Christ's power may rest on me. That is why; for Christ's sake, I delight in weaknesses, in insults, in hardships, in persecutions, in difficulties. For when I am weak then I am strong." 2 Corinthians 12:9-10

DON'S NOTE: We all fail and have weaknesses. The key to overcoming failure is how we live with it; how we react. In the NIV Bible, one of the notes about passages in 2 Corinthians that deal with failure and weakness reminds us that God often works best through our weaknesses. In this way, His power is revealed more clearly, and we are prevented from taking credit for what God has done. So, if you feel like a failure, take heart. God may be ready to use you to accomplish something very significant for Him. It's good during times of failure or ruination, to remember there's much evidence of the truth in the saying that whatever is meant for evil, God uses for good.

CHAPTER 32

My Friend from Utica

After leaving the nursing home, I thought about the first time I met this wonderful couple, Josh and Laurie. Often when I arrived home from work, I would get a vision or insight providing the need to go directly up to the cross. One day when this happened, I was feeling extremely tired and dirty—but still, I felt I simply had to go directly up to the sanctuary. Someone might as well have shouted: "Do not stop to rest, do not stop to wash." I had learned early on to obey these directives because there usually was someone there who needed prayer, or maybe just a friendly conversation. As soon as I got to the top, I saw a vehicle parked in the circular drive and two people who were sitting on one of the benches.

I asked, "What's up?"

He said, "We're just sitting here, hoping this place will still be here long after you're dead and gone."

"I hope so, too," I countered without equivocation, even as I thought *that's a strange thing to hear from someone I'd never met, but I guess it's quite a compliment, too. For the House of Angels, at least.*

When I introduced myself and welcomed them, they said they were from the Utica, New York area . . . about 150 miles away. They were visiting relatives in a nearby town, including his sister who

My Friend From Utica

told them about the House of Angels. When he mentioned how his sister knew about us, I remembered the encounter. She and a friend had been out for a drive when they had car trouble right in front of our property. Their exhaust system was falling off and dragging on the ground. I said I could do a temporary fix with some wire and suggested they might like to walk up our driveway into the woods.

"There's something up there I'm sure you'd enjoy seeing," I said. "The dirt road will circle around at the top where you'll find a special spot; and while you're checking it out, I'll see what I can do to get you back on the road."

They agreed and launched themselves up our dirt road while I got to work. I was just finishing my temporary repair job when they returned from their visit to the House of Angels. They loved it, of course; but at the time, I had no idea this encounter would lead to a lasting friendship with the driver's brother, Josh and his wife, Laurie. But it did.

The day after Josh's first visit, Ann called to say he and his wife had come back and had brought us some flowers to plant up back. They also blessed us with a gift, so we could acquire more flowers. It was Spring, and it turned out to be the first year we would be able to carry out an impressive planting.

We heard from Josh and his wife sporadically after that, mostly through telephone calls, but it felt as if we had known them for a long time. One year he called to say he was going to come to the area to help his brother who was having serious health issues and would have to be moved to his sister's home. He had worked on tugboats in the New York City area for most of his life, but it looked as though he would not be able to do that work anymore. As a matter of fact, they were not sure if he would be able to do much at all. I suggested that he be brought to the House of Angels for a special prayer session. He did not think it would make a difference, but I assured him all things are possible through God and I knew that God blesses many. He did agree to come, and we prayed up at the cross. Again, a year or two passed before we heard from them; but one day Josh called to tell us that although his brother probably would never be able to work on a tugboat again, he was traveling on his own and doing quite well.

DESTINATION D.C. A Modern-day Jonah?

Again, quite a bit of time passed before we heard from them. They called, giving us the option of a quick visit here at the House of Angels, or a chance to meet somewhere for dinner. We enjoy dining out, so we agreed to meet at a restaurant. And then, we had a pleasant surprise: Josh was good friends with Tim and Dawn Mead. Tim was the man who had that mysterious blockage; the one I had first laid hands on for healing, who showed up in church two days later, completely healed. So, the six of us got together for dinner. God works in mysterious ways. His wonders never cease—and neither do His connections!

By the time I finished my recollections about Josh, I returned to my parking space where I experienced a very short night. I was up early the next morning, wanting to get some miles in and make up for the time I'd spent visiting with people over the past couple of days. At one point a man and a woman stopped to say they had seen me on TV, and they had just come from a store and were kind enough to bring me a water and a soda.

I stopped at a store shortly after that and realized it was more of a renovated garage that was being used for selling beer in kegs and cases.

I went inside to search for a snack and mentioned to the man I thought was the clerk that I had diabetes. He apparently was the owner and asked if I would like a hamburger—he was about to turn on the grill. When it was sizzling hot, he cooked for me, the mail man and one of his friends that I nicknamed, "Keg." Seated on a stack of beer cases, the guy had consumed about six or seven beers in the short time I was there, so the name seemed to fit—especially since he was shaped like a keg and he was full of beer!

He wasn't belligerent, nor did he appear to be intoxicated. As we talked, he told me of a sick relative that was living with him. He also told me the store owner's wife was battling stage four liver cancer. I prayed for his relative and the owner's wife and gave them handkerchiefs. Then, I extended my thanks and headed back to my vehicle; but when I got there, I realized I needed ice.

When I returned to buy the ice, I noticed that Keg was looking troubled. I asked if he was okay and he said he was just thinking about all the sickness and troubling situations in the world and he wished it would all go away. I assured him that I believed most of us feel that way. Then, I thanked them for their friendship and generosity before heading back out.

CONNECTIONS: "All Scripture is God-breathed and is useful for teaching, rebuking, correcting and training in righteousness, so that the man of God may be thoroughly equipped for every good work." 2Timothy 3:16, 17

DON'S NOTE: Time and again, I concluded that there are divine connections that God has pre-ordained for our lives. They can become important, long-term relationships and sometimes, as in the case of Josh and Laurie, they can be associated with God-given assignments. I always feel uplifted after my discussions with Josh.

CHAPTER 33

Praising the Father Saves the Day

I found a secluded pond at the end of the day and then searched for a Walmart to park at that I had been told was a short distance ahead. By the time I reached it, I was totally beat, so I quickly settled down for the night. The next morning, I was just miserable. I hadn't slept well. I didn't feel well, and it was like the whole world was against me. On most days, I went down the highway praising Jesus, pronouncing "hallelujah"—sometimes shouting it at the top of my lungs—raising the cross high up and pointing to the heavens with my other hand. Well, not this day. I must admit it was grumble, grumble, grumble as I exerted myself, feeling as if there would be no end to the hard, continuous pavement or the oppressive heat. I was not in a good mood and I continued like that for about three hours, perhaps even four.

Eventually I came to my senses. I thought, *maybe if I stop grumbling and shout Hallelujah, praise You Jesus, things might change for this day.* I truly needed to thank the Lord for what I had! This has been such an amazing mission, surely my current attitude must change. I simply had to find my way back to the great state of expectancy!

"Alright," I said with an increasingly repentant attitude. "Hallelujah, hallelujah!"

Well, as soon as I did this and praised Jesus, my emotions changed like a switch had been flipped! I felt much better and what happened next was a big surprise. If you remember: to me, the presence of one dove represents the Spirit. Two are the Father and Son. And three doves represent the Holy Spirit, and the Father and the Son. And then, up ahead, what did my wondering eyes see? A whole flock of doves! There must have been a dozen or more. With a big smile, I decided these doves represented the Father and the Son and the Holy Spirit — and the entire congregation! And even more amazing? That flock of doves included one white one. That was incredible. Not only was one dove representative of the Spirit, but if you remember, when Jesus was baptized, the Spirit appeared to Him as a white dove!

Yes, this has been a hard walk, but not without reward. As I have said before, the presence of God was continually around me. Except for a short time that morning and when I felt the need for forgiveness, I truly felt Him 24 hours a day. Praise the Lord! Well, I did finish the day on a much better note than when I had started. Those glad-hearted thoughts led me to a memory that I still find astounding. When I think of the years when I defied God's principles, living a truly faithless life; I wonder again and again, why me? Why has God given me these wonderful moments and intense mandates? I feel so undeserving after being away from His ways for 40 years. Well after I recovered from the colon cancer, I came upon the last few verses in Mark 16, and realized they now pertain to my experience in this life.

Mark 16:15-18 states: "He said to them, "Go into all the world and preach the good news to all creation. Whoever believes and is baptized will be saved, but whoever does not believe will be condemned. And these signs will accompany those who believe: In my name they will drive out demons; they will speak in new tongues; they will pick up snakes with their hands; and when they drink deadly poison, it will not hurt them at all; they will place their hands on sick people, and they will get well."

I have been doing my best to preach to all creation that I come across. I do believe in Jesus. I was baptized. My prayers almost always urge God to drive out demons. One day, without a moment of thought while I was working up at the House of Angels, I suddenly found myself speaking in tongues. The sounds poured out of me as quickly as you could picture water pouring out of a bucket of water that had suddenly been kicked over. Regarding the handling of snakes? I picked up several snakes (especially the ones that appeared while I was digging the hole to put up the cross at the House of Angels) and I've had more than one encounter with poisonous copperheads. Not to mention the fact that during the time when I felt my cancer was gone, I took in the chemo which can be construed as a deadly poison when it is not needed to fight cancer cells. And I have placed my hands onto sick people, and they have become well. I truly feel unworthy, but when negative thoughts enter my mind, I also remember how my wife had explained to her co-workers that the Bible is filled with stories about unworthy people being chosen by God. How can I ignore the fact that all the signs mentioned in Mark 16, had happened to me?

As I started to settle in for the evening, I realized it was going to be another sweltering night, making it hard to settle down for a restful sleep. But even worse than the oppressive heat, there was an event that night that I'd rather forget. Something awakened me. Something was crawling on my back. It felt like a spider wearing combat boots! Eeegg, I gurgled with disgust as I twisted and turned, trying to get the thing off me. *What is it?* I wondered, frantically flailing around for my flashlight. "Where is it," I hissed, as my fingers finally latched onto the flashlight and I searched for the crawly creature. It was a tick. The biggest non-swollen tick I'd ever seen, it was literally the size of an eraser you'd find at the end of a pencil. I thanked God that it had not latched itself onto me and realized this experience gave good cause to my determination to avoid grassy areas near streams where I stopped to wash up. Otherwise, they'd have drained me of a lot of blood by now. All of it, judging from the size of that one!

Morning soon came. I had breakfast at a local diner and had come to Route 501, encouraged to realize I'd arrived at the Amish and Mennonite area. Fresh vegetables everywhere! I stopped at a Mennonite Market and got a six-inch sub for just $2.75. It must have contained a half a pound of meat and the whole thing must have weighed a pound and a half. I mean, it was so big, I only ate half for lunch and saved the rest for dinner.

Praising The Father Saves The Day

After eating my sub, I continued walking. Eventually a woman drove up and rolled down her window so she could ask me what I was doing. She said she was happy to see someone calling attention to Christ. I asked if she was Amish and she said, "No, I'm Mennonite." Soon into our discussion, I asked her what Bible the Mennonites use. She said it was a version of King James. She told me we need to have a heart for Jesus, and I agreed with her totally. She also said the Mennonites were following the footsteps of most other Christian people these days: some were quite liberal, and others were not. The Mennonites don't shun technology or education the way the Amish do. She said there was a Mennonite church nearby called the Church of the Brethren. I ended up attending a service there.

It was extremely hot, but I felt the need to keep going, despite the lack of shade. The road cut through cornfields like a hot black ribbon of tar. I had walked a long way, and realized I'd have a tough time continuing throughout the day; but at least there was a store up ahead and I could, hopefully, refill my water bottles.

A woman in the store asked, "Are you the husband of a woman who walked with her husband all over, carrying a cross?"

"No, that's not me," I replied.

Another man in the store said he had seen me on TV about a week ago. I was pleased to hear it, but I was so concerned about the heat I wanted to quickly head back toward my car. After a brief conversation with the man and having replenished my water, I realized I don't usually walk this far away from the car. A quick look toward the sky and a few steps onto the blistering roadside made me realize it was going to be a very long, very hot walk back and I was not looking forward to it. As I lumbered along, I quickly consumed both bottles of water and realized it hadn't gotten any cooler. If anything, it was much hotter. And the humidity! The sweat flowed and it was as close to unbearable as I'd ever want to experience.

"God," I said. "I don't know how Jesus walked in the desert with no place to refresh himself and having to rely on what a desert can supply." With a swipe at my dripping brow, I continued, "Thank you, Jesus, for the pain and the suffering You experienced on this earth to bring us Your teachings about the great good news." Then

DESTINATION D.C. A Modern-day Jonah?

I added, "God, I don't suppose there's a chance You would find me a drink anyplace around here?"

As I continued my trek back to the car, I surely didn't expect God to provide water where I knew there was nothing but cornfields; but our Lord has His ways. And right then, a car pulled up and a man held his hand out the window, offering an ice-cold bottle of water! "My daughter wants you to have this," he said.

I couldn't believe my eyes, thinking, *this must be a mirage!* But I knew it wasn't and, as I approached the car, I didn't see anyone else except the driver; but as I gratefully took the water, a glance toward the back seat revealed a beautiful little girl in a booster seat. I believe she was only four or five years old. This tiny girl looked up as I took the water and said, "God bless you." Choked with emotion, I said, "I don't need to say, "God bless you," because I can see God did bless you with a wonderful smile and a great heart!" I was just overwhelmed with emotion for two reasons: First, because this little girl of color had a great heart and secondly, God had once again provided for my need. That was so great! It was unbelievable! Of course, it was the answer to my question to Jesus about how He did it. It was through Godly provision.

I continued up the road and came to an intersection. A young man was approaching from the road that connected to the highway. When we met, he said his name was Levi and he was riding a scooter; but it was heavier built than a child's and it appeared to have been made from bicycle parts. He called what he was doing "scooting." He said he was Amish. I asked if he could stop a minute and talk. He agreed, so I asked him if he attended a church, and I asked what Bible they used. "I'm not sure what Bible we use," he said, "but most of the time our families get together at someone's home on Sundays".

I asked if the public harassed him, and he said, "Well, you should know. I'm sure you get a bit of harassment yourself."

"Yes, I do."

He said some people have been courteous, but others have laughed and sneered at him. At his religion. His manner. Sometimes giving him a hard time. I was impressed by his attitude, because he said, "It's all worth it. I believe in the things I do. And they don't have to."

Praising The Father Saves The Day

I agreed that we all have a right to believe what we believe. "After all, God gives us free will—but He also makes it clear in His Word that we should be following His Word." Before we said our goodbye's, he said he was scooting 12 miles down the road to see a girl and he would scoot home that night, making it a 24-mile scoot. I said I've been on an extended walk from Vermont to Washington, D.C. and offered him a prayer for a safe journey, assuring him that I believed he had God's blessing.

The next day, the humidity was, once again, nearly overwhelming. I started to walk as early as possible to get lots of miles in before the mid-day heat became unbearable. Once again, for whatever reason, I felt compelled to walk a longer distance than usual from where I'd parked and even before I turned around, I ran out of water. I looked upwards and said, "I don't suppose You would do that two days in a row, would You, God? Like, provide another water? I'm dry as a brittle bone in the desert and I'm not even heading back to my car yet."

I continued farther down the road, hoping to find a place to purchase a drink. To my great surprise, after walking another hundred yards or so, a station wagon pulled over; and when I approached the car, a woman thrust a soda out the window. "This is for you," she said. I offered my thanks, but sadly revealed, "I'm a diabetic and I don't think I should be drinking that right now—even though I do drink soda every now and then."

I began speaking with her because I had learned at the beginning of the trip that many people who stop to talk to me need prayer, for themselves or for someone close to them. I asked, "Are you sick? Or do you have someone close to you who is sick and in need of prayer?"

She said, "I'm not, but my father has cancer and that's where I'm going now."

I talked with her and prayed with her, and gave her a handkerchief, explaining what it was for. She extended her thanks and went on her way; but it wasn't long before she pulled up again. She opened her window and handed me a water. "God told me to go get this for you and I just felt I had to do it."

DESTINATION D.C. A Modern-day Jonah?

I was just overwhelmed with the power and willingness of God to use people to provide for me once again. I had been given a chance to pray for someone God had sent to me! I had traveled quite a way that day and it was just getting hotter, and hotter! I turned around and started back, but it wasn't long before that bottle of water was gone.

Once again, I was without a drink. Feeling like I was probably pushing my favor with the Almighty, I said, "God, I don't suppose you would do that twice in the same day . . .?"

Well, there was no one more surprised than I when I came upon two cars parked on the side of the road. A man and a woman were standing outside the cars, and as I approached them, the woman handed me a water and said, "God told me to give this to you." When I thanked her, she said, "I don't have time to talk, so I'll have to just go. I'm a little late for work."

I said, "May God bless you. Thank you so much—I really needed this!" I was just overwhelmed that it had happened again!

The man was still there, standing outside his car. "Aren't you with her?" I asked. He replied, "No, I'm not, but I'm a Christian, too, and I would like to invite you to come to my house for dinner."

I guess that was another day when God was just going to continue to bless me. I am still overwhelmed with the fact that God provided me with water two days in a row—not to mention twice on the second day! Moments later, I said, "Thank you, God, for showing me the provision you can provide and proving when we ask, we can receive!"

I decided to go back and get a shower at the truck stop I had found the day before. And then, I was going to return to the Walmart to stay for a second night. Imagine thinking that two showers in a row is a blessing. Makes you realize how fortunate so many of us are in this country. I planned to return the next day to where I had left off, to continue walking into Lancaster.

When the day ended, I got my shower and returned to Walmart as planned and as I parked my vehicle to get ready to settle for the night, there was a man who apparently had been living in his car. Sensing his sad circumstance makes me even more grateful for what I have. Yes, I've been living in my car, too; but I had a home to return to, thanks to God.

Upon awakening the next morning, I heard a train whistle. It was not just one blast or two, it was a continual sound and all I could think of was the sound of someone wailing, over, and over again with inconsolable agony. It sent chills down my spine. The train whistle woke me from a vision that I would rather not have had—a vision that was thoroughly crushing. The whole experience was enhanced by a dark stream of rain that flowed from the sky as if the whole world was weeping.

My pastor is the only one I have ever completely described that vision to. I told him about it a couple of months after I had returned home from this Heal America Walk. I wouldn't even tell my wife. It was about destruction and calamity and it was just an awful, terrifying scene of the devastation of everything. People were in dire straits. That train whistle reminded me of the mourning and the wailing that you read about in Lamentations. It was so dramatic, I was traumatized and began to weep. I had to sit there for several minutes to compose myself. It was the worst vision I'd ever had, and why I say that, is, I have had other visions during the trip. They were also of destruction, economic downfall and just a helpless situation in this country. But this one was so much more compelling, it made me sense the worst depression that America has ever experienced. Much worse! In one vision I saw a woman sitting on a cement wall next to a hamburger place. She was staring at a cell phone, wondering why it didn't work, seemingly disconnected with everyone as a hopeless expression creased her face. I felt the despair and helpless angst she experienced as she silently witnessed the chaos of the day.

It was the most vivid, traumatic thing I'd ever seen. Worse than any apocalyptic movie. Communications, provision, and hope completely unraveled, everything simply falling like dominoes. What caused the loss and destruction, I do not know; but, in my own feeling of gloom, I cried, "Oh, my Lord in heaven, what do You mean by showing me this, and the other visions of desolation?"

DESTINATION D.C. A Modern-day Jonah?

I can't help but remember a vision I'd had years ago that had been confirmed by an unexpected visitor at the House of Angels. That vision occurred while I was in bed, just starting to wake up. I saw myself walking at the base of the ledge where the cross stands at the House of Angels. I was surrounded by people. Some just standing, vacant and expressionless, others gathering in small groups, warming themselves around fires. I had white hair and a white beard. Now, that's no surprise since I already have the white hair, but I sensed it was occurring when I was much older. Still only half awake, I asked the Lord, "What am I seeing?" His answer was, "This is a time when people will come to the House of Angels in their search for a safe haven". I wasn't sure what they had escaped from, but I was told there would be several things—one being a great plague, and the other? Most likely, persecution.

Later that day when I had the chance to talk with Ann, I told her about the vision. Neither of us spoke of this to anyone. I guess we were both concerned about being tagged as zealous fanatics. However, one day we heard a knock on the door. It was a woman we had only seen occasionally, mostly at a Bible study. She said she had seen our sign many times and wondered what it was about. I said, "We encourage people to go up to the sanctuary we'd created and be amongst God's creation and have a place where they might pray and experience quiet time." I pointed toward the dirt road that extends from our driveway and said, "It's not far. You can drive or walk up that road."

I asked her if she wanted us to go up with her and she said, "Yes," so Ann and I accompanied her up to the House of Angels. As we walked, we told her about the place and some of the people who have visited and some of the miraculous things that had happened. We didn't have a clue that her visit would soon be added to our list of stories.

At a bench overlooking the cross, we sat and talked, and suddenly out of the blue, she declared, "My brother is going to help you. He is going to bring clothes to the people who are here."

"What people?" I asked.

"You know. The people who are going to come here that need protection and help."

Praising The Father Saves The Day

I almost fell out of my seat. I just could not believe that out of nowhere this woman seemed to be speaking about my vision. But it wasn't the last time we'd hear about the need for safe sanctuaries. Over the years, we've met other people who have moved to this area who believe they were directed by God to settle here.

I don't really know how they'll be "safe" or what the people will be escaping from; but what I've been shown to be true is that whoever seeks sanctuary will not be found if there comes a time when God desires to protect His people. It's to be a place that no others will behold.

I believe God had shown me these things so I could tell others to take warning of what might come; and the House of Angels is to be a place of sanctuary. Once I had the latest vision of torment and disaster, I knew there was a bigger purpose for my Heal America Walk than I even knew or could imagine.

I quickly began to head toward Letitz.

Eventually, I came to a second-hand/antique store. I thought, *I'll just window shop and see what they have on these sidewalk tables.* I quickly spied some plates with beautiful Christian paintings. One depicted Jesus healing someone. Another was Jesus being baptized. The third plate contained a scene of the Last Supper, and the fourth plate depicted His mother holding Him. I thought, *boy, would I love to have these plates. But then again, they're probably expensive. And besides that, I'd probably break them before I even get them home.* Even so, I decided to ask about them.

I entered the shop and found a man at his desk. "What's the price of those Christian plates," I asked, explaining, "the four plates with the Christian scenes?"

He said, "I don't know—they should be marked, though." And when I said I could not find a price on them, he went out to see for himself. That's when he saw my cross. "That yours?" he asked.

"Yes," I said. "I'm walking from Vermont to Washington, D.C."

"You are?"

"Yes," I replied. Then I explained why I was making the trip.

"Well, why don't you come back inside and I'm sure I can come up with a price that you would agree with." And before I knew it, he was sitting at his desk, saying, "You can just have those plates."

DESTINATION D.C. A Modern-day Jonah?

"Are you sure?" I was astounded by his generosity.

"Yes. I'm very thankful for what you're doing. I have a brother who walks all over with a cross. He goes from town to town on occasion."

I carefully packed the plates away and yes, I did manage to get them home safely. Three of them now hang on the mantle above my wood stove and serve as a permanent reminder of how good and gracious our God is, and of the kindness of people—especially those who believe in Him. The fourth plate, depicting Mary and the Christ child, hangs on another wall. I felt good when I finished walking that day and returned to the parking lot.

The next morning, I intended to go into Lancaster.

GRATEFULNESS: "Give thanks to the Lord, for He is good; His love endures forever." I Chronicles 16:34

DON'S NOTE: I cannot explain how exuberant I felt after praising the Lord, despite how terrible I felt during my cranky morning. And, then when I told Ann I'd had visions that tore at my heart, she told me later she had seen a quote related to trains and life by Joshua Robinson. She thought he was a former athlete who said, "When this train of life derails, God sends out the crane to put us back on track. This crane is like Jesus and His grace, and because of His grace, He picks us up and places us back on the tracks."

CHAPTER 34

Encounters on the Road

As I walked through Letitz, there was an old truck in front of a parts store. I asked the driver, "Are you sure they still carry parts for a truck that old?"

"Yes, I know they do," he said. "I've bought parts for it before." After he answered my question, I asked if he had a moment to talk. Of course, after seeing my cross, he wanted to know what I was doing and why I was doing it. Then he told me his wife had seen me the day before and she wanted to stop and talk to me, but she didn't and later she was sorry she hadn't.

He said, "What are you doing now?"

"I still have to walk a few more hours today—there's quite a bit of daylight left, and I have to walk as many miles as possible each day."

"Well, how about we meet up later and you come over to my house and meet my wife?"

"Sure, I could do that," I said. "Thanks!" Then I asked if I could park my vehicle in his driveway for the night.

"Yes, of course, that would be fine."

Hoping I wouldn't be pushing my welcome too far, I also asked, "Would it be possible to take a shower, too?"

"You'll be more than welcome." After he confirmed all this, we agreed to meet at a certain spot later that day, so I could follow him to his home. I made good mileage after that, then returned to my car and headed to our designated meeting spot. As soon as I reached his truck, he led me right to his house and introduced me to his wife. She was happy to have the chance to meet the guy with the cross and we talked for a while, then her husband said, "Would you like to go out to eat?"

I said, "That would be great."

I took a shower before we left for dinner; but his wife said she had something she had to do so it turned out to be just the two of us. And what a great meal we had; buffet style at its best. If I ever return to that area, I'll want to eat there again, for sure. Soon after we returned to his house, I expressed my heartfelt thanks and headed out to my vehicle for a good night's rest. The next morning, it didn't take long to find the place where I should park the car and head out on foot.

Now, a Lancaster newspaper had been notified about my walk and just before reaching the airport area, I received a call from the reporter who wanted to catch up to me. After seeing his story, I was quite pleased. He did a great job depicting the Heal America Walk.

At the end of the day, I had a tough time getting to the truck stop where I planned to take a shower. The directions were confusing and, worse than that, by the time I finished my shower, it was getting dark. I have never liked driving in big cities and searching for exits or whatever road I'd need. That night was no exception. Reaching the Walmart where I'd be parking for the night was a big problem. I'd get on a road that I couldn't get off from, and it would lead me to some place where I didn't know where I was. I'd get off that one and try again. And again. And at one point, I ended up going through the college campus in Lancaster! Then to my utter dismay, I found a gas station that I realized I recognized from years before! *Not good,* I thought, especially when I realized every window was boarded up and the doorways had bars on them. Talk about being flustered!

After driving around for two or three hours, I did finally reach my destination, and managed to settle down to get some sleep.

After breakfast the next morning, I decided to use up a few saved miles. I really wanted to get to a place that was more driver friendly for a country boy like me. I say, give me a dirt road any day!

I soon was walking down an area called Willow Street Park and had come to a supermarket. In one aisle, I heard a woman say to her daughter, "Go ahead. You can buy that. The world doesn't end until the 15th of September." She saw that I had heard what she was saying and began to apologize. "I'm sorry, I'm so sorry," she fretted. So, I told her it was okay. She seemed to be open to a discussion, so I said, "You must have read about the Shemitah." She said she had, and I realized she was mis-interpreting the message; so, at that point, I reminded her that the Bible clearly says no man knows when the end of life as we know it will come. I mentioned *The Harbinger* by Jonathan Cahn and said my wife and I believe that in his books he was trying to indicate the world would become even more topsy-turvy after that date because people don't follow the laws of the Shemitah.

And then I began to tell her I was an ordained minister and I didn't believe she was crazy. I ended our discussion by giving her some information before going off to buy something tasty for dinner.

At a shopping plaza, I came across a state representative's office and decided it would be a good opportunity to tell an elected official about my walk, and my efforts to raise money for an orphanage in Peru. I must say the visit was disappointing. He was not there, but the man minding the office did not seem to be supportive. He said the rep doesn't give to causes he did not support before his election. At that point, I told him I was not soliciting money and I had stopped to share with him my hope that he would be a man who would look to God for direction before voting on legislative matters. I could see the other people in the office were quietly chuckling, especially when I said I hoped he might find it in his heart to help a few starving children if he had a heart to serve people.

Thoughts of the man in that office remind me of an encounter that was quite the opposite. There was a man with a three-car garage who allowed me to park on his property. When I returned, I found a bottle of water with a twenty-dollar bill attached to it. A car pulled up beside me and I realized it was the owner. I asked him if he was the one who left the water and money and he suddenly broke into tears, barely able to speak. I guess he was tremendously moved by my efforts. He obviously had a big heart and I pray that God rewards him for his generosity.

After leaving the shopping plaza, I continued walking for another four and a half miles beyond the supermarket, then I walked back, feeling quite ill. I was tired, and my sugar level was low. I was beginning to think I'd never make it back to my vehicle. Thankfully, I did, but when I got there, I also had stomach trouble and laid down for half an hour or so. Ann tried to call, but I did not manage to answer the phone in time and decided to call her back later.

When I reached Ann, she told me some bad news about the condition of a woman we knew. It was my friend Roscoe's sister, who had been battling cancer. She was dying. I called Roscoe and told him that I'd dedicate my walk that day to his sister and that I would pray for her.

When I headed out on foot again, I saw a woman parked up ahead, on the side of the road that I was walking on. When I reached her, she said she didn't know why she was there. Boy, I've heard that one before! More than once, people have ended up at the House of Angels, asking me or Ann, 'why am I here?'

She said she was a nurse and she was on her way home and never chose to travel on this road because it was quite a distance out of her way. And then she said, "When I saw you, I was curious. I had to stop and see what this is about."

And so, I told her about my walk—how I was traveling from Vermont to Washington, D.C. And then I asked if she was a Christian. She said she was, but she found it hard to go to church, saying she works on Sundays and when she doesn't work, she has a hundred excuses why she can't go. She said she knew Jesus on a personal level, and I told her, "Well, that's a good thing." Then I told her she should consider the things that are most important in life, and to me one of the most important things in my life is my relationship with Jesus. I also encouraged her to take God and

Jesus Christ with her each time she approached a patient and to pray for them.

I asked if I could pray for her and when she said I could, I gave her a handkerchief and explained its meaning. When I finished praying for her, she wanted to do something for me. She gave me some water and then, as our conversation concluded, she started to cry and by the time we said goodbye, she was sobbing. I believe she was moved by the Spirit and by the time we parted ways, I was sure she knew why she had chosen to travel on the road that was so out of her way—God had used our encounter to send a message to her.

I kept walking and when it was time to stop, I decided to drive a bit to see what lay ahead. Maybe I'd find a place to swim or a place that would be safe for overnight parking. Well, I saw a campsite and decided to see if they had showers that I might be able to use. There was a person in the gate-house and I asked him about getting a shower and he said, "Well, if you rent a campsite of course you can."

I didn't want to rent a campsite and as I started to leave, a man who thought he recognized me, parked his car and approached. He asked why I was there, and I told him I needed a shower, but I didn't need a campsite. I explained that I've been sleeping in my vehicle at night. He said, "You're the guy who was walking with a cross, right?" I said, "Yes," and he said he saw me down the road a few hours ago. He added, "I'm the manager here and you're welcome to go in and take a shower."

I was grateful for his kindness and after getting a shower that evening, when I was on my way out, I saw him at the gate. I stopped to thank him once again and he told me if I needed a shower the next day, I was welcome to come back for it. I replied that considering the heat, there was a very good chance I would do that. And as you can guess, I did!

Now, sometimes, it was quite hard to find a place to park my vehicle, and it very seldom was where I had left off walking. One day, I came upon a woman at a vegetable stand where I asked if I could leave my car for two or three hours, explaining that I'm walking with a cross and need a place to park. She said it was okay if I pulled over to the side to avoid being in the way of customer parking. She said sometimes they get a lot of customers all at once.

"Are you the owner," I asked.

"No, I just work here, but I know the owner won't mind."

"Well, if you're sure, I'd be very grateful."

When I came back, she was speaking to someone, but I approached, ready to offer a thank you. It was her husband. He had long hair and resembled pictures that depict Christ. She introduced me to him and as it turned out, they allowed me to park in their driveway that night and I was able to get a shower. In addition to that, they would not allow me to stay in my vehicle. They insisted that I use their camper and when I got up the next day, they told me I could return and stay again the next night. I knew when I finished walking that day, most likely, I'd take them up on their offer. As it turned out, I had made a fair number of miles that day and was happy to have a place to return to—and to have someone to visit with! They fixed me supper. I got a shower. And once again I was able to sleep in the camper.

They were going to be away the next day and they were not going to be home that night, but despite this fact, they said I could return that night also. He said he trusted me as much as, or possibly more than, his own family! What a blessing to feel that trusted! I took them up on the offer; yet, although they were not present, I still had company—their dog affectionately welcomed me like an old friend, and they had a cute little fawn under their care that was a fun little companion to talk to. I love animals and having the chance to spend time with these two animals felt special.

I crossed the Susquehanna River the next day on the Robert Wood Bridge. It seemed like the bridge was a half a mile long or so. Whatever its length, it's a big, long bridge, and on my way across I could feel it sway. I realized the experience was bitter sweet. I'd enjoyed the time with the couple who trusted me stay at their home and crossing the Robert Wood Bridge was an interesting experience; but I must admit I was feeling mournful. You see, Ann called

Encounters On The Road

the night before to tell me Roscoe's sister had died. I called him again and told him how sorry I was and that I would not be able to make it back for the funeral—I was simply too far into the trip—and I felt even worse because I realized in the back of my mind, that if I returned home, I would not want to leave again—I missed home that much!

But, then again, I am quite sure the real reason I could not stop the walk was that it was not my decision to make. It was God's decision. And I knew returning home was not part of His plan. I think her passing was even harder to deal with because I knew I wouldn't be there for my friend and his family. Even during such a sorrowful mood, I managed to get about 12 miles past the bridge before turning back toward my vehicle.

It was while I was heading back that a state trooper pulled up. I immediately thought, *Hey, maybe I can ask what he knows about the condition of the road further down.* I was always trying to find out if it had a narrow shoulder or if it was brushy—or if there was some other condition that would make it dangerous or troublesome for walking. I was on the opposite side of the road when he stepped out of his cruiser and I called out to him, basically using sign language, pointing to him and myself. He held up a finger indicating he understood but I had to wait because he was on the phone.

As I waited to talk to him, an 18-wheeler pulled to a stop. It was God's provision once again! The truck driver got out of his truck, crossed the road and handed me a large bottle of ice-cold water. He pulled away shortly after that, and the policeman finally asked me to cross over to speak with him.

When I crossed the road, he asked, "What are you doing and where are you going?"

I explained I was on a Heal America Walk, from Vermont to Washington, D.C. Then I started to witness, explaining about *The Harbinger* and how it had played a part in confirming that I should do this. As I was talking to him, a car came and stopped next to us. The officer quickly asked, "Do you know him?" I said I did not, so he became quite watchful to the point of lowering his hand to his holster. All the while the car approached us, the officer kept his eyes on the vehicle.

The guy said his wife had seen me walking and they wanted to invite me to their place for lunch. I said it would be very nice, but I explained that I had to walk another mile or so down the road to retrieve my car and it would take a while. He gave me the directions to his home that happened to be easy to find. "It's on the next road down from here," he said. When he pulled away, I continued to tell the officer about my walk. I said, "I can't explain why God chose me to do this, but He did tell me to do it and to go to D.C. to declare Him to be the power, the blessing and the grace that made this country great. It was heartwarming and led me to understand that he believed me when he said, "You can't help it if you've been chosen to do something for God."

Then I asked the officer if he could tell me how far we were from Washington.

"I can tell you exactly," he said and quickly produced a GPS device. Seconds later, he said, "You are 91 miles from Washington."

Of course, I witnessed to him as much as I could, and I was surprised at how much time he spent listening. I explained further about my walk and Jonathan Cahn's books, *The Shemitah*, and *The Harbinger*; and I thanked him for his service, adding that I thought the police did a great job.

Once our conversation ended, I resumed the trek back to my vehicle. I was looking forward to a great lunch with the guy who had extended the invitation; but I was also wondering, *which one is sick?* It seems that most of the people I meet on this walk have stopped to talk to me either because they needed a prayer for themselves, or for someone they knew, usually because of an illness. I assumed the same was true this time. His name was John and his wife was Karen. As we conversed during lunch, he told me he was a truck driver; but he was currently on leave because his mom had a stroke and he himself had a few aches and pains; while Karen had been bitten by a recluse spider and she was self-treating, but the infection from the spider bite apparently had spread throughout her body.

He continued to tell me she had a young horse with an infection. "It's not eating or going out of the barn like it usually does to spend time with its mother," he explained. And then he asked, "Do you pray for animals?"

I said that I hadn't prayed for any other animals besides my own, and I had never laid hands on another animal to pray for them, but I was willing to try. And so, I prayed for the horse and I also prayed for my host's mother and for him and his wife, and I gave them handkerchiefs. They invited me to stay the night and I thanked them; but had to explain that I already had a place to stay for that night and it would not feel right to refuse the hospitality after I had agreed to return. Then I quickly said, "But, I'd love to take you up on your offer tomorrow, if that's okay." John and Karen both readily agreed.

When I returned to the other home where I had stayed prior to meeting John and Karen, I discovered that the house was empty; but there were reading glasses on the table alongside a book. A closer look revealed that it was the Bible. Later, when my host returned, I asked about it and he said he had been influenced by me and he thought it wouldn't hurt—and probably would do some good—to read the Bible that I had given him. I stayed that night and began walking the next day. At one point a car pulled up and the driver rolled down his window and said he was clergy. Thing is, he didn't ask any questions, nor did he say anything else. I bid him a good day and the blessing of God and continued along on my way.

Now, before the day ended, I stopped to ask a farmer if I could park in his yard for a few hours while I continued my walk, and he said I could. Then, at the end of the day, I called John to confirm whether I could still stay at his home that night if they were still willing to have me. He said yes, and he also said he knew where I was parked.

"How do you know that? Did you drive by and recognize my car?"

"No," he said. "I had gone into the town office and was inclined to tell the town manager about you. She said you had parked in her yard."

After spending the day on the road, I headed back toward my new hosts' house to stay for the night. As we were preparing to have supper, John and Karen told me their sick horse—the one I had prayed for—had come out of the barn in the morning and had spent the day outside, walking around with its mother. He seemed to be much better. We had supper and they invited me to stay as long as I wanted to.

"That's very kind of you and while I know I'll have to travel a little farther each day to return, I really appreciate it. All of it! The bed, the shower, the conversation!" Then I asked how his mother was doing and he said she was doing okay. At one point I mentioned how I didn't like big cities and I did not like trying to find my way around in them.

"Why don't we go down into Washington together," he suggested, adding, "I have the time, and I'd like to show you how to get in and out of the city and where you might be able to park."

"That would be great," I exclaimed, believing it would be wonderful and most likely would save a lot of aggravation. I've been dreading the thought of trying to find my way to and through the city."

"Well, let's do it then," he said, and I told him I had another day or two of walking to make the necessary mileage.

The next morning, I purchased a coffee, and then headed to where I'd stopped walking the day before. As I got out of my vehicle, a truck stopped across the road. I recognized the truck to be one that had passed me by a couple of times the day before. They had an intercom with a microphone attached to their vehicle and they would praise the Lord each time they went by. The man crossed to my side of the road and asked if I needed help. I explained that I was fine and said I recognized him from the previous day. I also told him I appreciated the fact that he stopped to offer his assistance.

After talking to him, I started off again, and before I got too far, another man pulled up. He said, "My wife called me from work, and she told me that you were walking along the road with a cross and she said to bring this to you." He handed me a plastic bag and some water. The bag had some change and some bills and a bag of cookies. I said, "Thanks, but I'm diabetic. I shouldn't have the cookies, but I can always use the money and water. He pulled away and I continued along until a woman pulled to a stop. She said her son had been on drugs and had been saved, but she felt a prayer for him to stay away from drugs might be good. *A good candidate for a handkerchief,* I thought as I handed her one, explaining that her son would benefit from the prayer if he would accept it. I told her it was in my heart that he would stay away from drugs and have a blessed life.

As I continued along, I thought about the oncoming traffic. I was facing them, and I was thinking I never would have made it this far and live to tell about it without God's help, considering the way some people drive. Just up ahead, on the opposite side of the road there was an intersection. A van had pulled to a stop and was about to come across in my direction. I watched as it cut across the road as if it would be coming to run me down, then it swerved back to its own lane, only to cross over again a couple more times.

Like a cat playing with a mouse, they forced me to the shoulder of the road, stopping just 15 feet away. There were two black men in the car. The driver opened his door and the first thing I thought was, *I need to put on my suit of armor.*

Of course, I was thinking about Ephesians 6, where it says, "be strong in the LORD and in His mighty power. Put on the full armor of God, so that you can take your stand against the Devil's schemes." I saw this guy was one and a half times my size. In a flash, I pictured myself holding my arms high over my head, slipping on God's armor like a woman might slip a nightgown over her head. Just as we came face to face, I felt myself armed.

He reached for my pouch. It was holding candy and two waters and a few other things. Everything was happening so fast, and yet in my head I've become armed and I was able to relax. A little.

Sort of.

Then the big—I mean *really* big—guy grabbed at my water, and said, "I'm gonna give you some trouble." Then, pointing back at it, he asked, "What's this?"

"That's just water," I said. "I need it for when I'm walking. It's real hot out."

He pulled it out of the holder, and I said, "I have another water here. Would you like this one, too?"

"What you mean?" he asked.

"Well, if you need it you can have it," I said.

DESTINATION D.C. A Modern-day Jonah?

"No, I don't need it," he said, and he handed the water back to me. Then he said, "I'm going to rough you up a bit." He studied my reaction through squinty eyes and asked, "What you doin' with Christ's cross?"

"This is not Christ's cross," I said. "It's one I use to remind people what Jesus did for us."

"Why you doin' this," he demanded.

"I'm not happy with the way things are going in this country and the way people are acting over certain things. I hope you don't mind like some people do, but I just want to tell you that you're my brother." He gazed at me with questioning eyes, so I explained, "You and I are brothers in Christ. I don't know if you're a Christian or not, but if you are, we're brothers in Christ. Do you believe in Him?"

"Well, yeah."

I held out my arm and pointed to my skin and explained as I had so many times on this trip, "I was whiter when I left home and I'm darker now and I'll probably be even darker when I get to D.C., but that doesn't matter". What does matter is that we all need the same things: self-worth, purpose, provision, and love. And these are all things that God gives us."

A crease formed between his brows. He snarled, "Like what? What'chu mean?"

"We all need purpose," I said, "and we need self-worth, provision, and love." And as I pointed up toward the sky, I said, "It all comes from Him. From God the Father." Then after a beat, I said, "Can I show you some pictures I have? They're here in my pouch." Without waiting for an answer, I pulled them out, explaining, "It's a place I spent seven years building. A place for prayer and healing. I'm an ordained minister." They were pictures of the House of Angels.

"Sure," he said, his voice softening slightly. "I'll look at 'em."

He's interested! I thought with jubilant surprise. So, I told him a little about it. A few minutes later, he told me he was from the D.C. area. And he asked, "What do you mean, God has given you a gift of healing? I like those pictures. Should I bring my friend Superman up to your place? He lives with me."

"Superman? Superman lives with you?"

"Yeah. He's a white guy who's covered with tattoos. All over his body."

"Well, he might be changed if you brought him up there and I prayed for him. He just might come to know Christ."

"Tell me about that gift of healing you said you had."

"Well, I pray for people and they might want to ask for healing of a sickness, or they might have a need in some other way. Here, let me show you." At that point I reached up, way up, to rest my left hand on his shoulder and I lifted my right hand to the heavens, asking God to deliver that which He has for this person, to be delivered to my right hand and that it would be distributed to them by my other hand.

I took a few steps away from him and before putting too much distance between us, I turned and looked at him and said, "And usually, the people I pray for feel exactly what you just felt."

His mouth fell wide open and he just stood there. Dumbfounded. I continued away from him and as I approached the van, I saw the other guy. And when I noticed his window was rolled down, I opened my pouch and retrieved two candies that I'd been carrying in case I had a low-blood-sugar-moment while I was walking. I handed them to him and instructed him to give his friend one when he got back into the van. As I did this, the big guy was still planted in the same spot. His mouth still wide open. I tipped my head in the big guy's direction and said, "It's to sweeten him up a little."

I continued to walk, but after a half dozen steps or so, I just had to look back. Mr. Big was finally heading toward the van. I chuckled more than a few times as I walked, thinking, *it's amazing what God's armor can do! The giant was slain!*

ATTITUDES: "Return, faithless people; I will cure you of backsliding." Yes, we will come to you, for you are the Lord our God. Jeremiah 3:22

DON'S NOTES: There was no way I could have avoided a bad outcome without God's help when I encountered that big man. Remembering my Lord's words and putting on His armor was, to me, a life saver, but I also understand that His Word is filled with multiple helpful reminders and words of wisdom that can fill a wayward heart with ease. Perhaps, if that aggressive young man remembers his encounter with me, he'll pick up a Bible, and turn to Jeremiah, and realize that his wayward heart can be healed and renewed.

CHAPTER 35
Getting Closer

Not long after my nerve-wracking experience with Mr. Big, my excitement grew. I realized I was getting very close to where I'd have enough miles completed to cover the trip to D.C. In just a day or two, I'd most likely come to the final tally.

On the next day, as you might guess, I encountered a few more people. One woman stopped to give me a cold water. Another woman took a picture. And yet another woman stopped to ask where I was headed. After I told her about the Heal America Walk, she told me about a function that was going to take place at the Mall in D.C. The next chance I got, I called Ann and asked her to look it up. It was called David's Tent D.C., but it would not start until the 11th of September. It was tempting, but I decided I would not stay in the area that long. I was more than ready to go home! Since then I've discovered it was reportedly the longest-running outdoor worship event in the country. They were staying there to worship God until the election the following year. They still continue to spread the word about Jesus and have a website at www.davidstent.net.

All I wanted to do was get into Washington, D.C. and make the declaration that God had told me to make. I was so tired, drained and homesick! So, I continued down the road, and after a few

DESTINATION D.C. A Modern-day Jonah?

more miles, I saw a state trooper who had an 18-wheeler pulled to the side of the road. He was talking to the driver, but as I came up across from them, the trooper looked my way, raised his voice and said, "I'm almost finished here, and I want to talk to you."

Oh boy. I nodded and said I'd wait. Once again, I found myself wondering why a state trooper would want to talk to me. A few minutes later, he crossed the road and said, "Hi, how are you doing?"

"I'm doing fine," I said, and then he asked, "What are you doing?" That's when I told him a little bit about my walk.

"Do you have any money?" he asked.

"Why? Do you think I'm a vagrant?"

"No. There's no such thing as vagrancy anymore. I was just wondering if you were hungry or if you need a few dollars. I'd like to help you if I can." And as he looked at me with friendly eyes, he added, "I could take you to lunch."

"Well, that's very nice and I'd like that, except I just ate not too long ago."

"Do you need any money?"

"No, I'm fine," I said, "but I really appreciate your offer." At that point, I told him I was thankful for the service he and his fellow officers provide and I offered him the blessing of God. *So much for the separation of church and state,* I thought. *Man's goodness and belief in Godly things still exist, especially, it seems, with the police that I've met.*

After continuing a little farther that day, I returned to my latest host's home. Once again, I checked the distance. Unfortunately, I realized I was a few miles short of the miles I needed, so I told them I'd have to go out and walk a few more miles the next day. We decided that after I walked those extra miles, John would take me to D.C. to scope it out. He would show me how to get in and out of the city and how to reach Union Station where I could park my car.

After a good breakfast the next day, I set out to rack up those last few miles, and even a few extra for good measure. I couldn't help but think, who would know if I walked the correct number of miles or not? Of course, I told myself: *God would know.* Besides, I had no intention of coming up short.

After walking all the miles required for the walk, I started to think about the trip. I believe that every person I met and the exact time and place we met, had been put in place and was meant to happen. I mean, I was so grateful that God had sent so many people in need of prayer to me. If you recall, before I even started this journey God told me many would be healed.

I'm not sure if all the people I prayed for were blessed with healing, but I did my part and I know God's plan is beyond my understanding. I only believe that whatever it is, God's plan always brings the right result. With these good thoughts in mind, I returned to my host's home. We had supper and he and I spoke for a little while before we all headed to bed.

We got underway the next morning. But it was Sunday, and John said he wanted to go to a church service either on the way to D.C., or in the city. He said, "I'm not familiar with any of the churches there. I've never attended any services in Washington."

"Well," I said, "God has directed me to the right church with the right message every Sunday since I left home. I'm sure it'll happen today, too."

It seemed that it did not take long to reach the outskirts of Washington, D.C. We were driving down Georgia Street when John looked at his watch and said, "It's about time for us to find a church. It's a little after 9, and a lot of them probably have services at 9:30 or 10 AM."

"Yes, you're probably right. We should definitely look for one," I said. And, just as I said that, I saw a building up ahead. It had been painted purple and white. I didn't notice the name, but it couldn't be more obvious that the colors represented white for purity and cleanliness, and purple for royalty. *Great*, I thought! But once we walked up to it, we realized the place had been vacant for some time. However, on our way for a closer look, we had passed a small window-front church. It was very small, but John suggested we go in. I agreed.

Before we even got inside, we noticed the parishioners were mostly people of color—probably 95-percent of them. I thought it would be great. When we entered, we received a warm welcome and saw they were very spiritual and not afraid to express themselves in worship and prayer. Little did they know, nor did I, that they were about to play a huge part in the purpose of my walk.

The service was about to start with singing and praise. There were no instruments. To be honest, they didn't have a big enough area for instruments, but it didn't matter at all. It was a wonderful worship time. When they finished that portion of the service, a young man approached the podium and was I blown away when he began to speak! His subject? Jonah!

It was about Jonah being directed by God. It caused me to reflect upon my answers to people when they would ask if I was still intending to walk to Washington, D.C. from Vermont. As you've read, I'd always think about Jonah when I answered. Of course, one of the best-known stories in the Bible is the one about Jonah and how he ran in the opposite direction when God told him to go to Nineveh; and his disobedience caused him to be swallowed up into the belly of a great fish.

After that young man ended his talk, the minister approached the pulpit and I was happy to realize he was a great speaker. He gave a sermon without referring to any notes. And what he preached was straight from the Bible. He had greeted me and John when we first arrived and had chuckled when I told him I was walking from Vermont to Washington. I wonder to this day if he thought I was joking.

When the service ended, we were invited to stay for a meal that was being brought in. So, while we waited for the food to arrive, we had time to speak with the minister and with some of the parishioners. I have to say I was awestruck by a conversation I had with one woman. It began when I told her about my wife and how troubled we were with the way things were going in this country. The unrest. The fear. The lack of trust. The prejudice! It felt as if there was no end to the influence of evil. And the complacency! "I feel so sad to believe most of us are living lives that are filled with complacency. We're falling out of God's grace. Too many of us are not compliant with His word." Then I told her how I wished people would turn back and look to Him for all their needs, adding, "I just don't believe there's ever been a man who could lead or rule in a righteous and just way without depending upon Godly wisdom."

When I stopped speaking, she said, "You remind me of a verse in the Bible that says something like, 'that which comes from your heart shall come forth from your lips and you shall speak it'". I believe she was referring to Luke 6:45. In the King James Bible published by the American Bible Society of New York, it says, "A good man out of the good treasure of his heart bringeth forth that which is good; and an evil man out of the evil treasure of his heart bringeth forth that which is evil: for of the abundance of the heart his mouth speaketh."

After she uttered those words, she listened to my testimony for several more minutes, and when I stopped, she said, "You also remind me of another verse in the Bible. It's 2 Chronicles 7:14. She knew this one by heart. And, when I looked it up, I saw that she seemed to be quoting from the NIV version, which states in verses 14 through 16: "Then if my people who are called by my name will humble themselves and pray and seek my face and turn from their wicked ways, I will hear from heaven and will forgive their sins and heal their land." After she said that, I asked if she knew the name of my walk and I said I called it the Heal America Walk. I was realizing that somehow, this was an incredible service and my presence in this church during this service, was playing a big role regarding the purpose of the walk. And as I sat there, filled with wonder, I remembered that around two weeks prior to this I had thought how great it would be to receive communion before I walked into Washington, D.C. And during this service? Communion was given—even though in most churches, communion is served at the beginning of a month. Yet, here I was—the end of August—in a church, literally hours before I'd be ending my walk, and I had just received communion!

After that memorable service, John and I continued down Georgia Street and found our way to Union Station. So, then I knew where I could park when I entered the city to complete my walk.

CONNECTIONS: "Praise the Lord. Blessed is the man who fears the Lord, who finds great delight in His commands. His children will be mighty in the land; the generation of the upright will be blessed." Psalm 112:1-2

DON'S NOTE: So many amazing connections have taken place throughout my story, it seemed like something that dreams are made of. And, I am so happy that I have worked hard to be obedient, whether it be through my work at the House of Angels, or, through my encounters during the Heal America Walk. Especially when I see the words in Psalm 112, listed above, for I truly hope I have made a difference in the lives of these people, and therefore in the lives of their children, and my own children.

CHAPTER 36

Declaring God's Grace

Back at the house, John and I told his wife Karen, about our experience. Her grin revealed to me that we were probably chattering like school boys who just won a state championship. But the effort had tired me out and I realized I needed a day of rest, so I took it easy the following day. Besides, I didn't want to enter the city without taking the time to notify everyone I knew I was finally ready to end the Heal America Walk.

When I spoke to Ann, I was pleased to hear she had just got off the phone with a woman who could help contact the press. The woman knew all the news agencies in D.C. and might even help me to speak to a senator or congressman. It was with her assistance that Ann was able to publish several articles online to promote Dr. Ben Carson while he ran in the presidential primaries, for Communities Digital News, a national digital news agency. I thought, *that would be great. I might get a chance to communicate on a large scale that we need to turn back to God and ask Him for wisdom and guidance and provision. And perhaps this nation would continue to receive His grace and blessing.*

When I spoke to the woman, she confirmed that she did know several TV news broadcasters who would be there if she could connect with them, but she said September 1st would not be a good

DESTINATION D.C. A Modern-day Jonah?

day for it and I should wait at least a day, if not more before ending my walk with an official entrance into D.C. I said I'd have to think about that. By then I had already called everyone I knew and had told them I'd be walking into the city on September 1st; and, I'm a great believer in being compliant with the Biblical direction: letting yes be yes and no be no. In other words, I believed I should do exactly what I had said I would do. With that thought in mind, I decided I would keep my promise to my friends and enter the city on September 1st and make a second trip on the second day of September as the digital news woman had suggested.

And so, on September 1st, 2015, I drove to the outskirts of D.C., walked across the city border, and gave thanks to God without any hoopla from the press. I was using the miles I had "saved up" as I drove to the outskirts of the city and walked into its limits as I had planned, and I would also return the following day to proclaim what God had told me to proclaim.

The next day, I was able to get up early and head out to accomplish what God had asked me to do. My press helper was not able to meet me; but she had helped to get me the phone numbers of some major TV stations and a major newspaper in the D.C. region. So, it was still possible to receive some coverage. But, what you expect, and what happens, are not always the same.

When I arrived at Union Station, I thought it best to check with the station attendant to see if there would be any trouble regarding my cross. I couldn't help but remember how I had felt totally unwelcomed and had been walked off the grounds of a major broadcast station in New York City. But the attendant at Union Station in D.C. said she didn't see any problem with it. With that assurance, I treated myself to a breakfast sandwich then retrieved the cross and hung the Bible onto my chest.

There were tour guides passing out pamphlets and one of them asked, "Where is Jesus? I don't see Him hanging from your cross." I replied, "No, you don't see Him because they took Him down and He is gone into heaven. Hallelujah! He has risen to be at the right hand of God our Father."

Approval flowed from her eyes as she exclaimed, "You're exactly right!"

Declaring God's Grace

I heard several murmurs concerning God's blessings as I continued down the last set of stairs leading to the street. One thing I did not notice? The press. None of them were lurking about, waiting for a story about the true faith that caused a 65-year old man to walk over 500 miles for God. But as you might expect from a city they now refer to as "the swamp", as soon as I went through the doors, I was approached by a con man who asked if I could help some needy people. He pointed across the way saying, "See the people over there? They need food." It was a group of homeless people in an area about halfway across the street near a group of statues. As I stared at them, he said he had cold cuts, but needed to buy seven loaves of bread.

"How much a loaf?" I asked.

"Bread is a dollar a loaf," he replied; so, I agreed to give him seven dollars, thinking, *if he's lying to me, it'll cost him more spiritually than it's costing my wallet.* I said, "You'll have to answer to God, if you're not telling the truth." He replied, "I know, but I am telling you the truth." So, I gave him the money and crossed to the area where the homeless were sitting.

One of the women pointed to the guy I'd been talking to and confirmed my suspicions when she said, "He's a crook."

Over the next few minutes, I called one news outlet after another. Just the day before, they said they'd be expecting me but could not promise anything. I guess that was an understatement. I got the same basic reply from them all, this time, like, "No, I can't cover you," and, "Sorry, today's a busy day after all," and "No, I just can't do it today." After being rejected by all of them, I was very disappointed, but it did not take long to get over the rejections. I just said to myself, God's in control and there must be a reason He had me choose this day, so I decided to head toward the entrance of the Capitol Building. On my way, I noticed there were police all over, many standing on guard along the edge of the Capitol property. Even so, I headed toward the front of the grounds; and as I stood there a minute or two, I reminded myself, *this isn't about me or the press. I've come to fulfill what God has directed me to do. That's all that really matters!*

And so, at the edge of the property, in front of the Capitol Building of the United States of America, I lifted the cross and proclaimed, "God is the power, the blessing and the grace that made this country great." I held the cross up for a few moments after making that proclamation. And, as I had professed to many people over the past several weeks, I didn't know if the sky would open or the earth would quake, and when I made the declaration none of those things happened; but as I stood in front of the Capitol Building, thoughts of God and the Bible swirled through my mind before settling upon Moses and I reflected upon his actions. Seconds later, I lowered the cross, pointed my finger at the Capitol and declared, "I hope it shakes you up in there."

Still nothing happened, but I did feel a measure of gratefulness for being used by God and being able to do as He had instructed. And at that moment, I was completely undaunted, feeling so blessed to have experienced God's presence in such a magnificent and powerful way, 24 hours a day, most every day, all the way here. It simply did not matter if any people paid attention to my presence. I had walked over 500 miles and had prayed for people and had accomplished what God had asked me to do.

By the time I got back to John's house, he and Karen were in bed, and most likely, fast asleep. I called Ann to tell her about my experience in D.C., and that I'd be heading home the next day. I got up very early, like around 3:30 AM, and left as quietly as I could. I regretted leaving in the night without saying thanks, or goodbye; but I was concerned about Ann and wanted so badly to get home. I knew she had not been feeling well and I also realized that she often tried to downplay the ailments that were troubling her—she had multiple health issues and had undertaken a lot of responsibility on the home front and at her jobs while I was gone. So, wanting to be sure she was okay, I drove with as few stops as possible and arrived back at the House of Angels in Vermont about 12 hours later.

Declaring God's Grace

It was so good to be home, to be welcomed by my wife and dogs and cat and to realize that Ann was not suffering from anything serious! The first few things on my agenda upon arriving home? A shower. A home-cooked meal. Time with Ann and our pets. And enough rest before attempting to carry on with all the daily things that needed doing on the home front. In all, I spent about a week not doing much of anything, except resting and feeling glad to be back. Then I started a list of things to do and errands to run. And the list grew. And grew.

There was always work on the grounds of the House of Angels along with lots of home maintenance projects, but I was thankful that God had directed me to bring in enough wood to heat our home for two years. It was great to realize there was no wood to split or stack!

OBEDIENT: "But the Lord said to me, "Do not say, 'I am only a child.' You must go to everyone I send you to and say whatever I command you. Do not be afraid of them, for I am with you and will rescue you," declares the Lord. Then the Lord reached out His hand and touched my mouth and said to me, "Now, I have put My words in your mouth." Jeremiah 1:7-9

DON'S NOTE: The joy I received from listening to my Savior's voice, from the time I was sick and refused man's treatment, to the development of the House of Angels, to the lengthy Heal America Walk, is, as Dean Braxton said of his time in heaven, beyond earthly words or descriptions. I feel so honored. So unworthy. So loved. And, so confident that anyone can testify for the Lord, too, if they work to soften their heart and listen for God's voice.

CHAPTER 37

Congregations Pray for America

I truly believe it has been under God and ordained by Him that this nation has been given so much. And so, like our forefathers, I look to Him and His ways for guidance. As you know by now, one thing I've been doing for the past few years before, during and after my Heal America Walk, is to lay hands on people and pray with a handkerchief, just as it has been done for centuries. It has been such a blessing to witness the healing and mending that happens in people's lives as the grace and mercy of God touches them. I heard great results from a high percentage of my prayers during the Heal America Walk, and I'm still being touched by people who have visited the House of Angels.

After I'd been home for about a week, our pastor wanted me to talk about the Heal America Walk, so I sat down to make a list of all the things I could speak about. As I sat there, I thought, "God, I know why I walked. It was because You asked me to. But I still don't know what it was for. I don't know what its purpose was."

As I sat there, wondering about the purpose of it all, I found myself getting up in the spur of the moment to cross the room and open the plastic box that held the two signed editions of Rabbi Jonathan Cahn's books.

I can't believe this, I thought, *I haven't even seen what he wrote!* I quickly pulled *The Harbinger* and *The Shemitah* out of the box. I opened to the signed page in *The Shemitah,* and read, "To Don, God Bless You." Then he added his signature and had written, "Jeremiah 33:3." I quickly grabbed my Holy Bible, King James Version by the American Bible Society of New York and opened it to that passage. To my amazement, it said: "Call unto me, and I will answer thee, and show thee great and mighty things, which thou knowest not." *This is incredible,* I thought. *I was just in the process of doing that!* Reading further to Verse 6, it says, "Behold, I will bring health and cure, and I will cure them, and will reveal unto them the abundance of peace and truth."

And then, I opened *The Harbinger*, to see what Jonathan Cahn had written there. Again, he wrote, "Don, God Bless You," followed by his signature. But on this one, he added, "Jeremiah 29:11." Quickly referring to that verse in the same bible, I read: "For I know the thoughts that I think toward you, saith the Lord, thoughts of peace, and not of evil, to give you an expected end."

Incredible! I am completely amazed at what that had said. He had also written the word, "confirmation." I had asked him to do that after telling him how things in *The Harbinger* had proven to embody multiple confirmations connected to what God had asked me to do.

Without a doubt, I know God has been speaking to me though the scriptures, and once again, Rabbi Jonathan Cahn has come into play. A moment later I remembered something someone from Jacob's Well had told me. They said Pastor Tim had spoken of 2 Chronicles 7:14 at a Sunday service during my walk. They also said that everyone who was able, had gotten down on their knees at the pastor's request, while he spoke the verse. I was quite sure that this was another act of God, showing His involvement in this whole thing. As soon as I could, I called Pastor Tim and asked if he knew when he had spoken 2 Chronicles 7:14. He said, "No," he could not remember; "but our services are filmed, and you can ask Don and Donna to look through the services to find when it occurred."

I called them and asked if they could look for it. They said it would be an awful lot of work to look through all those films to find the right one. By now, I was confident that God had a hand in what has been happening; and I had a strong feeling that the Chronicles verse was spoken to me on the same day in Washington, D.C., so I gave her that date and asked if she would please just look through the recording from that day. After doing so, she confirmed that it was the same day that I suspected. Precisely the same day I was hearing it spoken to me in D.C.! And I was convinced that it was during the same hour if not within the same moment, because, it was spoken to me when the D.C. congregation had ended their services, right around 11 AM, while Pastor Tim, had asked the congregation in Jacob's Well, to go down on their knees as he proclaimed 2 Chronicles 7:14, after his worship team had ended their portion of the service—right around 11 AM!

The amazing prophetic words filled me with renewed energy, and I felt I now could focus on the talk that my pastor had asked me to give. It would mostly be about the Heal America Walk, but it would include the spiritual connection between the two churches regarding 2 Chronicles 7:14. I turned to the verse and was inspired to continue reading and not stop at verse 14. As I read verse 15, I remembered how this church—Jacob's Well—was acquired and how it was being refurbished to a prestigious manner that would most certainly be worthy of a Godly house, and I was certain that 2 Chronicles 7:14-15 refers to Jacob's Well. For in Verse 15, it states, "Now mine eyes shall be open, and mine ears attentive unto the prayer that is made in this place." Who else but God would take a little congregation in a small business building in the middle of a cornfield and find a way to relocate it into such a beautiful building—through a dream/vision by the pastor and to have it be the setting of such remarkable prayers and readings?

I gave my talk about the walk and things got back to normal. And then, after a couple of months had gone by, I started to seriously work on this book. And as I did so, I marveled at the way God works. You see, for years, I tried and tried to work on the story about faith, my healings and the House of Angels. But no matter how much I wanted to do it, something always stopped me. Of course, now I understand: God did not want me to write this before the Heal America Walk had been accomplished. It simply had to be within His time. But, once again, I could not seem to write it. I felt as if there was a force field blocking the effort. It wouldn't be too much

Congregations Pray For America

longer, though, before I would know why I was unable to continue. After all, I had faith in the Lord, and I believed there were a few more pieces of the puzzle that God would have to put in place. All throughout my walk, the nation was focusing on the race for the presidency. It looked as though Hillary Clinton was going to be the prime candidate for the Democrats and the major press seemed to be pulling for the former first lady. The race seemed to be disappointing for many when Republican candidate Dr. Ben Carson stepped down, and before we knew it, business mogul Donald Trump was most likely going to be the choice for the conservative voters. An unlikely candidate for sure, according to the political pundits!

Sure enough, Donald Trump was the nominee to run for the Republican candidacy and Hillary was chosen as the candidate for the Democrats. As they campaigned, it looked more and more to most people, including myself and Ann, that Hillary would be the winner of the presidential race. Christians were alarmed, of course. We had seen time and time again how arrogant she was and how she had often seemed to be on the wrong side when issues involving the rights of Christians were in jeopardy. Even so, when people expressed to me their fear that she would win, I told them I believed something big would happen to disrupt her chances, prior to the election. I was certain of it because I was told so, by God.

One night, I found a way to communicate my belief in the messages I was receiving. Many churches throughout the nation were holding prayer vigils, asking for the Lord's wisdom. As a matter of fact, Jacob's Well was hosting a prayer night six days before the election. People from several churches showed up to pray for the nation. It was obvious to us that Mrs. Clinton was not a good choice for Christians — she was not a pro-life candidate, and progressive politicians like Hillary could be damaging for Christians and the Constitution; but many of the people attending our evening prayer session expressed their distress over the likelihood that she would win over Donald Trump. After all, he was such an unlikely candidate! So crass! So unpresidential! After several people voiced their concerns, I held up my hand and expressed my intention to speak.

I briefly mentioned my walk; and, despite my own fears, when people told me that Hillary would probably win, I said that God told

DESTINATION D.C. A Modern-day Jonah?

me something big would happen to cause her undoing. I said God had told me that He was still in charge. I also reminded them that Donald Trump had recently professed that he was a pro life candidate and he had chosen Mike Pence, a strong Christian, as his running mate. While I have never been a great supporter of Donald Trump, and was often disappointed by his actions and reactions, I did believe he and Pence would be a better choice for us, especially with the need for a new Supreme Court Justice. Ann and I were happy to realize that he was listening to and meeting with Christian leaders and promised to protect Christian practices in this country. If Hillary Clinton won, Ann and I believed her choice for a Supreme Court judge would most likely be a blow to the Constitution, to Christians, and possibly even to America's ability to remain as a sovereign nation.

Although God told me He was in charge, on election night when the polls were so highly favoring Hillary Clinton, I went to bed sadly believing she would win the election. But what wonderful news greeted us the following morning! Donald Trump had won the presidency. I believe the fervent prayers of Christians throughout the country moved our Lord. And the big event I had been telling people about? It was the release of thousands of Hillary Clinton's emails that put her in a bad light. A very bad light!

Congregations Pray For America

DOUBT: "As God's fellow workers we urge you not to receive God's grace in vain. For He says, "In the time of my favor I heard you, and in the day of salvation I helped you." I tell you, now is the time of God's favor, Now is the day of salvation. 2 Corinthians 6:1,2

DON'S NOTE: Stand strong in your faith in God and He will lead you to the right, Godly directed, conclusion.

CHAPTER 38

Destruction or Reprieve?

John, the truck driver who, with his wife Karen, had been so hospitable and had helped me navigate in D.C., called after the 2016 election of Donald Trump. I had not spoken much about politics during my time with them. Usually, when the subject comes up, I tell people that we should not look to the nation or the nations on this earth—we should look to the Kingdom of God for it's the only real thing we can depend upon. But during John's call, just as I was about to hang up, he said, "Wait a minute. You know what? I think your walk had something to do with the result of the elections."

I didn't ask why he said that, I just accepted it as being the truth because of my experiences before, during and after the walk. I had questioned the possibility that God was giving us a reprieve like He gave the people of Nineveh. After all, Christians throughout the country had gotten down on their knees and prayed for the election of a leader who would bring God back to our country!

But even as I agreed to the idea, my mind's eye returned to the destruction and devastation I had been shown in visions during my walk. I wondered about John's declaration about my role in the election—could it really have been a sign? A sign that God will give us a reprieve from such a fate? It's doubtful that it will come from the putting on of sackcloth and ashes as was done in Nineveh after God sent Jonah to them with His pronouncement regarding the need to stop their evil ways; but the Bible says it was a fact that when they changed their ways, God had mercy on them.

I can't help but wonder: if enough people hear about the multitude of prayers by Christians, along with my trek to D.C. and my visions of destruction, that they'll pray and honor Him, and walk away from their sinful flesh-minded nature and learn to once again love God and follow His ways. Perhaps my experiences in this book will also help them. More people need to understand that to focus on the pleasures of the flesh put before us by the Devil causes us to be defiant against God's wishes—and that defiance leads to death.

For instance, is it a coincidence that after several decades of legalizing abortion in the United States, a replica of Palmyra's Arch of Triumph was constructed in City Hall Park in New York City after the Islamic State militants destroyed the original 1800-year-old structure? That arch has historically served as the entrance to the Temple of Baal.

Just who is Baal? During the 17th century, he was recognized as one of the seven princes of Hell, and some referred to him as the primary God of the Phoenicians. Practitioners of the practices of Baal sacrificed their children. In just one instance, historical evidence reveals that throughout the years of 814 BC to 310 BC, hundreds of children in Carthage were believed to have been sacrificed to Baal. The Bible refers to Baal as Beelzebub. Baal worshippers connected him to weather and calamities, like earthquakes and drought and they would work themselves into a frenzy and sacrifice children to appease him.

Trouble is, Baal is not the only demonic-type entity to be unveiled in America. Hundreds of people gathered in Detroit to witness a huge bronze statue of Baphomet, the goat-headed wraith who is now considered by many to be a major symbol of Satanism. Almost nine feet in height, weighing about a ton, the horned idol sits on a throne adorned with a pentagram, disconcerting horns of a virile ram, biceps of a weight lifter, and hooves for feet. It's also disturbing that the figure is said to contain binary elements that celebrate differences of opinion, (perhaps leading many away from

DESTINATION D.C. A Modern-day Jonah?

the Bible?) and it's being idolized by statues of small adoring children. And supposedly, its followers do not believe in Satan—this world and the evil people in it have decided we need more demonic beings for evil and devastation and immoral corruption, thus being in direct disagreement with the Bible. Do these people truly want to reap what they are sowing?

On a good note, in 2012, state representative Mike Ritze gave several thousands of dollars to ensure that a marble slab with the Ten Commandments was installed in the shadow of the State of Oklahoma's Capitol dome, while lovers of Satanic temples were denied their petition to place a statue of Baphomet on legislative property. Unfortunately, the Supreme Court of Oklahoma ruled that the Ten Commandments monument violated the state constitution. I can't help but wonder—where does the Supreme Court of Oklahoma stand with their beliefs? If they do not want Biblical symbols displayed or Satanic symbols displayed, what does the Constitution of Oklahoma embrace—something in between, or nothing regarding righteousness and evil. And if it's nothing, what do they accomplish by not having a stand. As I think about it, I cannot help but wonder how many demonic idols have been erected in our country in recent years, and how many people have erected altars to them?

Are people trying to have the United States become a modern-day example of Sodom and Gomorrah, and therefore encourage God to come against us as He did with them? We have enough corruption and immorality without creating more symbols to encourage it.

I can't help but wonder if these belief systems are symptoms that reveal an increasing number of people are struggling simply to belong to something—anything, whether it be political activists or members of religious cults—to give them a feeling of purpose. It is truly sad for Christian believers to see this and know they are simply trying to fill a void in their lives—a void that only a relationship with God, the one true God, can fill. Like children rebelling against their parents, they are rebelling against their heavenly Father.

Destruction Or Reprieve?

It appears that disagreements will never disappear from politics or religion. Shortly after the election, Ann came home from work one night and told me about a discussion she'd had with a co-worker. That person had angrily pointed out Donald Trump's shortcomings: things that had occurred years ago that had not been good for his image, and sometimes perhaps, were not even honorable. They said because of his past actions he should not be president. But Ann had pointed out that Moses was greatly used by God, although he had killed someone. Prior to God asking him to lead the people into the desert to escape their bondage, Moses had killed one of the task masters. And then she pointed out that Saul had persecuted and killed many Christians, yet he had been given the name Paul and was chosen to do great acts for God and had written a large portion of the New Testament of the Bible. At least thirteen letters are attributed to Paul, and some believe it is possible that he also wrote the Book of Hebrews. Ann was stressing that the Bible mentions unlikely heroes. God looked beyond their earthly flaws and chose them because their hearts were filled with a desire to serve, and they had the will to be obedient when they heard His call. There were so many unlikely heroes to be found in the Book of Judges and the Book of Hebrews, some of whom were able to overthrow kingdoms by depending upon their faith in God, like Gideon, Barak and Jephthah. The only perfect person on this earth was God's son, Jesus Christ.

IMPORTANCE OF FAITH: "Open the gates that the righteous nation may enter, the nation that keeps faith. You will keep in perfect peace him whose mind is steadfast, because He trusts in you. Isaiah 26:2-3

"But the eyes of the Lord are on those who fear Him, on those whose hope is in His unfailing love, to deliver them from death and keep them alive in famine. We wait in hope for the Lord; He is our help and our shield. In Him our hearts rejoice, for we trust in His holy name. May your unfailing love rest upon us, O Lord, even as we put our hope in You." Psalm 33: 19-22

DON'S NOTE: Whether it be during my conversation with John long after I returned home from my Heal America Walk, during my work on the House of Angels, or even decades before while I watched the development of the melanoma on the back of my shoulder, I've always thought that God is the one who heals us, watches over us, and has the wisdom to rule us. I hope, so much, that those who are unbelievers or seekers read these words, understand them and learn to follow God's ways. Jesus the Christ, who never sinned, said belief in Him is the only way to keep the gates of heaven from locking you out!

CHAPTER 39

Shaking up America's Leaders

Think, please, please think about the blessings bestowed upon this country after our founding fathers turned to the wisdom of God for the inspiration to create the most glorious documents for the most glorious country in the world. And then, think about how our descent from Godly jurisdiction has brought us to a place where we are witnessing a growing tendency toward monumental governmental corruption, violence, flooding, hurricanes, fires, pollution, and invasive pests that are now plaguing us like never before. Could it be that God is giving us a series of warnings? Are we ripe for disaster; mirroring the destruction of the Israelites?

Or could we work to soften our hardened hearts and turn back to God and His ways? The answer lies within each of us. Won't you join the effort to repent and look to God for guidance and make this sinful generation an extraordinary one that glorifies God and His creation once again? I myself had lived a very sinful life for many years and can tell you I will live the rest of my life feeling most grievous because of my sin and for not living in compliance with God's laws. But He is a forgiving God. You only have to ask for His forgiveness with an open heart.

God was is and always will be the same. That is a fact that is revealed throughout the Bible. He was active in people's lives during Biblical times, He is still active in our lives today. There are so many stories throughout history to prove this; stories of virtually impossible situations that have been intervened by God and had miraculous outcomes.

I hope my witness throughout this book encourages you to go forth and find the love of God and the work that He has for you.

One thing I have not yet disclosed is that I have always had a desire to compose and sing a wonderful song of faith. An emotional song that would move hearts to the depths that would only be equal to the joy that God's love produces. Though I may never sing, I hope the words in this book might be the lyrics of my life's song. A song explaining that life is a journey to be enjoyed throughout one's entire earthly existence, not just with a great crescendo at the end—but rather, as a heavenly journey which begins as soon as you believe in Jesus as your Savior.

Pastor Tim preached a sermon several years ago and its message and lyrics-without-melody stayed with me. As I add it now, I find many verses seem to strongly pertain to the messages in this book.

I have helped readers to identify those specific verses by putting them in italics.

A NEW SONG
A sermon by Pastor Tim Bohley
Jacob's Well Fellowship, 12/30/01

The events of the past year make it easy to look to the Lord for a better year this year! America, and even the World, has been tried to the limit of its endurance. So much hatred, so much difficulty. How can we hope for a better tomorrow? If our hope is in this world and in the power of men to make things right, we will be quickly and inevitably permanently discouraged. Man will fail! But God, who has Heaven as His abode and the earth as His footstool shall not be turned aside from His plan for man. He has set in motion that which cannot be thwarted. He is not dismayed, He is not confused, and all that He speaks comes to pass! Praise God! So then, what must we do to bring our hopes in line with His will? The answer is simple: PRAISE HIM! SERVE HIM! LOVE HIM! TRUST HIM! FOLLOW HIS COMMANDMENTS! AND VICTORY SHALL BE OURS!! WE MUST <u>SING TO HIM A NEW SONG!</u>

One of the beautiful things about singing is that it begins deep within. It is not generated from without, but from within! As the Bible states: 1 Chronicles 16:23-27:
23 – Sing to the LORD, all the earth; proclaim the good news of His salvation from day to day.
24 – Declare His glory among the nations, His wonders among all peoples.
25 – For the LORD is great and greatly to be praised; He is also to be feared above all gods.
26 – For all the gods of the peoples are idols, but the LORD made the heavens.
27 – Honor and majesty are before Him; strength and gladness are in His place.
(NKJ)
Psalms 33:1-12
1 – Sing joyfully to the LORD, you righteous; it is fitting for the upright to praise Him.

**2 – Praise the LORD with the harp; make music to Him on the ten-stringed Lyre.
3 – Sing to Him a new song; play skillfully, and shout for joy.
4 – For the word of the LORD is right and true; He is faithful in all He does.
5 – The LORD loves righteousness and justice; the earth is full of His unfailing love.
6 – By the word of the LORD were the heavens made, their starry host by the breath of His mouth.
7 – He gathers the waters of the sea into jars; He puts the deep into storehouses.**
8 – Let all the earth fear the LORD; let all the people of the world revere Him.
9 – For He spoke, and it came to be; He commanded, and it stood firm.
10 – The LORD foils the plans of the nations; He thwarts the purposes of the peoples.
11 – But the plans of the LORD stand firm forever, the purposes of His heart through all generations.
12 – Blessed is the nation whose God is the LORD, the people He chose for His inheritance.

(NIV)
Evil men may have a plan; those who will not serve Him may have a plan; the terrorists may have a plan; but GOD is the spoiler of the plans of men. He stands in the way of the evildoer and brings to naught the counsels of the wicked. Though the evil seem to flourish now, God has not forgotten His people. Let God's people not forget Him!

The time when it is hardest to sing; that is when we need to raise up a new song in our hearts and in our mouths. Perhaps this last year has brought heartache and difficulty to you; maybe a loved one has passed away, or maybe the doctor has delivered bad news, maybe your finances are not what you would like them to be or your children have turned their backs on you or on the Lord. Maybe your marriage is in difficulty or a loved one is suffering. Life is full of

trouble and heartache, but God is the one to run to, not away from. He loves you! The new song is the song of Heaven. It is the deep within us reaching out to the deep within God.
Psalms 40:1-4
1 – I waited patiently for the LORD; and He inclined unto me and heard my cry.
2 – He brought me up also out of an horrible pit, out of the miry clay, and set my feet upon a rock, and established my goings.
3 – And He hath put a new song in my mouth, even praise unto our God: many shall see it, and fear, and shall trust in the LORD.
4 – Blessed is that man that maketh the LORD his trust, and respecteth not the proud, nor such as turn aside to lies.

(KJV)

The root of the word "Hallelujah" is *hallel.* **It means a shout of praise!! "hallelujah" means a shout of praise unto God!**
It's hard to be discouraged when you're shouting praises unto a Holy God! When we realize who God is, how much He loves us and what His plans are for those who love Him, a song begins way down within us and bursts forth to Him; a song of joy and praise. Not for the difficulties of life, but for the goodness of God.
Psalm 96:1-13
1 – O sing unto the LORD a new song; sing unto the LORD, all the earth.
2 – Sing unto the LORD, bless His name; shew forth His salvation from day to day.
3 – Declare His glory among the heathen, His wonders among all people.
4 – For the LORD is great, and greatly to be praised: He is to be feared above all gods.
5 – For all the gods of the nations are idols; but the LORD made the heavens.
6 – Honour and majesty are before Him: strength and beauty are in His sanctuary.
7 – Give unto the LORD, O ye kindreds of the people, give unto the LORD glory and strength.

**8 – Give unto the LORD the glory due unto His name: bring an offering and come into His courts.
9 – O worship the LORD in the beauty of holiness: fear before Him, all the earth.**
10 – Say among the heathen that the LORD reigned: the world and also shall be established that it shall not be moved: he shall judge the people righteously.
11.—Let the heavens rejoice, and let the earth be glad; let the sea roar, and the fulness thereof.
12.—Let the field be joyful, and all that is therein: then shall all the trees of the wood rejoice.
13.—Before the LORD: for He cometh, for He cometh to judge the earth: He shall judge the world with righteousness, and the people with His truth.

(KJV)

We can take comfort in knowing that the difficulty of life is only for a season. God inhabits eternity and we will be there with Him one day. So, let us sing!!!

What a wonderful sermon! It seems as we backslide from God's grace to complacency, we appear to receive spiritual amnesia. It is my belief that many have lost all sense of belonging and will seek belonging and purpose in anything even if they have no understanding of it or their part in a group or organization's evil deeds. The desire to belong and to have purpose has been going on since and before Biblical times. The angels that went with Satan wanted to belong, but surely made a bad choice. Many people seem to think they are above all things and know best and are the wisest. Or as Pastor Tim would say, "They think they are everything and a bag of chips."

Thank God this does not pertain to all men, but unfortunately it is many. Do some men think they were self-created? If they believe that, why didn't they create themselves greater than they are? I am sure they must know within themselves they have shortcomings. I know that God was is and always will be, whether you choose to believe it or not. You can accept my witness, or not, but this does not make my witness any less true. I would never ask anyone to accept God, Jesus and the Spirit without merit—but it seems to me it is what many do with so many other actions and beliefs.

I have heard and believe that Muslims are accepting Christ, realizing that it is Christ in the Koran who healed the sick and brought back the dead.

It would be my hope that you would at least seek Biblical knowledge and try to disprove it. As you do, I believe you will find the opposite happens. The more you try to disprove it, the more truths you will find in it. As for me? I have seen the miraculous over and over. I also have been blessed to see Christ, be in His presence, to serve Him and to witness His love and power. I was not born into riches or royalty in the earthly sense. I have come from humble beginnings and have obtained greater riches than worldly wealth, and contentment that money cannot buy.

Before earthly things are obtained, the anticipation of what they will be is far more pleasing than what they are when obtained. I only know one that has outshined the anticipation and that was God's love for me and mine for Him. As you've read in this book, my feelings for God sometimes just flow through tears. As I wipe my eyes, I remember a quote I heard. It was about tears being a sign of strength and not weakness. Of course, Ann and I looked it up. It was Washington Irving who wrote, "There is a sacredness in tears. They are not a mark of weakness, but of power. They speak more eloquently than ten thousand tongues. They are the messengers of overwhelming grief, of deep contrition and of unspeakable love." As for me, my tears are from the love for Jesus and the overwhelming grief I feel that He was crucified on a cross, even though this is an example of God's plan. Although it is not anything we can understand, we must believe it was necessary for the good of mankind. I do not understand why God created this earth or why He did things the way He did. I do know that without sadness there is no happiness; without sickness there is no health; and as it has been said many times, there are no flowers without rain. As I

DESTINATION D.C. A Modern-day Jonah?

reflect upon these things, I can't help but believe that it would be boring and downright uninteresting, if you went to church every week and every hymn was the same, like a mind-numbing hum, repeated over and over!

And as I think about my work and the years I have left on this earth, I know without a doubt that I will go wherever God sends me and do whatever God asks of me, for I know He will be there also.

Is it possible that I could have been used by God to be a modern-day Jonah? Could my obedient action—walking from a Godly place like the House of Angels to the Capital of our nation where our leaders have time and again ruled against Christianity—have given us a reprieve? After all, God uses ordinary people for extraordinary purposes!

*** INSERTS ***

Let Your Light Shine
Melody & Lyrics by Karen Gallagher, 2006
Worship Leader, Assembly of God, Granville, NY

The Constitution & God's Hand
Compiled by Don Duncan, Summer of 2010

I am a Christian Soldier
By Pastor Richard (Rick) Stetzer
2 BCT, 28th ID, 1/172 ARBN, Ar-Ramadi Iraq 2005-2006

A New Song
A Sermon by Reverend Timothy Bohley
Jacob's Well Fellowship, 12/30/01
Creator of the Living Waters Evangelistic Ministries with
Reverend Cindylee Bohley